...let answering go until...

First let me congratul... ...a
...unts and uncles the... ...a...
...he blessed parents of Katharine Jane. The...
...had reminded me to pray for P. and M. a...
...it was this expected news that made me ca...
...to hear from you today, partly.

The mail comes late on Thursdays because...
...fluke in the delivery system. I had been...
...for a letter from you since Monday (don't ask me...
...nd had almost concluded that you were...
..."desperate measures" to discipline our correspon...
...again. I was rather expecting today's pack...
...to contain a certain poem or two & I asked f...
...somehow (rightly) sensed you wouldn't send i...
So after lunch I headed for mount Tabor...
...lace where we discussed the letters that af...
...I had difficulty recognizing the exact spot...
...things are much more in a tangle since the fal...
...the leaves. This hindered considerably my sear...
...those bits of paper into which you rendered th...
...much disputed poem of March 22, 1947. I found o...
...few pieces, some badly soaked, some only shreds...
...rumpled and decomposed. You could h...

was glad. She left here Frida[y]
morning, & her boat was to s[ail]
that afternoon, at 4. I've ha[d]
word, so presume everything w[ent]
as planned. She is on a freighter,
ssensibly headed for Port Sudan,
[o]ne never knows on those things.

Now for your letter. Jim E, [you]
[yo]u are incorrigible. That's all [I]
[ca]n say. No man has ever treate[d]
[m]e like this before, and I don't [want]
[a]nother one to. And you needn't [be]
s[o] uppity about that, either! Se[eing]
[th]at you have forestalled the brillia[nt]
[re]ply I might make, by forbiddi[ng]
[m]e to make any quips on the ju[stness]
[o]f your phrases, what is there
[le]ft for me to say? Judging from
what you say, I'm persuaded
[yo]u know a lot of things about
[me] that I don't even know yet, and [you]
[t]o have access to a barometer of [my]
[f]eelings that I've never had a gli[mpse]
[o]f. Well, carry on, brother, it['s]
[f]ascinating.

You asked me to write my
[b]rother David. I don't see that
[it's] necessary. We've never disc-
[ussed] the matter at all, so I'll
[le]ave it up to you to defend you[r-]
[sel]f. He blew in here on Frida[y]
[m]orning, from Chicago, on his w[ay]

This book is riveting. It unveils something we've always yearned to see: the deepest recesses of Jim and Elisabeth's hearts. From the first few chapters, you become enthralled and fascinated by the worshipful way they turn every awakening emotion into a cause for celebrating Christ. Rather than allowing breathless passions to escape the stall, they prayerfully measure each desire against their devotion to their Savior. (Who *does* that nowadays?!) Jim and Elisabeth's amazing journey of love shows the reader what a sacred romance is all about. *Devotedly* is a should-read for those of us who grew up on Elliot books, but it is a blessed must-read for today's young Christian couples.

Joni Eareckson Tada
Joni and Friends International Disability Center

Tim and I had the privilege of studying under Elisabeth Elliot (and we still refer to notes from her class often, even after forty-five years). To us she was a woman of iron principles, one who did not suffer fools, gladly or any other way! What we learned from her has shaped my life and understanding of my role as a woman to this day. This book invited me to see an entirely new side of her, one of passionate commitment to her Savior and to Jim Elliot, in that order. I recommend this book to anyone who desires to know what a holy, fierce, and passionate love between a man and a woman, both committed first to Christ, could look like, as well as those who want to know more of Elisabeth Elliot.

Kathy Keller

Devotedly is a daughter's personal, powerful memorial to the love affair her parents cultivated between themselves and the God they served—from their early days together in college, their times of separation, their missionary journey to Ecuador, and continuing into their marriage. They wrote often, fortunately for us. And now, through their carefully preserved letters, we can share their commitment and insights directly from these two remarkable souls, gaining a window into the formation of power and love in their relationship and their work in the world. So I am pleased to recommend this compelling view of lives lived warmly. And well. Many thanks, Valerie. Well done.

Donna Otto

In a tinny time of tweets, emojis, and snappy chat, this book is a rich symphony of language and power, wit and wisdom, longing and passion, temptation and truth. Read it, and you'll find a feast for heart, mind and soul . . . one that you may not have even known for which you hungered!

Ellen Vaughn
New York Times bestselling author

Devotedly,

Devotedly,

THE PERSONAL LETTERS *and* **LOVE STORY** *of*
JIM *and* ELISABETH ELLIOT

VALERIE ELLIOT SHEPARD

PUBLISHING GROUP

NASHVILLE, TENNESSEE

Copyright © 2019 by Valerie Elliot Shepard
All rights reserved
Printed in the United States of America

978-1-4336-5156-4

Published by B&H Publishing Group
Nashville, Tennessee

Dewey Decimal Classification: 266.092
Subject Heading: ELLIOT, JIM \ ELLIOT, ELISABETH \ MISSIONARIES

Photography of the letters is by Randy Hughes.

Main Scripture reference is King James Version, public domain.

Also used: New King James Version (NKJV), copyright © 1982
by Thomas Nelson. Used by permission. All rights reserved.

Also used: New American Standard Bible (NASB),
copyright © 1960, 1962, 1963, 1968, 1971, 1972, 1973,
1975, 1977, 1995 by The Lockman Foundation

1 2 3 4 5 6 7 • 22 21 20 19

I dedicate this volume with deep love to the Shepard children:
Walter Dorman
Elisabeth (Martin)
Christiana Ruth (Greene)
James Elliot
Colleen Amy (McKinnell)
Evangeline Mary (Smidt)
Joy (gone to heaven in October 1990)
Theodore Flagg
Sarah Abigail (Ibanez)

With these words from my father's journal:
*Mayhap, in mercy, He shall give me a host of children that I may
lead through the vast star fields to explore His delicacies whose
fingers' ends set them to burning. But if not, if only I may see
Him, smell His garments, and smile into my Lover's eyes, ah,
then, not stars, nor children, shall matter—only Himself.*

Jesus, Thou art now my end;
Thou my starting, too, has been,
Oh, be Thou my present friend,
I would walk and on Thee lean.

I am indebted to him for the desire of a large family, which God
answered by giving me eight unique, intelligent, and beautiful
children. This book is dedicated to them, as well as little Joy, who
was stillborn at four months. God gave me the verse, "In Thy
presence is fullness of joy," when I was thinking of a name for her. I
trust we will all meet her someday and find out His purpose for her,
which will be, as ours is, to bring glory and praise to His name.

If there is one thing I know I'm most like my dad in, it is this love
of God's creation and the desire to show others how awesome
He is. I hope I have given this same love to each of you. May
this book show you God's glory and purpose too and encourage
you in following His leading. He is the Perfect Shepherd!

CONTENTS

ACKNOWLEDGMENTS

First, I want to thank God, and His Son, my Savior and Redeemer, for arranging and planning this wonderful union between my parents so that I could be their daughter and be given the privilege of delving into almost all their letters and journals. My parents have become even more treasured in my heart after reading through these marvelous writings of their walk with Christ as well as with each other.

I want to thank Marion Redding, my dear Maid of Honor, who chronologically organized and helped with many findings of quotes, the filing of documents in the right places, and patiently showing me what to do over the phone when I was falling apart! She also made some suggestions of how to write some of the sentences I struggled with, and understood the huge and precious legacy I carry.

I am so grateful for Margaret Ashmore (a dear friend of my mother's before Margaret and I even met) for editing, deleting, and rephrasing many words or sentences. I am just as grateful for Lawrence Kimbrough, my editor and collaborator at LifeWay/B&H. Lawrence and Margaret have been very patient with this "baby writer" and have shown only kindness, patience, and humility toward me in their suggestions.

When I first began the writing in 2013, another good friend, Samantha Caroway, found, marked, and labeled many sections of *Shadow of the Almighty* that I wanted to use in this book. She loved the book, as have so many, and appreciated my father's deep commitment to following Christ alone.

I also want to thank Anthony Solis who is working on a book of my mother's letters to her mother and is still helping me understand (because of my non-computer brain) how filing and folders work in a PC and has sent me my mother's letters from his findings at the Wheaton College Archives.

Two other friends, Julie Cochran and Shelley Hendry, have helped read through the journals and letters my parents wrote, and transcribed many of them for me, taking care and time to do it well for this book.

In reading these letters and journal entries, I hope each of you readers will be as affected and blessed (even awestruck) as we were, and as a result, give yourselves more fully to the cause of His kingdom. I also thank the many sisters in Christ, and my family, who prayed me through the last four years! There are too many to name, but each of you knows who you are and I am so very grateful!

How often, Lord, our grateful eyes
   Have seen what Thou hast done,
How often does Thy love surprise
   From dawn to set of sun.

How often has a gracious rain
   On Thine inheritance
When it was weary wrought again
   An inward peace.

Thou Who upon the heavens dost ride,
   What miracle of love
Brings Thee more swiftly to our side
   Than even thought can move?

Our love is like a little pool,
   Thy love is like the sea,
O beautiful, O wonderful,
   How noble Love can be.

AMY CARMICHAEL

PREFACE

Neither of my parents could have possibly foreseen their names becoming internationally known and beloved. Their hearts motivated them to higher ground. God desired to exhibit two lives melded into one, whose whole-hearted commitment to Him would influence the lives of countless souls.

They'd been born into quite ordinary, hardly well-to-do families on opposite edges of the United States. They didn't enter each other's lives until their paths crossed in the Midwest at college during the years following World War II. Yet even as adolescents and young adults, far more than most others their age, they held a singular devotion to Christ. They gave up any petty human desires for the sake of His kingdom, no matter the cost or implication—that He alone might receive all glory.

The Bible tells us, "In Your light we see light" (Ps. 36:9 NKJV). Because my parents walked in the light of God's Word, He gave them the clarity of their callings, directing each of them individually to the jungles of South America. They fully expected to serve Him the rest of their days in locations as obscure to the outside world as any other places on Earth, bringing the words of Scripture to unreached people who'd never heard the gospel spoken in their own language.

The *last* thing they wanted was to make a name for themselves.

But God ripped the curtain of anonymity from around them on Sunday, January 8, 1956. A primitive tribe of Ecuadorian Indians speared my father, Jim Elliot, and four other young missionaries to death while the men were attempting to communicate with them. His death left his wife of little more than two years, Elisabeth, alone. Widowed. At twenty-nine. With me.

I was only ten months old, so I never really knew my father, except through what I learned of him while growing up. Initially I watched my mother fearlessly minister to the very people who'd slain her husband in the same jungle. Later, after we returned to the States, I heard more of the story while I completed my education, grew into a woman, and became a wife and mother myself. By this time, of course, I became aware of just how extraordinary my parents' "ordinary" lives were.

My mother went on to give an account of her husband's life in monumental books like *Shadow of the Almighty* and *Through Gates of Splendor*. The Christian world came to know them as Jim Elliot, heroic missionary martyr, and Elisabeth Elliot, beloved author, speaker, mentor, and Bible teacher.

Through the years, the stories of their lives, along with some of their now-famous quotes, have inspired numerous books, articles, blog posts, and sermon illustrations, even feature-length films and documentaries. Their influence continues to reverberate throughout Christendom. To this day numerous men and women, sharing Christ within humble and difficult settings, point back to my parents' legacies of faithfulness as the spark that ignited their quest for serving in global missions.

In this book I want to share the untold part of this story. Even if you've read my mother's book *Passion and Purity*, you don't yet know the many colors and layers of my parents' love story.

In fact, I didn't either. Not all of it, at least. Obviously, some of it simply came out in conversation or in offhand comments through the years. My mother would often tell me with joy about my dad's personality, how he made everyone laugh, how his class-clown antics in college were, to her (the paragon of quiet, restrained, and studious devotion), horrifyingly intriguing. She would get a gleam in her eye whenever I asked about him, remarking how his masculinity thrilled her, his complete devotion to God inspired her, and his passion for the gospel, as well as for her, moved her. She hoped that one day the Lord would bless me with a husband who bore the same qualities she loved so dearly in my father. And He did!

I read my dad's journals (*The Journals of Jim Elliot*, which my mother compiled, edited, and published in 1978), so I also knew other details of their relationship that occasionally surfaced amid his otherwise daily notes of personal Bible study and insight. Theirs was a deep and delighted love, something they handled with extraordinary sacredness, even as it stretched and surprised them in ways they never saw coming—spiritually and beyond.

And for most of my life, such general knowledge of their romance and marriage always seemed enough for me.

But in recent years my curiosity reemerged, sending me on a mission to locate a special treasure my mother had once given me—a trove of all my dad's letters written to her from 1948 to 1953, the year they were married.

At the time she gave them to me, our houseful of eight children occupied my full capacity for both major and mundane undertakings. She realized this fact, too, and had told me—just as she'd done when bestowing her own private journals on me earlier—that I might find interest in them someday, "when you have more time."

In the passing years, as the house began slowly clearing out one by one, my mind returned to those letters again and to the love story I knew they contained, although sadly my memory of where I'd put them did not accompany the thought! But God knew. And He had plans which first began with my discovery of the trunk where I had stored them "for later." The time had come.

I began to pore over each word, which would reveal great and mysterious depths of that genuine and indestructible love born of God. The real-life interactions of two young adults would stir others. Jim and Betty modeled—not perfectly, but persistently—the way God intends us to handle love, steward it, and keep it continually under His guidance.

And, how they grew to love each other! What you'll see as you follow the progression of their relationship and the decisions they made along the way are the hallmarks of what I believe is *still* God's plan (and is even now just as possible) for young people in love. If they commit themselves and surrender to Him, they will be genuinely satisfied in their Savior.

Indeed, my parents' story is not unique to them. We read in 1 Corinthians 2:9, "Eye has not seen, nor ear heard, nor have entered into the heart of man the things which God has prepared for those who love Him" (NKJV). God loves those who trust His care, provision, and presence as devotedly as they did. He is still able to bless those who walk the all-too-uncommon path of purity and honor that He desires for His children. He plans for them a more profound joy when they are willing to prayerfully wait, work, and trust Him.

I recently came across a newspaper article that described the current dating trends among Millennials—a general label for those who have reached young adulthood in the twenty-first century. And while I know that our culture is far afield from the sheltered way I met and was courted by my future husband, I still was shocked by what was reported as customary practice. Nearly half of today's young singles say they typically have sex *before* the first date. What they now consider the intimate part of their relationship is what happens *after* they've been to bed together and are finally getting around to knowing each other in conversation and in meeting each other's family and friends. Worse, these poll numbers seem surprising to experts only because they contradicted the previous "rule of thumb" that people would save sex for the third date!

In sharp contrast, the story you're about to experience is much more than a testimony of how two people in love preserved their virginity for marriage and how people still do so today. Because as important as chastity is, the nature of my parents' words and actions reveal a couple defined not only by what they *didn't* do, but by what they *did*. The Lord permeated their thoughts with His love. They struggled mainly to ascertain His will for their lives with clarity and predetermined obedience. They kept each other focused on His never-ending promises, despite circumstances that could easily have spun them off into doubt, disillusionment, or despair. The Lord demanded of them extraordinary, inexplicable patience, which seemed daunting when watching others in their circle steadily become engaged and married. They could easily have chosen to justify their own timing, not the Lord's.

Instead, they gave up their own love for each other. They surrendered it totally to the One whose hand they trusted to lead them toward whatever future He'd created for them. And after valiantly and consistently returning it to His care so that they could more fully obey and follow Christ, they found their love given back to them in ways that—well, I won't spoil the story for you.

To grasp the scope of their adventure together, I should tell you that their words in this book come from several sources. One source is the letters from my father I mentioned, almost all of which have never been published, except sparingly in some of my mother's books. I've also drawn from her letters to him. Mysteriously, he chose not to keep her letters of 1948 and the first half of 1949, so I can only infer what she wrote to him by the comments he made within his return correspondence.

My mother, like my father, kept a journal during those same years, in which she captured some of her heart feelings, many prayers, and choice reflections on her reading and Bible study. In addition, she kept a five-year diary that she completed in 1951, using it as a quick, disciplined summary of each day's activities. Each calendar date (January 1, January 2, etc.) contains an entry for, first, 1947, then directly below it, 1948, and so on, allowing her to look back during each annual pass through the book at precisely what she was doing and thinking at that time a year ago, or the previous years.

As you can imagine, knowing my mother, even her most cryptic or humdrum reporting of details somehow seems weighty. We can even glean wisdom from the mundane details, which she knew were holy to the Lord.

Taken together, this combination of their letters to one another and their journals create several impressions. First, they capture the inquisitive, observant, highly thoughtful awareness of life that characterized the way they approached each day, and which kept them from rushing or reacting emotionally to things. They were sometimes impatient but rarely spiritually gullible.

Second, they frequently punctuated their writings with quotes from seasoned authors, stanzas of sacred hymns, memorized excerpts from creative poetry, as well as lines of their own original verse. They continually fed their minds with the insights of superior writers, both Christian and secular. They immersed themselves in the thoughts of spiritual giants, consuming a steady diet of classics that kept their thinking both broad and deep.

Only slightly less noticeable in their letters are, third, the unspoken realities of what long-distance communication required in the late 1940s and early 1950s. Like everyone in every generation, they knew only what was contemporary to their own time. But to understand the context of their story, some of us will need to suspend today's assumptions of having instant, international access to any person at any moment. Jim and Betty hearken back to an era when one wrote letters, stamped, and put them in the mailbox, aware they wouldn't arrive at the other's address for several days. Once the recipient read it (and reread it), he or she crafted a handwritten response. The next letter received might not provide answers to any questions that had been asked until a week later, maybe a month later, depending on how long it took for the person to sit down with his or her stationery. When my parents wrote more frequently, their letters would cross in the mail and refer to comments made in perhaps a previously written letter.

The rhythm of this reality—the unavoidably delayed gratification—was simply an accepted part of the world in which they live   It feels unbearable in comparison to the immediate response time we expect today, yet I can't help but wonder if what we've gained by accelerating life hasn't cost us the reflection that makes love stories like my parents' so unique.

When I read their words—even from the rare perspective of being their only child—my heart desires to honor Christ more with my best offering to Him. Even as a woman in my sixties, I'm inspired to rekindle my devotion and be willing to suffer and sacrifice for the sake of the gospel, as my parents did. I'm stirred also to pray for my own children and grandchildren and their generations, that they would catch an eternal vision for their lives. I pray they would experience for themselves the unrivaled joy of trusting God with every moment, with every question, with every hurt and confusing delay, knowing His way is always best, always better.

Being the daughter of such remarkable parents exposed me to many indescribable life lessons. They lived for Him, loved for Him, and persevered through His grace. I don't possess the same gifts or disciplines they shared and personified, at least not in the same manner. Yet I consider it my legacy to be faithful to Christ's calling on my life. I express part of that calling and responsibility in this volume that I am so honored you've picked up and chosen to read.

It is my way of returning to my mother and dad some measure of gratitude. And more importantly, it is my thanks to God for what He has so generously done for me. I hope it encourages you through their undying testimony. More than anything, I pray it results in praise to the Lord for allowing us all, by His grace, to share in the beauty of His holiness.

Valerie Elliot Shepard

Note to reader: My parents' letters and journals are generally presented throughout this book as indented text, in a different typeface. When I've included portions of their original writings within descriptive paragraphs of my own, their words appear as italics.

Hold Thou Thy Cross between us,
  Blessed Lord,
Let us love Thee. To us Thy
  power afford
To remain prostrate at Thy
  pierced feet,
Unhindered, holy channels for
  Thy purpose meet.

Set Thou our faces as a flint
  of stone,
To do Thy will—Our goal be
  this alone.
O God, our hearts are fixed—
  let us not turn.
Consume our heart's affections,
  let Thy love burn.

ELISABETH HOWARD

LOVE'S STIRRING

The opening line of my mother's diary for January 1 made clear her devout, single-focused faith in God, as well as her longing to be fully surrendered to Him, His Word, and His Spirit. Home from her senior year in college for the holidays, having just turned twenty-one a few days before Christmas, she [Elisabeth Howard] marked this first day of the year by opening the plain, navy cover of her five-year diary, where she wrote:

> Thursday—the beginning of another year in which "to walk humbly with my God." Oh that I might learn to love Him supremely and have no other desire but Him alone. "Teach me Thy way, O Lord . . ."

The words that had already begun to flow into this private little notebook of hers—though punctuated, of course, with the typical cares and crises of any young woman's life—would never shift from this due-north orientation. God was first; God was supreme; God was all. Indeed, her entry in this same little diary from the year prior, January 1, 1947, reflected the same unwavering commitment.

> What a wonderful year is behind, and I know that a more wonderful year is ahead. Truly I can raise my Ebenezer and anticipate great things from the Lord, Counsellor, Prince of Peace, Mighty God.

Yet on this crisp New Year's Day of 1948, writing at home in the Philadelphia suburb of Moorestown, New Jersey, her last lines of entry gave the first glimpse of an approaching figure that would truly make 1948 a year like no other—a development that, over time, would contribute to making her whole *life* like no other.

> Jim and I had another long talk tonight—oh, if only I were as sincere and genuine as he is.

Jim.

The first time "Jim" appeared in my mother's diary was an entry from nine months earlier, March 23, 1947, late in her junior year at Wheaton College, where she'd similarly noted having *"a good talk with Jim Elliot—he is a wonderful guy."* A friend, roommate, and wrestling squad teammate of her one-year-younger brother Dave, Jim was someone she began to notice at school occasionally from afar. Then in the fall, when their course schedules as Greek majors nearly all overlapped, the "afar" between them became much nearer. She began to become more familiar with this ardent underclassman who lived with such fiery devotion to Christ, who could write such things as:

> God, I pray, light these idle sticks of my life and may I burn up for Thee. Consume my life, my God, for it is Thine. I seek not a long life but a full one like Yours, Lord Jesus. . . . To that soul which has tasted of Christ, the jaunty laugh, the taunting music of mingled voices, and the haunting appeal of smiling eyes—all these lack flavor. I would drink deeply of Him. Fill me, O Spirit of Christ, with all the fullness of God.

Still, it was quite the surprise when Dave invited him home for Christmas break. That's how "Jim" ended up being at my mother's house, and in her diary, on New Year's Day 1948.

Jim Elliot.

My father.

The Howard household, though already filled with six children of its own (my mother being the second oldest), was like many others of its day, quick to welcome and make room for company. Still, she might have been

My mother's family at home, Christmas 1947. Back: Dave and Phil (as well as Phyllis Gibson, my Uncle Dave's future wife). Middle row: Elisabeth, Tom, Grandma and Grandpa Howard, Margaret and Kay Howard (Phil's wife and daughter). Front: Ginny and Jimmy. (My father is off-camera, but attracting attention!)

less than pleased initially to hear they'd be sharing their home and holiday with this "big man on campus" from the Pacific Northwest. Less than a month earlier—in one of the only other mentions of him from her 1947 diary—she recalled going to a party in the nearby Chicago suburb of Glen Ellyn with Dave and a few others. "Jim" was among them, and as forthright as ever, she recalled.

> On the way home Jim Elliott [notice the misspelling—two t's instead of one] told me some of the reasons why I have such a bad reputation among the fellows. I am terribly sarcastic, for one.

It wouldn't be the last time she'd hear this kind of critique and advice from him. (He was never one to beat around the bush or withhold sharing his opinions.) Her only recorded reaction to such revelations were mild sighs. But from what she later told me about the insecurity she felt during this season of her young womanhood, I can only imagine how it must have stung her, having her social demeanor challenged so directly by a mere acquaintance.

Some of her insecurity may have stemmed from her height—she stood a full 5'10-3/4". (If you wonder why she was so precise about the measurement: my father was 5'11", and she chose to accentuate this negligible difference as a deliberate means of expressing wifely deference.)

Another potential source of insecurity came from the fact that she'd rarely if ever received a compliment from her parents about her looks. The most flattering description she recalled her dad ever giving to both her and her sister as teenagers was about their being "two fine husky daughters." (I *guess* that's a compliment.)

No wonder, then, that her natural inclination was to be fairly withdrawn and critical of herself. She told me many times that she was a wallflower growing up. Yet even with that said, I'm sure this Jim-character's offhand mention of certain flaws in her appearance—such as later comments about her "banana nose and angular figure"—only added to her sense of insecurity.

But sometimes the teasing playfulness of criticism is a smokescreen that masks quite different, more affectionate feelings. The awkward interactions of young men and women, when unsure exactly how to express their hearts, can often result in conflicting messages. Perhaps his unlikely appearance at her home during Christmas break of 1947–48 was simply another way of his trying to send a message to her, a way of grappling with what his own heart was feeling.

The one thing both of my parents certainly shared was an equally intense devotion to the Lord. His zeal differed from hers only in volume, not in passion. He was loud; she was quiet. He was ultra-popular; she was more likely to retreat from the spotlight. He was occasionally confrontational, boisterous, exhortative; she, although decidedly tough at the core (and admittedly hotheaded and argumentative), was tender in comparison to his outgoing tenacity. But during the family meals, family worship, sledding, and skating that took place throughout these few days at her home, my dad later admitted to having feelings for her—Betty, Betts—at this Christmastime in New Jersey. *Love was stirring.*

Christmas sledding. Left to right: my father, Uncle Dave, Aunt Ginny,
Aunt Margaret and Uncle Phil. Little Jimmy in front.

Still, neither spoke of it yet. Nor did either write of it in their individual journals and diaries. Both had their minds on far more significant things than pairing off in a romantic relationship or competing against their peers, some of whom almost seemed to be racing each other to the altar!

In spring of the previous year, after spending time with a pair of couples who were engaged, my mother wrote of the relief she felt from any sense of distraction:

> How thankful I am that the Lord has kept me from any feeling of covetousness. There are times when I long for love, but lately I've not felt that way. It's a wonderful thing.

There had been boys before. Only recently a young man and college friend named George had asked her out. They had dated years earlier while students at Hampden DuBose Academy, the private Christian boarding school she'd attended in Zellwood, Florida, before each had moved on to

Wheaton. But after accepting this latest invitation for going out, she broke it the next day, consenting only to going on a walk with him . . . to break the whole thing off entirely.

She announced they needed to stop dating. Then she was surprised to see his eyes begin to pool with tears, to hear his voice break as he tried telling her how much she meant to him. *"Now I feel terrible,"* she wrote afterward—*"hadn't realized it would hurt him. I'm beginning to wonder if perhaps I acted rather hastily yesterday."*

Over the course of nearly a week, her diary swims with the changing emotions that resulted in the aftermath. She confessed to being *"positively miserable about George,"* working at *"getting over George,"* then trying to find George, only to hear he was *"afraid to come and talk to me, for fear I wouldn't speak to him."* Finally, after several days of this disquiet, she forced the opportunity to meet with him again, where she *"gave back his medals, explained a few things to him, thanked him for all he'd done for me."* It was hard to do, she said, but she hoped he understood. And she admitted in her heart that she missed him *"quite a bit."*

What she *didn't* miss, though, when reading back over those 1947 entries in her diary, was the unnecessary drama of it all. Several times in 1948 she spoke of being embarrassed at what she now deemed "immaturity" on her part. In March, for instance, after attending the wedding of two friends the previous night, she said:

> It used to be that when I went to a wedding I pictured myself in such a role. But thoughts of this nature seldom enter my head anymore. I have a calm assurance that I am not to be married. I am grateful to my Lord for winning the victory in that realm. Truly it is miraculous. I wept for joy during the ceremony, and the hymn kept running through my mind, "I Am Thine, O Lord," and "Loved with Everlasting Love."

I smile now in seeing this young, earnest woman go to a wedding, impressed with the thoroughly Christian center of it, yet in her own mind be assured that she was supposed to remain single. She was much more intrigued by the prospect of finding *"blessed happiness in Christ alone,"* she said . . . although I wonder how many times she wished throughout the next five years that she could recapture the same calm assurance on this subject.

My father, too, in his personal journal, which he began in mid-January 1948 and continued to keep with consistent regularity almost till his death, related similar convictions when thinking ahead to his future. Meditating on Genesis 31, he commented:

> Rachel and Leah manifest an attitude toward their family which I would have toward all earthly ties. There is now no longer an inheritance for me down here. I've been bought by the labors of that great Shepherd who came from afar to gain

me as His bride. Lead on, Lord, whatever God's command is or wherever He may
lead, I am now ready to go.

His father undoubtedly influenced some of his convictions on love and
marriage. My grandfather was an itinerant preacher knit from the same cloth
as the ultra-conservative tradition of Plymouth Brethren. He'd expressly said
in a letter to his son, "Jim, I am jealous of any thing or person who could
retard your progressive course to everlasting riches and a life completely
devoted to that supreme and glorious Man at God's right hand." My father
was also well-versed in Paul's writings from 1 Corinthians 7, which speak of
the benefits of remaining single and the cumbersome load of responsibility
a wife can bring.

Simply put, my parents—at similar times in college—each felt called to
being not only missionaries, but *unmarried* missionaries, singularly devoted.
And they maintained this near-certain conviction despite many pangs of
desire, impatience, and questioning that would later war against the spiritual
caution in their relationship.

What was it about being single and going to far-off lands that seemed
more appropriate and godly for them? Suffice to say, each of them bore
within themselves a burden for taking God's Word to peoples of the world
who'd never heard of Jesus Christ. And they were determined that absolutely
nothing would come between themselves and this honor-bound pursuit and
purpose.

My mother's first poem of 1948 (each of my parents was incredibly
skilled in writing poetry) reiterated her intention for keeping her heart
attuned solely to Christ.

> There is no other source of joy, Lord.
> In Thee alone I find deep, sweet, pure content.
> Forgive me for testing the waters of earth.
> They are not springs.
> They are stagnant pools.
> There is there no undefiled pleasure.
> It is all transient and frustrating.
> Oh, the blessedness of drinking long
>   and fully from Thy springs
>   that are in Thee, Lord Jesus!
> Thou knowest no limits—I take from
>   Thee all I can contain.
> Increase my capacity, Father!

My mother as a teenager (on bicycle), outside with
her sister Ginny and her brother Jimmy.

In another poem, written January 8, she echoed the same single-minded
resolve.

> "The Lord Jehovah is my . . . song" Is. 12:2
> No other song have I but Thee,
>   O Lord my God—
> The purest music of my soul
>   Bursts forth from Thee!
> Be Thou my only joy-note;
>   I, the instrument
> Incapable of any song
>   But Thine.
> O let me praise Thee, Lord!
>   O touch, and let me sing!

When not setting such devoted thoughts to poetry, she could write with
equally devoted prose.

FEBRUARY 18: My life is on Thy Altar, Lord—for Thee to consume. Set the fire,
Father. Now I begin to know that song! Oh, how can I call it sacrifice, when Thou

dost so richly repay—with song, with joy, with love. Bind me with cords of love to the Altar. Hold me there. Let me remember the Cross.

She could also state her case for singleness rather matter-of-factly.

MARCH 7: Translation work is a full-time job. I cannot see how it would be possible from a purely human standpoint to do that and raise a family. Of course if God should one day reveal His will for me to be married, He would supply the needed strength and grace to do both. But as I see it now, He would have me for Himself alone, that I might "care for the things of the Lord" (1 Cor. 7:34). I look ahead with joy at the possibility of a life wholly set apart unto God and the winning of His bride. . . .

I do not mean to say that I see the whole plan of my life. God may change it all. I only thank Him for the joy of resting in Him, and trusting Him for every step. He has given me direction and purpose. I shall not turn aside, even if it be for marriage, unless that is a part of His perfect will. God forbid that I should be satisfied with anything short of His highest.

My father, champion wrestler that he was, prophetically saw his situation in more violent, sacrificial terms.

APRIL 18: All other persons, places, and principles are false resting points for faith. . . . Father, take my life, yea, my blood, if Thou wilt, and consume it with Thine enveloping fire. I would not save it, for it is not mine to save. Have it, Lord, have it all. Pour out my life as an oblation for the world. Blood is only of value as it flows before Thine altars.

Therefore, everything was setting up inside them for lives spent alone, at least as far as marriage was concerned. To put it in my mother's words, *"Lord, I have said the eternal yes . . ."*

Let me never, having put my hand to the plough, look back. Make straight the way of the cross before me, guide Thou my feet therein. Hold me, Blessed Master, ever in Thy presence. Grant to me a steadfast singleness of purpose. O give me love, that there be no room for a wayward thought or step.

And yet . . . what if, as part of God's plan, human love came calling anyway?

SPRING

At some point in the spring of 1948, my parents began studying Greek together. I'm sure a stirring of attraction had been building, revealing itself in little ways, little overtures, little recognitions of noticing and being noticed— but again, not enough for them to entrust it to their journals yet. It was only

```
            BEFORE COMPS

Lord, let not this day be one of
        earthly striving,
For knowledge puffeth up. O let it be
A quiet time of study in the Spirit,
My realm of intellect controlled by Thee.
As Thou didst use the hands of the lad Jesus
Plying His carpentar's trade as given of Thee,
So use my mind. Through all this human learning
Hold Thou my thoughts in focus. Let them be
In earnest concentration, permeated
By the deep consciousness that I am Thine.
Direct my thinking. Give to me, O Father
As Thou didst give to Jesus, such a mind.
```

My mother's earnest prayer-poem before her senior exams.

———

enough to make them want to gravitate toward places where the other was located.

But should they? Was it wrong? they wondered. Were they allowing this stirring of affection to drive a harmful, distracting wedge between themselves and God? Even by entertaining the mere thought of romance, by giving unspoken consent to its emotions, were they compromising precious moments of Godward devotion that were critical to their callings?

As usual—reflective of a trait that I'm sure would surprise no one familiar with my mother's life and teaching—her sensitivity to sins of the heart was keen and acute. As the oldest daughter of strict parents in a large family, she became quite naturally hard on herself. (Too hard, perhaps.) Subtle offenses that most people would never stop to notice or contemplate in themselves could convict her to the core. She admitted, for example, that she was a bit overly devoted to excelling at every school subject. By early April in this final semester of her senior year, nearly two months before graduation, she was already working on her term papers *"so that I might get all A's in them, and hence have more time in which to work for a distinctive rating on comps [comprehensive exams],"* to which she added, *"I have an intense and unholy desire to graduate with high honor."* Most might see this as healthy ambition. She saw it as misguided ambition, interfering with the greatest ambition of knowing Christ.

My father, too, wrote often of how he feared *"offending the heavenly Dove"* by some thought or impetuous act. He would remark of being *"wholly dissatisfied with my present powerlessness"*—this young firebrand who was probably the most spiritually fervent person most people had ever known. *"My love is faint; my warmth practically nil,"* he sometimes confessed in his journal. *"I don't love; I don't feel; I don't understand; I can only believe."* Neither of my parents could bear the idea of allowing a rival interest to divert their attention from the Almighty.

This new struggle, however—this love attraction—created something else altogether with which to torment their tender consciences. And neither of them knew exactly how to handle it.

"The Lord knows I have had a struggle today," Mama dared confess in her diary during this time. *"I cannot write it even here,"* she added, although I suspect her "struggle" was related to something that involved my father. In whatever subtle ways she'd perceived herself having given in to her flesh, however innocent it might have been by less stringent standards, she nonetheless felt the waves of conviction. Yes, with a fervent heat—to the point of not wanting to go anywhere near its root causes again. *"O God, purge me, take away all desire! I have been severely tried on two accounts, and have not rung true. Forgive me, Lord!"*

Yet her inner turmoil continued . . .

APRIL 2: I am seized with fear that my own will is to be given place, and I will thus ruin my usableness for God. It would be easy to follow my feelings, to interfere with the voice of the Lord when He says, "This is the way, walk ye in it."

APRIL 13: I feel the tremendous importance of this particular time in my life. I am twenty-one—only six weeks left of seventeen years in school! I face an uncertain tomorrow, with the certainty of Christ. Perhaps I face a life of complete separation from all I have loved. But blessed will that be with the Lord, who is my sun and shield. How I pray that He will hold absolute sway.

APRIL 24: How subtle is the flesh! I think that my whole life is utterly lost in the Father's, and then comes a suggestion that perhaps He would lead this way, and immediately I rise up, almost unconsciously, in objection! I know not my own heart—He alone sees all the reservation, all my wishes, all the mistrust. When I think that I am longing to know His will, I find that my own heart is choked with human desires, and He cannot speak.

My father, too, though expressing himself with a bit more objectivity, as if dealing with a more general principle, still revealed a glimpse into his own personal dilemma.

APRIL 16: Lord, Thou must put an end to my fleshly issue. Stop it, Lord. Staunch the flow of this defilement which springs from rotten flesh. Instead, flow Thou through me, today, yea, for seven days, until Thou dost see me to be clean.

APRIL 18: The pattern of my behavior is not set in the activities of those about me. Don't follow the example of those left in the world or those found in the church. Rather, the law of God, found in His Word, shall be my standard, and, as I see it, there are few examples of this sort of living anywhere. God gives commands to abstain from all enormities and confusion.

One of the "confusions" my father had long chosen to abstain from—and had exhorted others of his Wheaton classmates to avoid as well—was *dating*. Yet at the end of April . . .

Tonight Jim Elliot took me in to the W.E.C. conference at Moody.

It amounted to their first "date"—a term my mother intentionally placed in quotation marks when she inserted this item of note within her edited version of *The Journals of Jim Elliot*. This gathering of the Worldwide Evangelization for Christ organization at Moody Church in downtown Chicago was *"a blessed, encouraging meeting,"* she said, where her heart was stirred afresh for *"those 100,000 souls who perished in 'blackness of darkness forever' today! What am I doing about it?"*

Notable too, however, from this diary posting of April 30—in addition to its genuine reflection of her missionary heart—was the strength of character she had grown to admire in my father. *"Jim is without exception the finest fellow I have ever met."* And how nice it would've been to know him better, perhaps, if she wasn't due to graduate in a few short weeks and presumably never again see him in her whole life.

Wheaton Student Council 1948. My father, middle row, third from left. My mother, front row, second from right. (Uncle Dave is next to my father, second from left.)

She did, in fact, excitedly tell her mother about a little trip she and some other students had recently taken as a gospel team to Taylor University in northern Indiana, on which my father had invited her. The following is from a letter sent home around Memorial Day:

The usual procedure has been to take just men, but after some persuasion from various sources, Jim [Elliot], who is in charge of the teams, consented to take girls. The thing is, the fellows always do the preaching, but girls are needed for personal work, in dealing with other girls. So Jan and I went along.

It was a wonderful trip down. The fellowship was truly in the heavenlies. We sang "Sunrise Tomorrow," etc., as the sun came up. Then there was a great deal of prayer and hymn singing on the way. The Lord opened my eyes to what true Christian love can mean. I saw it exhibited in the four fellows as I have never before seen it. Just to be a witness of such fellowship was blessed, let alone to partake. In a wonderful way God undertook to keep our minds and conversation stayed upon Him. We earnestly sought to keep our motives pure and holy, and to go forth in the power of the Spirit. Praise be to God!

When we arrived, one minute before time, we had the morning chapel service. It was a time of heart-searching for us, as well as for the students there. Jim gave the message—a powerful challenge to the mission field. Some told me afterward they had never heard such a message in all their years at Taylor. . . .

The evening meeting was one of the finest things I've ever been to. Hatch had charge, and Jim, Bill, and Art spoke. Their messages dovetailed perfectly, though they had not been previously outlined. There was power there which one rarely sees. . . . The trip home was a similar time of real communion. It was practically a brand new experience for me. I've never spent a day like it in my life.

Saturday afternoon we spent in a special meeting of the judiciary committee. Officially, this consists of the deans, the president of the Council, and two members of the student body. These latter are Jim Elliot and I this year.

But despite whatever flutter of affection she may have felt from these up-close encounters with my dad, she focused her attentions on other things, as this journal entry from late May suggests:

MAY 24: I have just finished reading Frank Lawes' *The Sanctity of Sex.* A fine presentation of one of youth's gravest problems. But instead of firing my desire for such a channel of fulfillment, I am brought to my knees in worship and adoration of Christ, for whom my whole love-life shall by His grace alone be poured out.

I am thankful for the power and beauty of love, but I only pray that it might be directed wholly to God, and as an offering acceptable unto Him. All the love poems which I have heretofore written—let them be claimed by Christ. All the desires of my heart are toward Him. All the dreams of my younger days—let them be fulfilled in a life lost in the love of Jesus. In the power of the Cross be my dynamic, in the glory of God my sole motivation. Accept all this, dear Father, in Thy holy name.

She then closed with this original poem.

> Let me burn out for Thee, dear Lord,
> Burn, and wear out for Thee,
> Let me not rust or my life be
>   a failure, my God, to Thee.
> Use me, and all I have, for Thee—
> And draw me so close to Thee
>   that I feel the throb
>   of the great heart of God
>   until I burn out for Thee.

The short burst of weeks she'd spent dealing with *"this new thing"* had now seemed to fade behind more pressing plans for her immediate future.

> **APRIL 20:** I have just spent an hour with the Lord in His Word, seeking to know His will about my life—teaching at PBI *[Prairie Bible Institute]* next year, or PSOB? *[Philadelphia School of the Bible]* Or neither? AIM *[Adventures in Mission]* or SIM *[Sudan Interior Mission]* or neither? How abundantly He has answered, and promised to show me. He tells me to wait, fear not, for He is the Lord. My mind is so clouded, my eyes so dim, my understanding so human—and He says, "I know the things that come into your mind, every one of them" (Ezek. 11:5). "In the shadow of His hand hath He hid me" (Is. 49:2).

Yet my father decided a scant week before graduation to go ahead and make his feelings more visibly plain. On June 3 between classes, he handed my mother a leather-bound copy of the *Little Flock* hymnbook, on which he had inscribed the flyleaf, directing her inside to a G. W. Frazer hymn which opened with the following lyric: "Have I an object, Lord, below / Which would divide my heart with Thee?" The clear implication, now discreetly yet intentionally addressed, was that they somehow (before it was too late) needed to talk this thing out.

What we see next is a very flustered Betty.

"It is terribly difficult to study," she captured in her diary the next day. *"I could not get to sleep last night, and then I woke at 2:30 a.m. and stayed awake! Could not eat much breakfast."* And as to her history final, which kept her up studying all night the next night, *"I shall not be at all surprised if I flunk it."*

My father, waxing poetic, was faring no better, struggling through final exam preparations himself with a mind made *"muddy about Betty H. lately,"* causing him *"trouble in concentration."* He composed the following on June 5:

> O Lord, against this bosom blast
>   of coiled and seething feelings,

Battering passions, ebbing yearnings,
   oozing aches of inner man,
Raise Thou the flinty walls of stuff
   of which Thy Son was made.
Yea, build in me the buttressed
   bastions of faith.
That shall resist the undersucking flow
   of selfish tide,
And make me to endure this late attack,
   I pray, in Jesus' name.

This was all setting up for a dramatic showdown.

The vivid events that followed in the next week my mother has already told more capably than I could ever relate them, captured in her classic work *Passion and Purity* as well as in her fuller account of my father's life, *Shadow of the Almighty*. I'd rather step back and let her tell you the story herself in her own original words, taken directly from her diaries, just as it happened.

On June 7—a Monday—they took a long walk *"from 9:00 to 11:00 p.m. The evening was cool and beautiful, the heavens spangled. Talked of many things, very seriously."* Writing the next day in her longer journal, she expanded on the events:

JUNE 8: It was a time of serious heart-searching and an overwhelming sense of responsibility, to each other and to God. I honestly believe that both of us are yielded on this point—or we at least were. Now what? Have we gone back? Have we turned our eyes from Him who alone can satisfy? O Lord, let it never be!

Strange that two should have their whole patterns of thinking so intermingled. Strange, too, that we should have seemingly been led in opposite directions as regards the mission field. Each of us has built up a sort of code, his on Matt. 19:12, mine on 1 Cor. 7 and Is. 54. Now what about these? Have we failed? Have we lost our vision?

Often, we are startled that our ideas so perfectly coincide—things which neither of us has discussed with anyone before. But are we taken by this "coincidence"? Is it only a case of proximity? Has God allowed this as a test of our stand with Him for a single life, and we, in the crisis, have not rung true? If we have fallen in failure and loss, forgetting the glorious gain of the Cross, it is nothing short of tragedy. How will we know this? Yes, how little we know our own hearts! Neither has felt any conviction, except wherein we have allowed our love to become selfish—when Christ has been dimmed by our own sinful "earth-born clouds."

We can only pray earnestly, and wait patiently, asleep, as was Adam, in the will of God. We need to heed the solemn warning of Song of Sol. 2:7, and live in the power of Romans 8.

She spoke in words far wiser than her young years, words that young people would do well to ponder when their emotions vie for rule and want to get ahead of God's best for them. She thought of words that many other faithful, hopelessly-in-love souls would wish they had stopped to say at such a moment.

> God has shown me very clearly that this is all to be left—untouched—in His hand alone. We cannot go further. We have not, I think, done wrong so far, but now we wait.

Two days later, they took another evening walk, realizing more sharply than ever how brief was their remaining time together.

> **JUNE 9:** Tonight we walked out to the cemetery and by chance (!) sat beneath a great cross. How symbolic it seemed! . . . There was a great struggle of heart for both. Long spaces of silence—but communion. "What is to be done with the ashes?" It has cut very deep—therefore we dare not touch it. O, inexorable Love!

Without doubt they sensed the sparks of young passion in that place. Yet they had long allowed God's Spirit to lead their hearts and they did not react to sheer emotion. Their many hours of humble surrender before the Lord and His Word caused them to recognize this moment as something extremely sacred. And in case they didn't, the holiness of it certainly came into view when the moon's glow upon the headstone where they sat caused the shadow of a cross to align itself strikingly between them.

I went to find that cross this past July at the Wheaton cemetery, and I think I found it. I imagined them sitting in front of it in silence. It still makes me shiver with awe at their emotional, intellectual, and spiritual unity. Whatever goose bumps of excitement might have enchanted them both throughout the past several weeks now calmed to a settled, sobering hush. They knew better than to move.

> To wait on the Lord is to stand perfectly still. It is not to make even a tentative step. Because we are not led to continue, we stop. We cannot take any of this thing into our own hands. . . . Surely this torrent would sweep down the walls, if it not be founded upon a rock. So, Lord, until it is firmly grounded in the will of God, let us not build.

My father recounted the evening this way:

> **JUNE 10:** Came to an understanding at the Cross with Betty last night. Seemed the Lord made me think of it as laying a sacrifice on the altar. She has put her life there, and I almost felt as if I would lay a hand on it, to retrieve it for myself, but it is not mine—wholly God's. He paid for it and is worthy to do with it what He will. Take it and burn it for Thy pleasure, Lord, and may Thy fire fall on me as well.

They arrived, then, at a decision. The cross of Christ would be their point of surrender. They would die to their desires and live for Him alone. They would give up their own human attraction in order to follow Christ singly. The cross which demanded their whole hearts gave them the *"liberty of obedience"* (interestingly, the title of a book Mama wrote). So rather than press forward and make plans to keep in touch, they would allow silence and distance to be God's winnowing tools to sift out what should stay and what should go.

They loved each other, yes—undeniably so. But even more, they could not deny that God had been setting them on a path that hardly seemed to include each other (or *anyone*, for that matter). And despite this unexpected wildflower that had appeared in the carefully tended garden of their souls this spring, it was difficult not to discern it as a flirtation with temptation compared to what God had been growing there all along.

I will say, though, if my father had not taken the active step of making his feelings known, the likelihood of their maintaining a close relationship from that point forward was quite low. And because of his openly professed doubtfulness that God's will would ever be for him to marry, I've often wondered if he was right in expressing his fondness for her, especially at such a late hour of their time together. Yet both seemed prepared, despite the anguish (and we will see what their waiting would cost them!) to walk on at this level of trust and understanding. *"It is on the altar,"* my mother wrote. *"God will set the fire or stay the hand."*

Her diary went on to say . . .

JUNE 12: Tonight we walked out to the lagoon. Perhaps we will not be together again—ever. We don't know about tomorrow night—should we be together? He will decide. "It is going to be hard . . . harder than we'd like to think."

JUNE 13: Our last night together. The "dust of words." There were very few. Only quietness—and peace of spirit.

In the end, my mother captured it well—with a measure of hope, contentment, and gratitude that seemed to silence her trepidation for the time being, even if not always enough to hold back the flood of perceived loss and the pangs of loneliness that ensued.

JUNE 17: These have not been days of barrenness. But they are utterly inexpressible. God has taken me apart, wholly unto Himself. He has let me see His face. No word can be written of it. I stand silent, and wondering. O blessed Lord "that will not let me go, I rest my weary soul in Thee."

And with the kiss of a distant prayer she closed, *"Keep him thus, too, Lord Jesus."*

SUMMER

There was hardly time to dwell on the gravity of what they'd just experienced, amid the hubbub of my mother's graduation festivities, the influx of family, the snapping of photographs, and the many sidewalk farewells with dear friends made over four indelible years. But how quickly, almost within hours, did the sudden shock of silence cause all other goodbyes to melt into a single goodbye—the fixed gaze from only one pair of eyes, left behind in memory, both to ponder and perplex. *"What passed between us cannot be spoken or written,"* she said, recalling that final moment together at the train station. Could it really be over so soon?

My father took their parting equally as hard.

JUNE 15: Wept myself to sleep last night after seeing Betty off at the depot. Wistful all day today in spite of outdoor exercise. Feel a concentrated pressure in my throat even now. Homesickness partly—but I never felt it until after I left her.

Yet indeed, she was gone—off to the Summer Institute of Linguistics, a partnership with Wycliffe Bible Translators—ten weeks of intensive training held on the campus of the University of Oklahoma. But the real intensity of those weeks and months would be what happened outside the classroom, where daily she would wrestle with the whys, what-ifs, and what-nexts. How was it all supposed to fit together properly with everything else she knew about life: her single-minded faith in God and the unswerving certainty that she would doubtless follow Him wherever He led?

On most days throughout the summer, particularly in the evenings and on Saturday mornings, she would ascend the steps in the football stadium, where she could be alone with the Lord amid its echoes and emptiness—the vacant bleachers below, the vastness of the heavens above. With every prayer and Scripture reading uttered at that height, her heart continued to come down consistently on total surrender to God, His will, and His plan. Yet the flight on the way to that landing spot could often be turbulent.

JUNE 16: Climbed to the top of the University Stadium this morning and had my devotions. God met me there—wonderfully. And He has been with me. He keeps my heart at peace, but when I pray for J. the tears must come.

JUNE 17: It is impossible for me to dismiss all thought of ever seeing him again. I find myself thinking of how I will talk with him. Each time the future comes to mind, he is there.

On nights when *"memories would sweep over me with a strange forcefulness,"* she would sometimes bemoan *"how easy it is to give place to myself, my own moods and feelings. The Lord save me from belonging to the Order of the self-pitying. No man hath a velvet cross."*

JUNE 19: I cannot even pray any specific prayer for either of us, except that he be not hindered in his purposes to wholly follow the Lord. I can say "Thy will be done," or "Do Thou for us," and He restrains from my mind any speculation as to how this will be accomplished. There are many things which I see not.

Have I the proper perspective on the past three weeks, or have I been blinded somewhere? Do I see the lessons God has for me now? Surely I do not at all see what He will reveal. O, that Christ might "be the object bright and fair to fill and satisfy the heart."

Perhaps she felt at times as my father did, who wondered to himself if *"the Lord gave me this affair with B.H. to try me, to see if I were really in earnest about the life of loneliness He taught me."* Just as God tested the ancient Israelites *"to see if they would walk in the ways of their fathers or not, perhaps this is His plan with me,"* he wrote. *"The Lord wants to see if I will follow Him regardless."* And without question, that's what he would do. Against the pulsating tide of missing and wishing for my mother, he sensed God must be telling him to *"lose the fondling touch. Rather, open my hand to receive the nail of Calvary—as Christ's was opened—that I, releasing all, might be released, unleashed from all that binds me here."*

Yet as soon as either of them steeled their souls against physical longing, forsaking even each other for the clarion call of a life spent wholly in God's service, the pendulum might swing back the other direction.

There was the day, for instance, when my mother received what she called *"a very perplexing letter"*—from her father—presumably advising her not to consider it tantamount to disobedience if she were to consider a future with Jim Elliot. Was it possible, she wondered to herself in response, *"that by my own determination not to make one un-commanded step, I might be allowed to miss God's best?"*

This was obviously no easy path to navigate.

Truly, in her undivided mind, *"God forbid that His highest purpose should be checked, in any degree, by the fleshly determination of my own will. Not mine, but His, is all I want."* But if she could only receive some kind of specific answer from Him on where He was leading—some way of coming to a settled conclusion on what to do, one way or the other. *"Give me grace to follow, for my heart and flesh are weak."*

JULY 10: Spent several hours in prayer and study up in the stadium this morning. I am distressed that it is so difficult for me to direct my whole mind and heart fully to God. I find it very easy to spend much time thinking of J. Why should this be? Oh, to know more of the law of the spirit of life in Christ Jesus! Oh, for that burning passion whose sole object is Christ!

One thing she knew for certain, however, having spent this time so fiercely seeking to ascertain the will of God concerning their relationship:

she was ruined for anyone else. When a fellow classmate asked if she'd like to go out one Friday night, *"of course I refused. Odd to think that I should probably never date anyone again. How could I?"* She was far too taken with my father by now. For if the Lord in His sovereign plan had determined she should keep her romantic distance even from *him*—from Jim Elliot—she certainly wasn't about to consider another in his place.

Interestingly, though, in God's curious providence, one of the mercies He extended toward her during the summer was that my father's older brother Bert was involved in this same linguistics program as well. The two of them would often talk, sing hymns around the piano, and compare notes on their spiritual insights. It was like getting a peek into the family home where my dad, like his brother and other siblings, obtained such an intense love and grasp of the Scriptures.

The Elliot family, Portland. Front: Jane, Jim, Bob, with Bert behind them.
Back: Clara and Fred, their parents (my grandparents).

In some ways, seeing him there made things hard for her. The physical similarities (the cut of his profile, the sound of his laughter) almost hurt when she'd catch sight of him. *"He reminds me so much of J."*

JULY 12: Bert sits by me in nearly every lecture. Strange. How I wish he knew. I doubt if he has any idea whatever about us. I have to catch myself now and then about the way I refer to Jim.

JULY 13: There has been some talk about Bert and I being together so much. Oh—people—how they love to talk! If they only knew the circumstances!

And yet being near him made her feel nearer to my father too. He was to her a source of unexpected, unsolicited info on the real object of her interest. *"Bert had a card from Jim today which he let me read."* How cagey she must have felt, not wanting to be the one to divulge that this kid brother of his was frankly a bit more than just a college acquaintance.

However, being around Bert so much—despite the wonderful guy he was—only served to bring into sharper focus just how exceptional a man she'd found my father to be. *"He [Bert] has not the strength of character nor force of personality which Jim has . . . or nearly the self-discipline. In J., I see all that I think of as true, pure manhood."*

And to my mother, "true, pure manhood" was hardly a nebulous concept.

In May of the previous year, long before developing any sense of affection for my dad, she had written down eleven qualities of what she termed "My Ideal Man." Perhaps these would interest you. She never published them, to my knowledge. I give them to you in their entirety.

1. Depth of spirituality such as I have never plumbed. Missionary.
2. An iron character—strong, deep, consistent, enduring.
3. Towering intellect—a wide knowledge of many things, with a special knowledge of several. Love for books.
4. Keen personality, cheerful and thoughtful, able to get along with all kinds of people.
5. Appreciation of the aesthetic—love for beauty of nature, love for good music and poetry.
6. Considerate, courteous, well-versed in social graces, at ease with society of any sort. All of this, if genuine, is from unselfishness.
7. A tremendous capacity to love—tender, strong, ever-deepening, warm devotion.
8. Strong jaw, searching eyes, healthy body, masculinity.
9. Sense of humor—clever, not clownish.
10. Ability to sing and speak beautifully.
11. Equal social background.

No one who didn't possess these qualities (or wasn't growing in them) would ever be of interest to her. My father's heart was much the same. They understood early that if God were ever to draw them romantically toward each other or toward any other person, part of the proof behind the relationship's legitimacy would be a recognizable pattern of spiritual fruit in bloom. And throughout their long odyssey of waiting on Him to confirm and permit their own love for one another to lead toward marriage, each of them remained doggedly more concerned about the other's conformity to God's will. In fact, this priority was visible already, this first summer, in my mother's prayers.

> O, may the Lord set His love upon him, and lead him up higher. I only want to know that he is daily learning more of the Lord Jesus.

> Almost every time he comes to mind, I pray that his thoughts may be directed wholly to God.

> I would rather be blotted from his thoughts forever than for one moment to stand between him and his Lord, or weaken his power with one soul.

This final line—praying for the effectiveness of his ministry to others— referred to a month-long preaching circuit that my father embarked upon between mid-July and mid-August. After completing a summer school session at Wheaton, he and three other team members (including Dave, my mother's brother) volunteered for a four-week itinerary with Foreign Missions Fellowship that took them to several states throughout the Midwest. They spoke at camps and Bible conferences and college campuses in Michigan, Minnesota, even as far west as Montana, seeking to energize the church's passion for unreached people in other lands. *"Often the Lord brings to mind the F.M.F. team with which Dave & J. are traveling,"* my mother wrote in her diary, more than once. *"I pray that God would keep them low at His feet, open, and usable."*

Ministry team at a church in Detroit. My father is second from left. Dave Howard at far right.

From all accounts it was a most fruitful time. It inspired many young people to commit to missions. Still, my father confessed privately a couple of times in his journal of being *"frail in contending with myself,"* saying that *"unchecked inordinate desire will make even a king's son sickly."* My mother, of course, busy with her own work, was similarly struck in quieter moments with an ache of bewilderment. *"Six weeks ago tonight that we made our decision. Never a day passes without my remembering with mingled pain and pleasure those two unbelievable weeks."* Her Scripture reading and journal writing from an August day said it like this:

> **AUGUST 4:** Psalm 106—"He led them through the depths . . . They sang His praise . . . They soon forgat His works; they waited not for His counsel: but lusted exceedingly in the wilderness, and tempted God in the desert. And He gave them their request but sent leanness into their soul."
>
> Solemn warning indeed. He has led us through the depths, and we have sung His praise. God forbid that we should ever forget His works, and haste ahead of Him. God keep us from making any request which springs from the lust of self. O Lord our Father—stay our wills in Thine. Keep us ever trusting, resting—as Thou hast so wondrously done.

Yet among my favorite images of them that summer, cobbled together from their various writings, is picturing them sitting alone at nightfall somewhere—my mother high above the football field in Oklahoma, my father perhaps overlooking a still lake at a Minnesota campground—perhaps observing the same sunset from four states away.

> **EH (JUNE 30):** Went to the stadium again to view the sunset. How wonderfully the clouds reflect the glory of the sun! This, my cloud of uncertainty, flashes His glory even now. I wonder if I could go on in peace if I know that all hope was gone of seeing him again? Although it is all committed to Him, that hope cannot be dispelled. Scatter it, Lord, if it hinders. Prepare me even for *that*.
>
> **EH (JULY 4):** A golden evening at the top of the stadium—great reaches of golden paths sweeping up to Him who is the giver of all light.
>
> **EH (JULY 26):** The sunset tonight, viewed from the stadium, was unspeakable. The most brilliant red I've ever seen, I think. At times I wonder how it would be if we were to meet again. Would it be possible to pick up where we left off? Is it possible that he could feel the same? But I don't feel the same—it is different now. Deeper and more pure, even than before. Have Thine own way, Lord.
>
> **JE (AUGUST 15):** Oh, the sunset last night! It was as if the dying sun sprawled gory riot in the western sky, wallowing in its own bloody throes, warming the folds of the clutching darkness with the heat of its passion, and moving even mute cloud forms to flush crimson with the huge horror of its passing. But clouds are fickle.

For it was only an hour or so before they had turned their faces to reflect the grim glory of a ghastly grinning moon.

Looking up from his reverie, he added as if in apology, *"Enough—that sounds overworked, but it's fun writing."* Little could he have known how much his daughter wishes he would've just kept on writing.

After the completion of his summer tasks, he headed home to Oregon. His stay there with family could only be brief; he was due back soon in Wheaton for the beginning of his senior year. Yet he faced an unclear future. Not surprisingly, however, he bravely held his chief ideals and ambitions intact while continuing to battle this new inner conflict.

> **AUGUST 23:** Was sensitively touched at reading [Hudson] Taylor's love victory. I cannot understand man, even godly man. Having been conquered by a power unseen and willingly owning the sway of the Absolute, thus "finding himself" and satiating the ultimate longings of his breast, he can ache with a perfect fury to be subjected still further to the rule of woman's love. Or perhaps it his desire to possess, having been strangely dispossessed by owning Christ as Lord. And within I feel the very same.
>
> Oh, that Christ were all and enough for me. He is supposed to be, and I dare not say, "Why hast Thou made me thus?" Oh, to be swept away in a flood of consuming passion for Jesus that all desire might be sublimated to Him.

My mother's ten weeks of summer translation study concluded in mid-August as well, and she caught a train going the opposite direction, to New Jersey, including a two-hour layover in Chicago—*"Union and Dearborn Stations, sites of such memories. God forgive me the weakness of 'nostalgia.'"* She also made a scheduled stop in Wexford, Pennsylvania, just north of Pittsburgh, to spend a few days with Eleanor Vandevort, one of their favorite missions-minded friends from college. (Van later lived with us when we came back from Ecuador.) While there, Van showed three letters she'd received from my father over the summer. *"This gave me a strange feeling,"* my mother wrote, to be reading his correspondence again over the shoulder of someone else.

As lovely as it was to spend time with Van—(*"She asked me a lot about J."*)—she was thrilled to finally reach home, making blessed reunions with family and friends. And yet she arrived feeling troubled concerning her future.

> **AUGUST 30:** It is the first time in my life when plans have not been laid out for me far in advance. I am cast only upon my Lord. Oh, that "Christ, the wisdom of God" might have full charge. Never have I felt so completely helpless and ignorant of the way I should turn. I turn, O God, in faith and love, to Thee.

One opportunity that immediately presented itself was with the Sudan Interior Mission, which she seriously considered. She approached it with arms wide open, wanting only God's will, confident that He would providentially lead. *"I can think of two times just last year,"* she wrote, *"when I did everything in my own power to go a certain way, but God withstood me—and as I look back I praise Him for His way. How much better it was."* But in the end, she chose to enroll for a year of further training at Prairie Bible Institute (PBI)—a common feeder program for those who, like herself, attended Wheaton for undergrad. Located in western Canada, it meant another extended season away from home—likely not even back for Christmas. But it meant useful study while waiting for clearer direction on the specific part of the world in which God was calling her to serve Him.

And it furthermore meant, on the long train ride from New Jersey to Alberta, she would pass right through Chicago again.

SEPTEMBER 19: Should I stop in Wheaton on my way to P.B.I.? I would love to— in fact, today my need seemed more acute than ever. O, what it would mean! But is it God's way? Could things be the same? *Should* they be?

My father, hearing word of her coming, was an equal mix of hopeful anticipation and frustration.

SEPTEMBER 20: I cannot explain the yearnings of my heart this morning. Cannot bring myself to study or to pray for any length of time. Oh, what a jumble of cross-currented passions I am—a heart so deceitful it deceives itself. . . .

Possibility of seeing Betty again brings back wistful thoughts. How I hate myself for such weakness! Is not Christ enough, Jim? What need you more—a woman—in His place? Nay, God forbid. *I shall have Thee,* Lord Jesus. Thou didst buy me; now I must buy Thee.

But those five or six days proved liberating and refreshing to both of them. How good to be together! As often as he could tear himself away from the classroom and other responsibilities, they revisited all the sites of their most significant encounters. They walked and talked *"of divine things, and things of home and family. Precious time."* Going out to the *"same stone cross of fifteen weeks ago"* was *"beyond words,"* she added.

SEPTEMBER 22: But oh, how acutely aware I was of all that he needs that I could never offer. O to be *holy!* God, give me a heart like his.

SEPTEMBER 23: I long to enter in more fully to the things which Jim seems to understand so well.

Maybe that's why she dared to make a rather bold request. *"Betty asked me last night if she could see this thing"*—his now remarkably well-known journal—at the time simply an old notebook containing its first nine months of material. *"I guess it's all right,"* he said.

Turns out, this entry of September 25 would be his last in that particular volume. But to my mother, it was like experiencing a brand-new beginning to their relationship. It opened a window into his being, making her spirit soar at his resemblance to the "Ideal Man" she'd envisioned in her prayers. *"Today I have been admitted into some of the inner sanctum of his soul,"* she wrote. And what she saw therein were *"the yearnings of a man for God—the heart-cry of a naked soul."* She would be leaving soon—much too soon—but this stirring revelation of his heart she would never forget. When they said their second painful goodbye of the year, only two days hence, it would now contain a knowing that was almost as heavy as the unknown—a knowing made even more plain when on the following night he just came out and said . . .

"I love you."

I should probably interpret for you the import of this statement, particularly as it related to my mother. In many cases (in most cases), the words "I love you" that pass between a smitten boy and girl can mean anything from an intense, excitable emotion to almost nothing at all. But she knew from her parents to expect to hear those special three words only when he was ready to follow it up with a proposal for marriage.

My father, though not flighty at all in the seriousness of his speech, did not feel the same restraint. Understandably, I'd say. He just said it impulsively, though not without believing it to his core. Still, the openness of his expression would have entered her ear with a more intense sensitivity than might have been received by most. She needed to be able to overlook what, to her thinking, those words should have meant, and simply be able to accept them for how he truly intended them. He was in love with her. And, oh, how ecstatically she must have felt it. But she understood full well that *"neither of us can reconcile ourselves with the thought of marriage."* Too many noble, spiritual, kingdom-of-God-sized obstacles stood between their love for each other and their freedom to act on it.

They could agree they'd been wise to let the summer's distance do its winnowing work. They could even agree, at this point, to begin writing letters to one another—*"yes, God led us both separately to that decision,"* she recorded. This alone would make their separate lives more bearable. It wasn't much, but it was something—a thread of future communication, strung like a thin lifeline between them, even as she *"caught a glimpse of him just as my taxi pulled out,"* leaving her feeling *"so incomplete now—my very soul seems torn in two. Why should it be thus? Why must I miss J. so?"*

The hope and encouragement he'd penned into his journal earlier in the week were still there the morning he knew she'd be reading later in the day.

That's why he cast the following excerpt as if he was writing it as a letter to her.

> **SEPTEMBER 25:** Betty, we shall behold Him face-to-face, much the same as you and I have looked with longing on one another these last two nights—eye to eye— and He will tell us of His love in those looks as we have never known it here. . . .
>
> He knows our love and is touched from a sympathy within, and I feel He holds us from each other that He might draw us to Himself. Let us pray *individually,* "Draw *me.*" It may be that then we will be allowed to say *together,* "*We* will run after Thee."

AUTUMN

She hadn't traveled more than a few hundred miles from Chicago by train before she dropped a postcard in the mail from a stop in St. Paul, Minnesota. Its inscription contained only two words:

"*Miss you.*"

Her next, another postcard from farther up the line in Moose Jaw, Saskatchewan, continued the thought with only one word:

"*More.*"

I think my father was a bit shocked by the effect of these messages on him. The thrill of her unexpected visit, as well as the unavoidable certainty that they would be parted from each other for the near future—these competing feelings that bombarded him appeared to mystify him.

He tried untangling them in his first letter to her, dated Saturday, October 2. Since it's the first we have of his, I quote it in its entirety so you'll get a clearer sense of his heart at the time.

> Beloved,
>
> It's hard to pull out of the nebulae that has collected in thinking about this letter some clever point with which to impress you right off, so I won't attempt it but proceed as if I had been writing in my present capacity for a good long time. Got your card Wednesday afternoon; clever . . . devastatingly so. I wish I had here a "feel-o-meter" to transcribe what has been going on inside for the last few days. It began with that word I think I spoke to you when we were together in chapel the last morning—"trembling."
>
> And what should a tuffy like me be trembling about? Three things: You, Me and God.
>
> You: Remember, Betty, I have already upset one girl's life to the extent that I know that if she ever misfires in her life for the Lord, her biggest excuse for doing so will be Jim Elliot. I tremble to think that my forwardness in declaring my feelings to you is actually affecting your entire life. I have an idea that it will be almost

impossible to discern the Lord's mind for you without your struggling through a maze of thought and feeling about me. You must know a bit of this already in putting in your application to SIM. And what if, in a real test, your feeling should overcome your faith? Whose then the responsibility? *Not entirely yours.* For this I fear, that I, stepping out of the path of the Lord for just a moment, should draw you with me and thus be accountable for the "loss" of two lives.

Me: I cannot for the life of me understand my heart. Somewhere down deep in the murky pools of consciousness, there is a great monster whom I will name "Want" for just now. This is the only constant thing about me—Desire. Much to Freud's consternation, I cannot name it "Sex Urge," for I have found that such will not glut the maw of the brute. He demands more of a varied diet, and one not so easily obtained as that either. I am very thankful that the Buddhist Nirvana is not the apex of the spiritual life or I should be the least spiritual of all men, if absolute satiation were the ideal. The brute is not the spirit nor the soul, least of all is he the body; rather, he is the ME that talks about these other things, argues about them, laughs and asks for more. He is Life. He is submerged down there a-lusting after something he can't name. The nearest He can get to it is with the word *God*. And God feeds him when I allow it. Silly, isn't it? For who, then, am "I"?

Well, I didn't intend that this should run into metaphysics, but what I want to say is that there is within a hunger after God, given of God, filled by God. I can only be happy when I am conscious that He is doing what He wills to do within. What makes me tremble is that I might allow something else (Betty Howard, for instance) to take the place that my God should have. Now something tells me that I can maybe have them both, as both you and Billy have ministered to me lately. *[Bill Cathers was a mutual friend of my parents.]* I am not averse to this, understand, I only tremble that I should think wrongly in supposing that you are one of the ways in which God intends to come in.

God: or, better, the Lord Jesus. I tremble lest I should in any way offend my Eternal Lover. And whatever passes between us let us take note of this: all shall be revoked at His command. I am such a great, cumbersome boor to be "Dove-driven." Oh, how delicate are the tuggings of my Beloved, and how calloused my responses. Above all else, I will that He might find in me the travail of His soul and be satisfied. But this is a hard thing when I speak to you, for somehow the pleasing Him and the getting you are in conflict. I don't pretend to explain it; I can only describe what I feel, and that not very adequately.

Since you left, it has been as if a film has been over my soul. My genuine fervor in prayer was gone for two days—too much rubble so that I couldn't get to building the wall. (See Neh. 4:10 for this.) Notice, it was not the outward opposers that hindered the work so much as the inward clutter. Not "destruction" from outside forces so much as "decay" within. But the proof of God's hand comes in the affirmative answer to Sanballat's mocking in verse 2: "Will they revive the stones out of the heaps of rubbish which are burned?" The zealous Jews did. Apply this to us and imagine a little while. Are we willing to build with a trowel in one hand while our other hand grasps the sword? The building (God's work) must go on, and if there is to be battle as we build, very well, let us strengthen the "lower places" (v. 13). And I say to you the words of Nehemiah to the nobles: "The work is great . . . we are separated . . . God shall fight for us."

I must confess to you, Betty, that I have had regrets about going even as far as we did in our physical contact, and that was very little as most judge. We must guard against this if we are ever together again, for it gave me a whetted appetite for your body that I have found to be "rubble" in getting to the work. You must be hard on me in this. I know we do not have the same mind or makeup, and I feel that I need more of yours than you need of mine. Nietzsche has a word for us here: "One must discontinue being feasted upon when one tasteth best; that is known by all who want to be long loved." Do you get what he means by this: "For too long hath there been a slave and a tyrant concealed in woman. On that account woman is not capable of friendship: she knoweth only love." This is what I found in Billy, neither a worshipper (though he loved me) nor an over-lord (though he was most esteemed). We met as equal dogs at the feet of the Omnipotent. I would have it this way with you and me. Fear not to hurt me with the Living Sword; yea, strike to this purpose. Be more than a lover; be a friend. We spoke of this at the moon-rising tryst. "As I have loved you . . ." Remember?

But how shall I praise the Lord for removing the film this very morning? Confession is good for the soul; it was imperative for mine this morning. I cast it all upon him, and John's truth about "cleansing from all sin" was very precious. Oh, how He sweetly "preached peace" to one that was far off (Eph. 2:13, 17). And Heb. 10:16–22 lived afresh. What a power is in that word! Nearness was the theme of my song, and the thoughts seem well expressed in 136, *Little Flock* (LF from now on). And LF 10, as well. Oh, Bets, let us "undistracted be" in our following.

Just to show you what a poor journalist I am, I will quote my time in composition of this letter: two hours. Part of it is due to typing, I'm sure!

Have you been delivered after the fashion of Ps. 116:8?

Tenderly, Jim

It was in this spirit that their letter writing commenced at a rapid pace. Soon after his first one arrived, she spent two hours the next evening composing her own. In some of these early letters, you can tell they were sort of feeling each other out, trying to navigate what to them was untried territory. Both were accustomed to writing frequent letters as a common practice—home to parents and family, away to grown siblings, relatives, and friends. But this kind of writing was new and different, drawing on a heart muscle that wasn't yet as well exercised or fully developed.

Part of the adjustment they were experiencing was the amount of time each letter required to write. My mother, noting the hours it took to collect her thoughts to him on paper, realized the two of them couldn't sustain this

Example of my mother's five-year diary. Greek writing in the 1948
entry translates to the text of Philippians 1:21—"For me, to live is Christ."

pace interminably (*"We cannot write often at that rate!"*) and keep up their
studies and other responsibilities. Writing, she said, was *"a difficult task, in
many ways, though joyous."*

Another contributing struggle was the acute effort needed to read
between the lines, to interpret nuance and intention, a skill that other letters
from other people didn't as often elicit. *"I sense somehow a little depression
in your last,"* my father once commented, *"as I suppose you have felt in
one or two of my previous ones."* In another instance, he apologized for
captions he'd inscribed on photos he'd enclosed to her, saying, *"I think you
misunderstood a couple. . . . I used those in utter simplicity and with not the
least intention of low connotation—you must believe me."*

Some of it, too, as they got further along, came from learning how to
incorporate this new, added facet of their lives into the whole of what God
was daily working to accomplish in their individual hearts. *"Often I have a
desire to write,"* my mother said in her diary, *"but limit myself to once every
eight or nine days,"* believing that in exercising measured restraint, *"we will
be glad of every discipline we learned, though it is not at all easy now."* She
was discovering, she said, in lieu of constant writing, that *"intercession is*

the highest expression of love—it is pure giving. Teach me such love, dear Lord."

As his October 2 letter had said, they saw reason to begin their budding correspondence on a "trembling" note, which I think is a wise word for young men and women in love to heed. The typical alternative, both then as now—the silly, superficial, even irreverent flippancy in a couple's speech and communication—only reveals how little of lasting worth they are investing or expecting.

From the beginning, my parents treated their relationship seriously. They viewed each other as a special friend to encourage, counsel, and pray for, as well as to challenge, both lovingly and directly, to seek ever harder after Christ. They didn't see the point of squandering the attraction they felt for each other if it wasn't helping them bring out each of their absolute bests. *"Otherwise, it is nothing short of a waste of time,"* my mother wrote. There was *"no future in it,"* she said, *"except eternally."* Or as my father wrote to one of his friends, *"We prayed that God would give me tenderness, and He replied by giving me Betty."*

Again, her letters are missing from this period. All I have are her personal journal and diary. They speak of the joys she was experiencing in fellowship with Christ and in the fine teaching she was receiving. I hear in them as her daughter the gracious, grateful, submissive hope she ruggedly maintained in God's faithfulness and goodness. But she tended to be harder on herself in private writing than reality would probably have revealed. For this reason, my father's letters provide the more accurate window on the gems they were likely sharing with one another during this time.

October 19

You are His particular treasure, Betty—something He paid for at a terrific cost to His own person. . . . He is bound to display you to principalities and powers as a trophy of His searching. For that eternal display-day, He is making sure you are the best possible piece He can make of you—and, glory to His name, He will perform it!

Meanwhile, He keeps you for Himself, hidden away, forming you in secret ways that you don't understand. Much the same as I keep your letters, laid flat and secret in my drawer at hand to scan when I want to feel loved, so He keeps the pious for Himself. . . . Christ loves, even though seeing, hating, and condemning our sin. He shows us how much He hates it by an enormous sacrifice, and then continues to love when we are smitten with guilt.

This is not how we love ourselves. Oh, we say we don't like us very well, but we put up with ourselves. This is the old economy—getting along with "covering up" the sin (animal sacrifice only *covered*) until the sacrifice of Christ does away with it.

I have asked you to be a friend of this sort—mercilessly wrenching out my pet darlings which I cannot see as idols, and then, seeing me sad at bereavement, still love the heart that can cherish the memory of such things. This is love of another sort than we humans experience.

October 24

Betty, my dearest sister, stop struggling and believe! The confidence of Phil. 1:6 assuages all doubt for me just now—He cannot fail us. Oh, He may lead us oceans apart (and we can trust Him for that, too, can we not?), but are we so childish (I do not say *child-like*) as to think a God who would scheme a Jesus-plan would lead poor pilgrims into situations they could not bear? Dost thou believe that God doth answer prayers, my heart? Yea, I believe. Then will He not most assuredly answer that frequent cry of thine, "Lord, lead me.". . .

Stop this nonsense of your "making it difficult" for me—you have made it scores of times more wonderful—all praise to His grace in you. God is answering your prayers for me, so thank Him in those early morning wakings as you think of me. He will accomplish His own purpose in all our ways. Believe, Bets? I know you do.

Many know my father's now famous quote, paraphrasing Matthew 10:39: *"He is no fool who gives what he cannot keep to gain that which he cannot lose."* However, *my* absolute favorite entry from his journal comes from a year earlier, back here in 1948. It's one that most people have never heard, but to me it exemplifies his sincere prayer to be obedient, no matter the cost.

OCTOBER 28: Prayed a strange prayer today. I covenanted with my Father that He would do either of two things—either glorify Himself to the utmost in me, or slay me. By His grace I shall not have His second best. He heard me, I believe, so that now I have nothing to look forward to but a life of sacrificial sonship (that's how my Savior was glorified, my soul) or heaven soon. Perhaps tomorrow. What a prospect!

Didn't God answer that prayer in both ways? Did He not bring much glory to Himself by my father's life as well as in his tragic death? My dad lived out his own code: *"Wherever you are, be all there. Live to the hilt every situation you believe to be the will of God."* And at this point in each of my parents' journeys, the will of God and His divine directives for their next step were precisely what they were seeking to discern. To which part of the globe was He leading them?

My mother, having felt adequate assurance to make application in early October to SIM, one of the missionary sending agencies, was sensing a calling toward Africa. My father, in one of his October letters, mentioned spending *"three hours today with a missionary to the jungle Indians of Peru,"* a man who was *"doing the type of work I would like to think of doing. . . . I would pray that I might be in S. America a year from today."* For now, though, they each labored faithfully at their respective locations, prayerfully navigating the future, regardless of whether it might be alone or together. *"It is as if two pilgrims see the fork in the road ahead,"* my mother said, *"and walk."*

My mother's situation in Canada was obviously the more unfamiliar to manage than my dad's at Wheaton. Yes, she was blessed to be rooming with a college friend, Phyl Gibson (who would eventually become engaged and married to her brother Dave). But the strict schedule the school leadership imposed on students during that era left it *"very difficult to find proper time to meet the Lord alone. We are given only a half hour before breakfast, and of course Phyl is in the room then."* It was her *"eighth year of dormitory life,"* she calculated, and perhaps the hunger for being more in control of her time and priorities was wearing on her. It had reached the point of becoming exasperating. *"The 'social' set-up"* at PBI, for example, *"seems to me somewhat overdone,"* she wrote in her diary.

> **NOVEMBER 5:** It is perhaps good to have a certain amount of segregation, but it becomes an unnecessary strain at times to have to avoid walking past a man, etc.! So much here is judged by outward appearance. I wonder if God is "annoyed" at trivialities.

> **NOVEMBER 15:** One of the things that makes it difficult here is that the schedule is positively adamant. Not one minute of the day can be called one's own. We have to do everything exactly at the appointed moment, and there is no possibility whatsoever of readjusting one's day to fit the time. This is a situation most trying for me.

Or to use another of her words from this diary posting—*"tribulation."*

In addition, the regular correspondence she was keeping with my father was just barely above the line of what the school considered appropriate behavior. A female classmate, who apparently had been called to account for the letters she too was sending and receiving from a young man at Wheaton, tried explaining to a woman in the administration that the two of them had met over the summer and had recently started writing. According to all accounts, my mother's friend was told *"this is forbidden, even during summer, for those who meet after they come to P.B.I.—I do not understand it."*

But for my parents, the letter-writing continued between them throughout this most interesting, enlightening autumn—back and forth, happily and with difficulty. As my father summarized the process:

November 20

> Letter writing is such a heartless method of communicating. First, one has difficulty putting into words what he really feels—then he must worry for fear what is written is misunderstood—and that for a good long time, since he cannot erase once the post-box has banged shut, and then he must wait—*and that is worst of all.*

Being so far off the beaten path up there in Alberta muted my mother's expectations of an arriving letter somewhat. The train that delivered the mail to PBI only ran on Tuesdays, Thursdays, and Saturdays. My dad, however, spoke of *"unreasonableness in my waiting—going to the box three or four times extra a day—even on days when I have no right to expect it."* The anticipation was almost maddening. *"Waiting word Thursday would surely bring something. No? Then Friday afternoon for certain. Well, Saturday cannot help bear fruit. (Monday is miles away . . .)"*

Then when it does come—the first hurried reading (in which you get practically nothing) and then the utter woe of finding it *so short*, then the slow, careful going over it, reading everything possible into every syllable—yes, I know, the gentle rebukes, the hard little things sometimes—but "to the hungry soul even the bitter is sweet."

You would have laughed to see me read yours yesterday. I save your letters till last (though not till evening by a long shot), skim the Record *[the campus newspaper]*, race through the more commonplace mail, then with a mind free to soar, I huddle somewhere to exercise anxious eyes over your fine hand—wishing I could answer *that* sentence right now as the thoughts pour fresh over me, or add a verse to this idea here. But half a continent and fountain pen ban the aspirations, so things aren't as real now as they were twenty-four hours ago.

My father, reading letters at the college post office.

After the second reading, I sprawled in the bed to editorialize and felt all the feelings rush to my throat, leaving the pit of my stomach empty and weak, with little convulsive sobs pushing at my belt-line in jerky, irrational tempo. No tears—just a quiet, sinking agony, as if crushed by a vacuum. I cannot tell you how I felt, but this in no way reduces the feeling.

Oh, Betty, what is it makes me experience such tenderness toward you? And if your words affected me so, what would your presence have done?

In truth, her presence could be almost too real sometimes—a tangible result provided by another of those unique advantages of written correspondence, as opposed to phone and email messages. *Scented letters!*

Your letter exudes nostalgia with every breath of thought—perfume, I guess it is—which seems so familiar just now. It nearly embarrassed me in Fisher Library when I was reading it this morning—and I am not easily embarrassed!

While there was indeed a hint of Tweed on the letters (Tweed was the name of a perfume she wore for years!), the true aroma came from the sincerity of their faith, the fullness of their surrender to Christ, the free sharing of deep truths unearthed in their study and meditations, and—to me—the added perspectives it provides on their legacies and personas. I see her vulnerability and questioning, along with her depth of knowledge, character, and conviction. I see his gentler, softer side, along with his brash, ever-onward exuberance and candor. Amid their own distinct yet corresponding challenges, they provided for each other an inspiring interchange of genuine friendship, empathetic understanding, and biblical perspective.

Not all of it was quite so reassuring. There was the time, for instance, when he wondered *"if you were telling the truth in speaking of the thirst God gave for Himself while you were with me. I didn't feel aware of much piety those nights—far more aware of something else."* Then this stinger of a statement: *"If He actually made you hungry for Himself those times, I must say—He is indeed a miracle working God."*

I can just see the expression on her face when she was reading that!

Still, for the most part, she found it refreshing to be dealing with someone who was so *"transparently honest,"* as further evidenced in this next letter from my dad:

December 9

If Betty Howard is a block of ice, Jim Elliot is a hunk of marble. Ice melts ultimately; dissolution in stone is a bit more slow. I know a little something of this yearning for gentle tenderness, dear sister. Still the yearning is more real than the tenderness.

At the midnight-noon of Calvary, the final cry of the Man nobody knows split solid stones. But I have heard that cry—yea, preached it, awed others with it, but my own heart remains in one piece—my eyelids, iron. Not to be moved at the realization of Calvary love is to have a heart more obdurate than those stones—but still I am not moved.

What lovely writing.

Those are what I call *real* love letters.

As the hard frosts and snowfalls of December arrived, so did the memories and recollections of what had happened only a year before: Christmas together at Birdsong, the affectionate name given to the Howard home in western New Jersey.

"Yes, I have recalled several times this week last Xmas time," he wrote, specifically mentioning a night of sledding in nearby Philadelphia.

December 22

We called each other brother and sister every time we'd cross paths—and I recall aching to get you alone, though I'm sure I don't know what I would have done or said had such an occasion arisen. It doesn't take vacation to recall late sessions in the kitchen and front room of Birdsong.

This Christmas, however, would be markedly different. Neither would be going home at all—to their own or the other's. *"It will seem somewhat new to spend Christmas alone,"* my mother wrote. *"At H.D.A. there was much fellowship and celebration, and of course I went home during all four Wheaton years. Wonder where Jim will be spending his vacation?"*

If he'd wanted, he could have spent it at Birdsong again. My grandfather, Philip E. Howard, on campus for trustee meetings at Wheaton in late October, had met Dave and my father for breakfast a couple of times and extended the repeat invitation. He might have taken him up on it, too, had it not required travel money he didn't have, and had it not been for the InterVarsity convention (the first of what's become a once-every-three-years gathering, now called Urbana), scheduled to begin Monday, December 27. It was a rich opportunity for high school and college young adults to hear missionary speakers and possibly hear God's call to the mission field.

My other grandparents in Oregon invited my mother to spend Christmas at their home too, had it been feasible. When she first heard of it in my father's letter of November 1—*"Something else: Mom wonders if you could go to Portland for Xmas"*—he was also planning on being there himself for his brother Bert's wedding, an event which ended up being postponed into January. Two weeks later, even her own mother wrote asking why she hadn't accepted the invitation. *"That would surely seem strange if I should, for he was at our house last Christmas. Little did I know then of his feeling."*

She did, however, receive a letter from Mrs. Elliot on December 1. *"I was really surprised—five pages, telling me about the family, her interest in me, and inviting me to come to Portland for Christmas vacation, which of course I cannot do for lack of time, money, etc."* My father understood but was disappointed. *"I had pictured you in all sorts of places at home—and even yet wonder if you might not be able to route home that way in April."* Maybe so.

In the end, though, she spent a quiet Christmas on the prairies, *"alone with God. Yet not alone at all, in comparison with the loneliness I may be called upon to face in some little missionary hut far afield."*

She expanded on these sober thoughts in her larger journal:

DECEMBER 25: I am alone, in the evening of a strange Christmas Day. My heart seems to be full of unnamed yearnings mingled with praise and at the same time an aching void. How to describe it? Someone in the opposite dormitory is playing "Jesus, Keep Me Near the Cross." [*She and I would later sing this song often when I went to bed.*] It strikes home. For shadowing that joy to the world which the incarnation brought was the inexorable, eternal purpose of Bethlehem—Calvary. Yea, Love is strong as death, His Love led to nothing else.

The world goes on. Nearly 2000 years of hollow gladness, pitiable shells of joy, for those who at this season know nothing of its Christ. And we who know Him—how much do we understand? How much do we live our thanks for God's unspeakable gift? O, if we could know His price! The world is weary—they look and long for some "sunrise," some faint ray of truth. Even all creation groans for His appearing. What will it be when He returns?

O, to see Thee, Beloved—make haste and be Thou like to a roe or a young hart upon the mountains of spices. . . . Accept my grateful thanksgiving, blessed Lord, for meeting me on this, so especially Thy day. Far on the barren prairies I have spoken with Thee, so near, so dear to me. Be Thou ever more so. Amen.

And so ends 1948, with my mother at PBI and my father in Wheaton. Her quiet Christmas, characterized by an "aching void" both for family and for him, made her cry out to God for understanding and peace on *the last day of a very wonderful crisis year in my life.* Meanwhile, my dad's continual longing for the pleased look of his Master, as well as his longing to hear and see more of my mother, kept a thread of conflict running through his thoughts on the future. Yet his thirst to remain staunchly at the Lord's business overcame all.

December 27

What a year, eh? Remember last New Year's Eve? I can't say I recall all the details—maybe you can help me in your next. Seems like last month, though, instead of last year.

If what happens in '49 is as momentous and unexpected as what '48 held for us, we shall look back with ogle-eyed wonder a year from now—half-scared, half-eager to see what '50 will hold. Whatever it is, the confidence of knowing the will of the Most High brings great rest of heart.

And, as they would come to know well, more waiting. More questioning.

I sought song inside
But found a heart of brick unused to singing,
And the words came very slow.
It seemed as if the gentle
Pressure of the Father's finger
Had caused a slight crevasse midst all the hardness,
And there, down deep, there bubbled up a quiet spring.
But still no song,
Just risings which never reached above the surface.
And though there was no singing, somehow there was a
Harmony not often heard among clattering temporalities.
Love was the keynote of the deep spring's song.
A major key that lent fullness to the pool.
Peace and joy chimed softly,
And other little recesses opened in the hardness,
And gentleness, born of the fractures of sorrow,
Flowed unhindered to fill the rising pool.
And as the music played, the brick dissolved,
And my soul was happy,
Though there were still no words.

JIM ELLIOT

Wheels carried her into silence
Out of my reach.
I feared lest darkness, closing round us
Might gain our souls,
And we lose sight
Of real things.
But nay, the sun that ruled our days
Has lit the moon to rule our night.

JIM ELLIOT

Perhaps some future day, Lord, Thy strong hand
Will lead me to the place where I must stand
   Utterly alone.
Alone, O gracious Lover, but for Thee!
I shall be satisfied if I can see
   Jesus only.
I do not know Thy plan for years to come;
My spirit finds in Thee its perfect home,
   Sufficiency.
Lord, all my desire is before Thee now.
Lead on, no matter where, no matter how—
   I trust in Thee.

ELISABETH HOWARD

LOVE'S QUESTIONING

A year that would lead to more questions, concerning both their future missionary work as well as the future of their relationship, at least began with some settled answers—each of which would ultimately come to pass.

"The Lord has done what I asked Him to do for me this week," said my father's note of December 27. It was hand-delivered to my mother in January by way of a female classmate who'd attended the same missions conference in Champaign where my father had been.

> I wanted primarily a peace about going to Peru—or at least into pioneer Indian work—and as I analyze my feelings now, I feel quite at ease about saying that tribes work in South American jungles is the general direction of my missionary purpose. Also, I feel quite certain about Wycliffe—though I don't know yet whether it will be next summer or not.

It would actually be the next. Summer 1950. (Wycliffe, of course, meant the Summer Institute of Linguistics program in Norman, Oklahoma, the same ten-week intensive language study that my mother attended the summer of '48.)

But there was yet another answer he wanted to share—*"one more,"* he said, *"and this paragraph will end"*—though he would soon admit he wrote of it far too carelessly. You might even say heartlessly. Simply this:

> I am quite confident that God wants me to begin jungle work, single. Those are some good-sized issues to get settled finally in a week, but just now I feel quite happy about all three.

Happy?

She entrusted an immediate response to her daily diary. *"How I praise God for this. We both prayed much for this conference, and God met him!"* I have no doubt in my mind, knowing my mother, that she meant every word of that praise. And I'm struck by the contrast between her heart and mine. Perhaps you are too. Whenever I have a hard time understanding a decision made by someone I love, I often demand logic and justifications. How different her response from those of us who would likely have cried out for an immediate and lengthy explanation! She kept her mouth closed for a long while, not giving any kind of written reaction to him during what my father termed *"nearly a three-week siege of silence."*

But underneath, the conflicting heart continued. A day after hearing of how definite he now considered his plans, her inevitable feelings (and questions) began leaking out.

> **JANUARY 5:** A letter came yesterday which forces me to face the Cross anew. I stand now in darkness—the only glimmer of vision into the future is the faint apprehension of a road I do not care to tread. But what have I to which I would cling? Nothing, Lord, nothing. . . .
>
> I guess I should be unaffected by the news received yesterday. After all, was it a surprise? Surely not. Surely it is the way we expected God to lead. Somehow I feel strangely more cast wholly upon Him. Was I not fully trusting before? . . . I had asked earnestly for faith. How else could I have expected to learn it? "I'd rather walk in the dark with God than go alone in the light."

In her intellect she wholly believed in God's sovereign control. She was also not surprised by the likelihood of God's leading my dad this direction. He had never shied away from speaking quite consistently along these lines, even when my mother's parents expressed worry that he was somewhat leading her on, knowing full well his conviction about remaining both single-minded and single-status.

But her heart did vacillate. She knew of her love for him; she knew of his love for her. Even in an intervening letter that came from my dad, he spoke of her love as *"a thing so undeserved."*

January 3

> Oh, Betty, you cannot know me and still desire me. None of us knows each other as we ought, as we are, but I suppose it is well or I would be very lonely. Gripped today with a sense of my unworthiness—of grace, of my family, and of you. How can I call you such things as I do in my prayers and guilty thoughts—how dare I presume?

In his next letter, he sought to define their relationship and declare his feelings even further.

January 8

> Let me tell you a story. When I returned from Birdsong last January, I had fallen—or grown very much in attachment to the girl you know better than anyone else. Because of heart-searching I had had regarding God's use of those who have made themselves eunuchs for the kingdom's sake, I determined that none should know of my affinities with that girl—even though it was evident we should be much together. I can remember confessing to the Lord what I called "my love

for her" and striving daily to forget and swallow hard, though I was aware that I allowed myself liberties one who is earnest about "forgetting" should not enjoy.

In those days of decision to keep silence, it seemed as if I had sealed the course for my whole life—and I must confess, I felt as if I were somewhat of a martyr. There came to me this song:

> Why should I droop in sorrow? Thou art ever by my side!
> Why, trembling, dread the morrow? What ill can e'er betide?
> If I my cross have taken, 'tis but to follow Thee.
> If I scorned, despised, forsaken, naught severs me from Thee!
> (Little Flock hymnbook #16)

And in my hymnbook, there is a blue line drawn with the date as I have indicated. Dearest Betty, I charge you in the name of our Unfailing Friend, do away once and for all with your waverings, bewilderment, and wonder! You have bargained for a cross. Overcome anything in the confidence of your union with Him, so that contemplating trials, enduring persecution, and past all these you may know the blessings of the "joy set before."

"We are the sheep of His pasture. Enter into His gates with thanksgiving and into His courts with praise." And what are sheep doing going into the gate? What is their purpose inside those courts—to bleat melodies and enjoy the company of the flock? No—those sheep were destined for the altar. Their pasture feeding had been for one purpose—to test them and fatten them for bloody sacrifice. Give Him thanks, then, that you have been counted worthy of His altars, and enter into the work with praise.

She found these admissions from him *"a new cause for wondering— he expressed things he had not said before."* Still, in light of the recent pronouncements about his future plans, *"I cannot help but wonder,"* she said, *"what right we have to write at all. Yet I feel no compunction to cease, though I am willing."* Her only certainty in the matter was the assurance to ask, *"Lord, rule my will and affections."* As long as she devotedly maintained this point of surrender, she knew everything was sure of working toward God's desired ends.

When she finally did write back, expressing her reaction to the decisions he said he'd made, my father appeared dumbfounded—if not by what he had said, surely by the way he had said it.

JANUARY 17: Stung with a regret that almost brings me to sobbing as I received Betty's letter of the twelfth. I wrote carelessly that I felt God was leading me singly to the field, and it has touched her far more deeply than I supposed.

O God, how *can* she desire me? Have I played the part so well that she actually thinks me worthy of woman's love? I tremble, Lord, at what surprises she shall know when all secret thoughts of men shall be manifest. Perhaps then she will believe that I am not worth her while.

I'd love to have the actual letter she sent him, the one from January 12 to which he referred. I can only assume it spoke openly of her trust in God's good purposes, but also (based on a line of hers he repeated back) of what she termed *"vague bewilderment."*

January 18

Had I known how my casual statement of going singly to the field would affect you, I seriously doubt I would have been so casual. And even now I wonder if I should put it more softly. My decision was based on seeing a man from central Brazilian jungles who has done a work comparable to the sort I feel exercised for and hearing him tell of the impossibility of marriage in this particular context. That was all—no voices, no scripture, just the settled peace of decision which often comes to the exercised soul.

I will not say God is leading me to a life of celibacy. I only know what I need to know for now—and that is that the Lord does not want me seeking a wife until I have His definite sign. In reality, Bets, that was our understanding when we talked in front of the North Hall after the Lagoon episode.

Oh, I wish you were here sitting on my bed so that I could talk sensibly to you—this sounds so harsh. Betty, if you only knew. I cannot say it as I want to.

Perhaps that's why he couldn't keep himself from continuing to try. As early as the next day, he was already writing her again.

January 19

Had a talk with Dave about you today. . . . He said he had wondered how you would take my "decision" to go to the field unmarried, and when I told him I felt it had upset you, he replied, "I doubt if she will think it worthwhile to keep up a casual, pointless correspondence. Betty loves you."

I don't think I've ever doubted that last, but you never had told me in so many words, and it startled me coming so bluntly from him. Betty, if last night's letter connoted anything different than what I said in this regard about my feeling for you that night at the Lagoon, please discount the letter.

I came home today earnest about finding out my own soul in this matter. Do I really love her, or is this to be a "casual, pointless correspondence"? As honestly as I could, I faced it, and it is answered. I do, and it can never be casual. As to the "point" or end of our corresponding, I have no revelation from God, but this I am settled on: He has led us together in writing, and I have no sign that His will is anything else than that we continue. If such a course leads ultimately to a more bitter renunciation than withdrawal just now should mean, the more bitter way is to be God's way. Remember Marah.

What they shared together, even knowing the strong possibility they would spend their lifetimes apart, was more than worth it, he said.

I would have it no other way, were I to choose again, as I did last May 30, whether or not to tell you my feelings, seeing all the future months of loneliness and struggle. I say I would not have it otherwise even if I never saw you again.

So there you have it—the depth of his love, the depth of his trust. Perhaps he still wasn't sure if he'd succeeded in being able to "say it as I want to," but his heart had come shining through, and my mother received it as bright encouragement. It landed on her heart with refreshing peace and confidence. She said in a series of diary entries:

JANUARY 22: Two letters from Jim tonight, to my great surprise, for he has finals at this time, and I had not expected to hear, though it had been over two weeks. They were beautiful letters. He has been led the very same way I have. God has given me much peace about our correspondence, as well as confidence in His lovingkindness to do what is better for us than we can know.

JANUARY 23: I have never heretofore had such peace about my relationship with Jim—somehow those letters of yesterday left me inexplicably calm and glad, when they should have made things the more difficult perhaps. O, how I thank the Lord for such a one—He only knows how undeserving I am of him.

JANUARY 25: Though my manifold questions are not answered, they have ceased, and when I remember him, there is greater thanksgiving than ever before for what he has done for me and all he means to me now. If our renunciation must come and must therefore be the more bitter because of the continual growth of our friendship, that is God's way. Remember Marah.

My father (in center, on table) with the Foreign Mission Fellowship group at Wheaton.

We can almost feel the sigh of relief from them. God led them both so similarly, one step at a time, each of them convinced they loved each other, wanting to do only what He would want from them. Their correspondence was not just casual; they believed He had a purpose for the true fellowship they shared with each other.

The average person in this situation would find it tempting to talk more specifically of marriage. Young people, my mother told me, often think they need to discuss every issue thoroughly. But it simply isn't necessary, and it wasn't necessary for my parents. The most important thing is to know Who's in charge. This was their foremost desire, to be obedient to the Captain of their salvation.

Two important things are worth mentioning at this point concerning their deep hunger for knowing the will of God, both in specific matters as well as in general principles for life.

First, his comment about waiting for a "definite sign" was indicative of their attitude in prayer and their sensitivity in all things spiritual. They expected God's Spirit to show them what to do and when to do it. In everything.

Here in January 1949, for example, my mother found herself wrestling with another substantial decision. Having not been able to make an introductory trip to meet my father's family in Portland during the Christmas holiday, he'd encouraged her to consider routing her return trip home through Oregon later in the year. As usual, she sought God's will only.

> **JANUARY 27:** Yesterday as I prayed about going to Portland, I almost asked that a little money be sent tomorrow to be for a sign. Knowing that I had not yet fully come to the place of "crucified desire" and not feeling sure it might be God's will for me to go, I refrained from asking.
>
> But A.C. [one of my parents' favorite writers, Amy Carmichael] speaks of our Lord's hearing our wishes, sometimes, and lovingly giving the thing wished for. Tonight $1 came from Aunt Anne—first time in my life.

What a blessed encouragement! For if going to visit the Elliots was truly the will of God, He would surely provide the funds for it, right?—just as He would provide answers for all the other questions she faced. So on Sunday, January 30, she asked God for another sign: *"Asked that He would send money for trip home before folks do."*

Imagine what arrived on Monday:

> **JANUARY 31:** This evening word came from Mother that she will finance a trip home via Portland and California.

Admittedly, the fact that the money came from her mother *"perplexed"* her a bit, she said, since she'd asked God that it would arrive from someone else besides her parents. Yet here again, He answers according to His good pleasure and was merciful in His provision, no matter the source.

I think His kindness toward her childlike prayer is so tender. *"Lord, I am but a little child,"* she wrote at the time, *"and know not how to go out or come in."* She was somewhat hesitant to ask something so temporal of Him because she was afraid her own fleshly desire to be with my dad might outweigh her overriding prayer about constantly dying to self. But nothing outweighed being in moment-by-moment alignment with God and His purposes.

This reminds me of a principle that both Brother Lawrence and Fénelon taught which comforted her many years later—how having the intent alone to know and do God's will is pleasing to the Father, and He honors those who come to Him as a little child wanting to follow His bidding. He knows how much we fail, just as He knows our forgetfulness, but He's given us His promised Holy Spirit to empower us to seek and do His will.

This call to be still and wait on Him for guidance was very real in my parents' hearts, and I'm thankful for their example of spending at least an hour each day (often more) doing nothing else. Every letter and journal entry of theirs reveals this longing to be serious about prayer and sincerely seek God's face. Therefore, I'm not surprised at all to read of my father's continual watching for some kind of confirmation or direction before feeling free to pursue marriage.

In fact, this observation leads to my second point, more general in nature: their devotion to Scripture. They focused on Scripture always, of course, but the opportunity for my father to travel home at the end of January for his brother Bert's wedding reinvigorated his sense of dependence on and confidence in the Word.

Much of this rededication came from spending some rich, significant time with his father (my grandfather, Fred Elliot) during those brief days, focusing on the subject of yielding to God's will. His dad inspired and led him in all knowledge of Scripture, and it was certainly the case in this instance. Here's how he related these parental lessons in a letter sent to my mother from Portland.

February 1

Had a discussion with Dad last night on the fullness of the Spirit. He says mere "yielding" is insufficient. Plenty of those who have presented themselves are not filled, because both filling and consecration are lifelong processes which involve *knowledge*. I must know what God's will is before I can submit to it.

Thus, progressively as the soul is enlightened *in the Word* (Dad's stress is here), he comes to know what is demanded of him and can choose. Submission without a clear definition of what one submits to is empty mockery and accounts for so many dissatisfied, yielded souls. All filling is conditioned by the Word.

"By the Word." If I could express my one hope for compiling this book, my prayer is that these entries of theirs would call us to search faithfully for God in His Word. And upon discovering His unchanging, faithful, merciful, and loving character, I pray we would be more fully moved in obedience to Him that we too might leave a lasting legacy of faith as my parents did.

But such a life of faith is not without its struggles, as my mother wrote in her diary one day in February: *"Today I found severe temptation (and I yielded) to laxity in prayer and Bible study. Oh, I am conscious more than ever of my desperate need to know the Word—my only offensive weapon—but how very difficult it is for me to concentrate upon that only and wait upon God."*

Yet it was their mutual love for God and for each other as expressed in their letters that kept them challenged in their devotion to the Word. In the following letter from my dad we see a mingling of his love for the Bible, as well as his love for *"a girl"* who drank from it often!

February 7

My day has been one of genuine joy. Woke this morning to Jeremiah 33 and this promise, "The days come when I shall perform that good word which I have spoken."... And tonight from Psalm 87, "All my springs are in thee." (You used that verse in Ancient History devotions last year. Remember? I do, for I was watching for a girl who had found such a Source.)

Not long afterward she remarked in her diary:

FEBRUARY 21: Seven pages from J. tonight. It never ceases to amaze—he spoke of how he was impressed with the phrase "Quicken me according to Thy word" in Psalm 119. That is the very phrase which has run in my mind for several days! We both have been studying the psalms, unknown to the other.

Here is his response to *her* letter, in which she must have shared her delight that they were both thinking along the same lines spiritually:

February 22

Yes, we were both studying Psalm 119 last week.... "Quicken me according to Thy word" occurs several times and seems to be about what Dad said of powerful life in the Spirit. "Quickening" can only come from the Spirit (Jn. 6:63; 1 Cor. 15:45) and that according to the Word.

Now I've known in my own experience a quickening that is as the false fire of Nadab and Abihu—that which does not come as a direct commandment from the Lord (Lev. 10:1).... Often I've been possessed of a fiery idea which I've preached with impassioned force but which did not profit because it was sparked by fire other than the Word gives. It is all well and good to tell others to abide in Christ—but remember Christ did not leave it in that flowery generality. "Abide in Me, and My words abide in you . . . if you keep My commandments ye shall abide."

So then, Bets, be not discouraged if you do not feel full power—that comes when the entire counsel of God's will has dominated us for a lifetime. "Those that be planted . . . shall still bring forth fruit in old age" (Ps. 92:13–14).

How differently young men and women's relationships would grow if the Word of God, rather than changing emotion, were their source for guidance and godliness in an ever-shifting culture. My parents saw God's Word as the North Star, fixed and always pointing the way to freedom and joy.

Sometime during this period of late winter, my mother received a letter from home, in which her mother shared *"some of her thoughts re: Jim and I. She feels strongly that I should confess my love for him, and that we should see more of one another."* I can imagine for most college-age singles, such a timely and desirable word coming unsolicited from an authority source, as from a parent, would have rung with unquestioned confirmation. It would have seemed like God's outright endorsement and permission to act on it. And yet she laid it immediately before the searchlight of the Word, particularly before some passages from Philippians 3, which had been the focus of her previous day's reading from Amy Carmichael's *Though the Mountains Shake.*

> **FEBRUARY 28:** I besought the Lord to know whither my friendship with Jim was really "conformable unto His death" *[verse 10]* . . . My prayer was that at any cost God would teach us how the Cross applies here. He teaches through His Word, so I read on in the passage quoted (Phil. 3).
>
> The principle of death and resurrection is brought out. This gave new light. And then, to my question, "Lord, have we so much as begun to know the Cross? How long must it be, if not, that we go on in an uncrucified relationship? Was last summer's experience of any profit?" came the gentle answer: "Not as though I had already attained . . . the *one thing* I do . . ." *[from verses 12–13].*
>
> "Lord, have I missed Thy signs anywhere? Has my imagination deceived me? I do most surely long to do Thy will." *[Her answer, from verse 15]*—"Let us therefore, as many as be perfect, be thus minded, and if in anything ye be otherwise minded, God shall reveal even this unto you."
>
> "I thank Thee, Lord, for this strong assurance. Now how shall I walk? How 'follow after'?" *[verse 12, answered by verse 16]*—"Nevertheless, whereto we have already attained, let us walk by the same rule, let us mind the same thing."
>
> After this word, the peace of God which passeth all understanding kept my mind and heart through Christ Jesus.

Always going to the Word, letting God guide her thinking and responses. This was her model and pattern. His too.

Basically then, the way for her to love my father best and most appropriately—most biblically, she determined—was by more and more loving the Lord Jesus. *"It is to love Him just for Himself, yes, but it is to love when we are in total darkness and He has turned His back upon us. It is to love transcendently, in total detachment, abandoned, drowned, as it were, in that vast sea of the love of God."*

Throughout the 1970s and '80s, as she began to speak to greater numbers of people, she frequently meditated on this biblical principle of love for God and total trust in Him. Many times when I would ask to go hear her speak, she would tell me she spoke on the same thing everywhere she went, that her message of the cross being the gateway to joy never changed. God was always saying to her in every experience, *Will you trust Me in this too?* Whether unwitting or not, she was heeding those final words my father spoke to her before he was killed by the Aucas—*"Teach the believers, Darling, teach the believers."* And this she did to countless numbers of those who have read her books and heard her speak with that redoubtable conviction that we are to trust God even when He seems the most silent.

As far back as the winter of 1949—far beyond, in fact—I see her doing it already. Led by the Spirit. Led by the Word.

> After I got into bed last night, I simply confessed to the Lord all my desires and hopes of seeing Jim this spring, all my despicable hesitation in obeying Him for this summer. But He was tender and understanding, reassuring me that since I had asked Him to lead me, He would do just that and I could trust Him, for His "wisdom is unerring and we are fools and blind." Lord, Thou knowest all things. Thou knowest that I love Thee.

Surprisingly, her "hopes of seeing Jim in the spring" revolved around, of all places, Florida. The family was planning an Easter reunion of sorts at Hampden DuBose Academy, the boarding school near Orlando where my mother's younger sister Ginny was currently enrolled. And on a thirty-five-below-zero Thursday at PBI in mid-January, the prospect of visiting Florida in the spring couldn't have sounded better. Or could it?

> Letter from Dave tells of his desire to take Jim to H.D.A. this Easter vacation. Immediately my thoughts fly to those scenes, picturing us there together, and I wonder if anything so perfect (it seems) could come true.

But in the end, neither Uncle Dave *nor* my dad went to Florida, pressed by the need to study for exams. Nor did my mother—for reasons that would deeply trouble her heart throughout the first two weeks of March and which colored the direction of her entire summer.

She was determined to spend the upcoming summer doing something in preparation for her life's calling in missions. Though she continued to be prayerfully leaning toward a future in Africa, experiences over the past several months had opened her eyes to the needs in South America. *"Brazil is the largest unevangelized field in the world. There are Indian tribes far up near the headwaters of the Amazon who have never seen a white face or heard the name of Jesus."* Besides, PBI graduates working in Africa already numbered a hundred or more. *"How I would love to do some truly pioneer work. . . . In Africa (S.I.M.'s field) no mission station is a day's journey from the next."* Still, for the time being, her application remained in force with SIM, though no word had yet been forthcoming on the immediate opportunities awaiting her.

On a single day in March, however, she felt her decision abruptly made.

MARCH 3: Talked with Miss Phillips this p.m. about Jim, the S.I.M., etc., and she advised me strongly to withdraw my application and go out in Canadian S.S. Mission this summer.

Miss Phillips was like a spiritual guide/director, who counseled students according to PBI's expectations. Her word was well nigh a command. True, the idea of remaining in Canada on this kind of assignment (visiting families and inviting children to Sunday school) was not pleasant to my mother, yet she felt she should comply in order to grow and become more acclimated to missions work.

But the personal cost was great indeed.

The next morning she *"woke at five and could not refrain from a few tears at the thought of having to tell Mother that I will not see her for at least six months."* She worried how to break the news, especially after receiving a letter from home a few days later, *"with all kinds of plans for my going to Florida—she is so sweet, joyfully anticipating all the happiness I would have there!"* Imagine the dreaded waiting for her disappointing letter to reach New Jersey, then for her mother's response to be written and make it all the way back up to Alberta. It wouldn't arrive for nearly ten days more, though thankfully with the sweet relief that *"she understood and rejoiced!"*

But, of course, there was the added sadness of being kept longer from my dad, whom she likewise wouldn't be able to see for at least six months. He, too, however, answered back with encouraging words:

March 19

Think of the privilege, Bets, to be made ministers of this message of reconciliation! What should be our wonder and praise that we be known as those "approved of God to be entrusted with the gospel" (1 Thess. 2:4). Throw all you have into it for the Lord's sake, and I will pray that His hand shall yield abundant increase. Faithfulness in that which is least brings:

1. "Well done" . . . praise
2. "Be ruler over ten cities" . . . honor
3. "Enter into the joy of the Lord" . . . glory (1 Pet. 1:7)

Your faith is on trial! He comes quickly, His reward *with* Himself. Indeed, what need we beside Himself?

And so she went from grappling with levels of sadness and trepidation about the upcoming summer to being able to say with surrendered confidence, *"The Lord has granted wonderful joy in the contemplation of Canadian S.S. Mission."*

Something else that my father said, however, further down in his letter, *"left me cold."*

SPRING

A day before this March 19 letter had arrived from Wheaton, my mother had written in her diary, *"I have been praying earnestly that the Lord will guide Jim as to what he is to do for the summer. Wycliffe or British Guiana?"* The "British Guiana" option (the South American country now known simply as Guyana, situated along the northern coast) had entered the equation while he was home to attend my Uncle Bert's wedding. In his letter of February 1, he had said,

> [My father] is seriously considering a trip to British Guiana where some local brethren from here are establishing a lumbering business. There are about thirty small, English-speaking assemblies and a British missionary who needs a furlough but has no teacher to take his place. Dad may fit in, as he is both millwright and teacher.
>
> If he goes this summer, he wants me to go with him, and if God so allows it, I would drop Wycliffe plans in a minute. We've had some happy times together, and I cannot estimate what enrichment a few months working with him might do for me, practically and spiritually.

The possibility remained viable throughout the spring.

> I sometimes think that three months of real, practical experiences would be better for me just now than three more in the books. . . . As you are praying for me, do think of this, Bets, as I feel much constrained to go.

So, on March 22 she was praying for my dad, saying, *"Oh, how I long to see him—if I could just talk with him for ten minutes! Have not had a letter since March 5."* Then on March 23, his letter arrived. And it struck her as though a whole other person had written it. Here's a little of what it said:

> The Record will inform you of the high old time we had on Reverse Day this year. Arlene Swanson—onetime moll of the great Dubbins Norbeck . . . invited me as evening guest. Charming time, I must say. I dated her for a wrestling banquet the first year here—mostly for her appearance, I think.

He went on to add other names of guys she knew (including her brother Dave), listed alongside the girls who'd asked them out on "Reverse Day," a Wheaton tradition from a simpler time when gender roles were reversed for a single day.

Crazy antics at "Senior Sneak."

———

Reverse Day.

———

The whole outfit looked like a gang of fugitives from New England attics. Lace, bustles, hoop skirts, sun bonnets, top hats, spats, cases, pipes, complete with three-week beards—wow. (Yes, I had three weeks' growth—it was red, believe it or not, and I still maintain a moustache, but public opinion is getting unbearable.) . . .

Seniors had a party following with pie throwing and water dunking in the baptistery of lower chapel . . . the wildest, most raucous, absurd set of loveable hoodlums I have ever known.

And rather than signing off with his more customary "Lovingly" or "Tenderly," he closed with the relatively generic, impersonal "Sincerely."

Scenes like the ones he described in this letter were the beginning of what my father dubbed his "Renaissance"—a time at the end of his senior year when he threw off all the shackles he'd placed upon himself in order to prove to the class that he was freed from legalism. He'd seen how Paul in his New Testament letters had taught of our need to be conformed to Christ and not to rules. As a result, my dad set out to create a *"disruption of my previously pious 'code of don'ts' that used to motivate much of my action."*

He'd concluded that some of the rigorous standards he held over the course of three college years had essentially turned into *"a legal bondage that was developing into critical prayers"* and *"a general attitude of spiritual superiority. Missionary candidacy became my standard for spirituality, and my fellowship was limited to those of that sphere."* He felt as if his *"good, consecrated attitudes"* and *"priggish little laws"* had alienated him from many of the students, and he therefore decided to start acting a little more *"normal"*—normal to his natural self, and normal to those in the rest of the student body who perhaps thought he was just a tad too spiritual. Before the spring was out, his Renaissance would contribute to a Senior Sneak unlike any other in Wheaton's history—the weekend when seniors "sneak" away for a time of fun without letting the juniors know. The antics were crazy and different enough that even he would later admit, *"My pendulum swung too far."*

But my mother, upon hearing the first waves of these shenanigans shared with such glee in letters from both my dad and her brother Dave, became very upset—confounded at him as well as worried for him.

MARCH 23: The foolishness and clowning left me cold. Jim actually led FMF dressed up in an outrageous '49er outfit. I had been faced with eternity today, reading Revelation 15 and 16 and A.C. *Things As They Are*—and could not but weep my heart out at the disappointment all this has been. His letter was strangely empty. O, has he kept his promise to be honest? Have I been a drain on him?

The next day brought no relief. In fact, she sat down and wrote a letter not only to him—a brief, curt one apparently—but also to their friend Bill Cathers, *"asking him to pray and, if he deems wise, to exhort the brother along the line of Titus 2:6."*

Not J., not Jim, but "the brother."

This notable change in tone reveals how hard she'd taken the news of my dad's Renaissance, feeling a greater distance from him spiritually than the 1,500 miles that separated them physically. *"Have no idea how he will receive it,"* she said, *"or if he will understand at all."*

She waited to see.

Less than a week later, March 28, she presumed that *"Bill and Jim probably received my letters today."* It obviously had its effect. My dad's lengthy, seven-page return letter was dated, not surprisingly, the same day.

March 28

I think it very difficult to explain why I wrote as I did last week—but remember, the fact that I change my tone does not indicate another "Jim" who signs his name "Jim," prefixed by "Sincerely" rather than by "Tenderly" or something other. The "Jim" is the same, and if you are to love him, you must love him, whether he be sincere, tender, or sarcastic. I live with him all the time and can assure you (as I've tried to maintain from the beginning, but am only now getting convincing), you do not know all of him yet—and he has far more deplorable aspects than signing "Sincerely."

What I wrote was from my heart—I was sincere. You must accept me that way, or leave me alone. I cannot give you anything but what I am, and if now you see for the first time what I really am, and you choose to defer, you do only as I feared you might do when you found out, and will incidentally fulfill prophecies I voiced to you from the beginning.

Continuing on, he broached a theme that would reappear in several letters throughout the year—a struggle within his own heart, not knowing if he was even capable of love.

To explain psychologically what I was thinking when I wrote, which so changed my tone, is impossible. I can only attempt an apology.

I don't remember whether I ever said this to you or not, but I have been very conscious of it since breaking up with Wilma *[a childhood sweetheart]*. The very fact that I began going with her at fourteen and wouldn't look at another girl for four years warned me that my affections go out very easily and are jealously tenacious.

Recognizing this fact, that I would lose my heart at every turn if I didn't discipline myself carefully, I withdrew from dating and even close association with girls whom I knew attracted me, or to whom I was somehow attractive.

Love, like his own heart, remained mysterious to him. In later letters he would mention how he *"loved too easily and not deeply enough,"* noticing how his love tended to fluctuate through *"cycles of warmth and cold,"* how he was *"impetuous in nature,"* how he could *"swing to extremes which make me either too nice or too brutal."* If my mother felt him untrue and unsteady, it's because he felt untrue and unsteady himself.

I'm surprised at how bold, brash, and uninhibited he could be, especially after knowing the constancy of my mother's love. Yet he wanted to be real with her, admitting his love was capable of waning and waxing. I love him for it, because I also am often too bold with my words, but the Holy Spirit tempers everything.

He then ended with a dismissive flourish:

If you don't like the tone of this letter, send it back, and I'll re-edit another time. Just now, I feel as if this little rift is tremendously inconsequential, and I can *sincerely* sign my letters . . .

Lovingly, Jim

"*Should all be revoked?*" my mother was already wondering, even before this letter arrived and as her school term was wrapping up. "*Just now there is a great longing to be home. . . . Still much exercised about the matter spoken of Tuesday.*" Yet gathering herself in the Word and in prayer, she summarized the following thoughts in her journal, spiritually bracing herself for whatever was coming next.

MARCH 30: Lord, this night I do earnestly ask of Thee:

1. Grace to perform without hesitation Thy whole will.
2. Discernment, that I may know a self-imposed Cross when I am faced therewith.
3. Restfulness and unquestioning love when Thou art silent and the way is not clear.
4. The will to do away immediately and thoroughly with all that is only fleshly entanglement, weak indecision, or "earth-born cloud."
5. Holy Ghost wisdom to know the difference.

Therefore, when his letter came, she was eager to hear his heart but was also secure in wanting God's will alone. She thought he was being ridiculously obtuse, the way he was excusing his behavior and his lack of reticence, but she rested in the clear truth of Scripture, that God would never leave her and would always be her refuge.

APRIL 1: I have thought of several ways of replying to Jim's letter. I could quite successfully answer some of his arguments and include some choice retorts. But, oh, how petty and foolish! . . . What wonderful rest there is, I remind myself, that this whole business is not mine to hold or secure, but His all.

APRIL 2: I have asked a definite thing of the Lord—that He will either give perfect place re: J., or make it unmistakably clear that I am to forsake the whole affair. And as I leave this in His hands, I ask for power to center all my thoughts on Christ, uninstructed by a concern which is not mine at all.

What's interesting, as I hold his letters here in my hand—not just the one of March 28, but several others that follow (April 18, April 25)—are little comments my mother scribbled in the margin as she read. For example, where he mentions "*one or two girls*" he'd dated in the past, as well as one or two others in his current class who were wanting him to go to spring functions, she wrote things like, "*Who are these? Did you accept? Why all this? Should I be interested? Or jealous?"* Or where he says, *"My recently acquired moustache brought a well-signed petition to have it removed from several 'attentive' girls,"* she remarked, *"You were duly flattered by this?"*

> April 25 — 1949
> Wheaton
>
> You left out one concept in your poem which I have only now discovered at the very core of your love — craft — an excellent trait, even in love, if it is not too obvious. However am I to believe you — or when know that you are really being honest? No less than three times in your letter of April 11 you refer to your attempts "to be wholly transparent." Then, in today's you write of "impure motives" in a sentence following one of those three references in that letter. Please — Betty. how am I to take these? One letter reads with a tone of marked surprise, "Why, Jim, you write as if you assumed there were something between us — a shadow of a claim we have on one another." Jim is simple so he bites — hard — and responds in appreciation of your "ease & naivete." And the next letter returns with poet-talk of deep-seated, inevitable, powerful heart-passion ... a passion of love which I interpret, because of its dynamic nature, to have a very real "claim" upon me. Does "this go" with a sentence written in one of your October letters, "Never have I felt any claim of any sort whatever on you"? No claims? Then why all this stir... what's the difference if you have "no claims"? To me that poem might have been an acrostic spelling POSSESSION. She talks of holding a loose grasp and then of "never-turning, ever deepening, warm, powerful, fathomless devotion." Stuff! There is no such thing as possessionless love. And now you ask

Notice my mother's penciled commentary in the margins of my father's letter.

Here are a few others, with her commentary in brackets:

On re-reading, I see that I have made myself beautifully obscure. *[no, only too clear]* I can't seem to put on paper in a few—or many—words what I really want to say. Incidentally, that was why I said "I wish you were near" in my last, for I sense that the constancy of my warmth of affection is determined by proximity. *[so that's all we have?]*

This tendency to love quickly, combined with a natural desire for flattery and a yen for intimacy with anyone and all, will doubtless make me a "problem-husband." *[thought you weren't getting married]* Last week it made me a "difficult boyfriend." *[who calls you that?]*

I cannot help but tell you—and for the last time, I hope—my love is not constant. The brute is too much with me. "Our loves as humans must be nourished by response"—quoted from your letter of February 13. *[taken out of context—not referring to our particular love]*

Are not your letters something like mine—at times vivid with a subtle passion, at other times not committal to the point of dullness? *[this only because I turn off my heart at such times!]*

Please—Betty, how am I to take this? One letter reads with a tone of marked surprise, "why, Jim, you write as if you assumed there were something between us—a shadow of a claim we have on one another." Jim is so simple, he bites—hard—and responds in appreciation of your "ease and naiveté." And the next letter returns with poet-talk of deep-seated, inevitable, powerful heart-passion—a passion of love which I interpret because of its dynamic nature to have a very real "claim" upon me. Does this go with a sentence written in one of your October letters: "Never have I felt any claim of any sort whatever on you"? No claims? Then why all this stir? What's the difference if you have "no claims"? *[No, we have no claim. If it is selfless, love has no "rights." Had I a claim, I should have said, "all, or nothing at all."]*

I want you to take me up on anything I have written—condemn, criticize, question until you're satisfied. Before God my heart is pure, *[that to me is ALL that matters]* and I will tell you all I can if it will help. Somehow I sense that your brevity has been far more loquacious than my ramblings.

I don't wish to paint my father in too unfavorable a light for things we observe here in his tone and behavior. He was young, like all of us were young. He was flawed, like all of us are flawed. Nor was my mother innocent of displaying pride and immaturity in some of her reactions. But my dad was also aware enough to realize he didn't like a lot of what he was seeing in himself during this time. One night, for instance, while at the campus snack bar . . .

APRIL 6: Decided to follow Peg Rodgers and Arlene Swanson home . . . and decided to have a party at [one of the girls' dormitories]. . . . We all went over for pop, ice cream, potato chips, stories, folk dancing, and cutting up generally. Wish my heart were more condemned. I am worse than a social animal; I'm a social fiend—I love to be with a gang.

Not long afterward:

APRIL 23: Dorm party with Florence Kelsy tonight. Got to cutting up again. Oh, when will I ever mature? How I despise myself when I get home here in quiet and think of the noise I've made.

It led him to a prayerful, penitent place:

Fellowship with the gang is enticing fun. But I feel carried away tonight with soul enticement. Nothing bad, just nothing good. . . .

Son of God, purger of the inner parts, discerner of my sittings down, my risings, wilt Thou hallow this soul of mine? The choice is mine, You say? Ah, yes, the choice is mine.

Reflecting on one of these nights, in fact, he composed the following poem:

> God of the strangest ways,
> Who silent watches Thy son
> While away rollicking days
> Playing 'til day is done,
> A son who, sobered at silence,
> Loves the sound of a joke
> And drowning the surging quiet
> Seeks consolation in noise,
> How *can* Thy love remain fervent,
> Father of this careless child?
> How be still in Thine ardor,
> A stillness which hankers me wild?
> Son of sound-ridden mind,
> Question no more of "How?"
> Silent or saucy, crowded or lone,
> My love rests on Thee now.

Meanwhile in Canada, my mother was seeking rest in the Lord as well, dealing with all this unexpected drama as she prepared for her summer mission work.

APRIL 22: Last night, after receiving the first letter in three weeks from Jim, my soul was nearly torn apart. Oh, I cannot write of all it meant, but my heart was desperately wrung. My soul cried out, "Why? How can it be?"

Then I remembered. I had prayed, *"No matter how"*—it is only for my Lord to choose my cross. Can He not give grace and enable me to go in peace? I have asked to be broken, to be dealt with in any way, only that I might be like Jesus, fit to be His witness. "Though He slay me, yet will I trust Him."

And the Lord Himself stood by me. He spoke peace. He held me in His everlasting arms and loved me with His everlasting love. He reminded me of the "weight of glory" ahead and gently rebuked me for looking at myself and my own selfish interest.

Apparently, this sense of surrendered peace was evident in the next letter she wrote. Perhaps her words were still pointed enough to sting him a little, but they must also have hinted at a softening. His response didn't carry now the same fiery, defensive flavor that had dominated his most recent letters of the spring.

May 3

All right, all right, put up the buckler and I'll lay down the sword. Yours of this morning with what I've been getting from above the last week has sufficiently beaten my spears into pruning hooks and left me with a plow handle cuddled into my fist rather than a sword held.

Her letter must also have included a refusal to send him any more of her poems, since he'd been hard on the last one. *"Never did I dream the only man I ever sent this poem to,"* she'd written in one of those personal sidebars, *"would tear it to pieces, laugh, mock! But somehow I love this reaction, thrive on it!"* He playfully answered:

If you refuse to send me poems, I'll get mad again and then you'll be sorry. The one of March 23 lies quite intact in my drawer—a thing of beauty and a joy forever—in spite of itself! I haven't got time to write anything, as I hope to finish a seminar term paper on Thucydides tonight—more with you later, young lady.

He wasn't yet in full agreement with everything she might have been challenging him about, nor with all she'd interpreted from what he'd been saying. But even in disagreeing, he now said he did it *"smilingly so."* He was *"quite game"* to restore peace between them. So as she left PBI on Monday, May 9, traveling 125 miles north to the tiny community of Patience, Alberta, at least she was warmed to some degree by this thaw in relations.

Patience, a rustic village near Jasper National Park, home of the Athabasca Glacier, was the site of her summer work with the Canadian Sunday School Mission (CSSM). Her job, as I've mentioned, primarily involved going out visiting families and inviting their children to Sunday school. She lived in a drafty, cheaply built trailer on a local farm, traveling many miles by bicycle each day, both to find meeting locations as well as entice people to come. *"It is a new and strange experience for me,"* she wrote, *"and I feel keenly my tremendous need of a mighty Fortress."*

First day:

> **MAY 10:** Awoke at 4:30 with the farm fowl. Made a small breakfast and cleaned up my little home. In the hot stillness of the afternoon, felt desolate, helpless, lonely, discouraged. Was helped by Deut. 1, especially verses 3, 17, 29, 30. And this from Hudson Taylor: "It is not what we set ourselves to do that really tells in blessing, so much as what He is doing through us when we least expect it, if only we are in abiding fellowship with Him." Walked with children in the woods.

And so she worked and witnessed. Here are a few more of her struggles through that spring:

> **MAY 12:** Visited two homes this p.m.—one Christian, not sure of the other. Both consented to send children to S.S. Wept as I rode along the road on my bike.

> **MAY 13:** Letters from Phyl, home, and Jim last night. I do not think I have ever been so overwhelmed with my own helplessness as today.

> **MAY 16:** Rode my bike 15-1/2 miles today, up to Conjuring Lake. Had to see three men about using the school for S.S. on Saturday afternoons, since that is a more convenient time. Finally got permission. The wind was terrific, coming from NW, so that I could scarcely pedal. Had to walk part of the way—came home to my dark little house, cold and very tired. "No reward save that of knowing that I do Thy will."

The families she saw were mostly very poor and extremely uneducated, having had no Christian influence. The men gambled and drank; the women gossiped and used foul language, tending to the farms without many of the men taking their responsibility seriously. There were bright spots, like the Brinks family who would often invite her to their home for Sunday dinner. But most of her days were purely hard work, trying to serve people who couldn't have cared less for the gospel.

Thankfully, letters arrived from home and elsewhere with comforting regularity. The bundle she received on Saturday, May 21, came with exciting but homesick news: *"Letters from Mother, Mrs. Elliot. The Elliots are going to Jim's graduation—Mother is hoping to go, too* [my Uncle Dave was graduating as well] *so perhaps they will have a chance to meet. I do hope so."*

Her next letter from my dad was quite newsy as well.

the street. He always wheezes on that harp when walking—as do I and Billy occasionally, too. Well it turned out to be Bill. He said he felt constrained of the Spirit to come here and talk to me... You guessed it, it was about your letter. Bob came in after awhile and we talked til late. One of those frank, heartening talks like we used to have so often. I was glad for it, tho' it will make this letter a couple of days late.

Bill Cathers, one of my dad's closest friends, coming to talk about
the letter my mother had sent, asking him to "exhort the brother."
Bob Weeber, another good friend and roommate, joined them.

May 26

You must be experiencing some close companionship with the Savior being so very much alone these days. I had read [the letter you sent] to the family, which your mother typed and sent around. Dave gave it to me last week, and so I was prepared for the note coming from "Patience." I confess fears for you at times, but then I know I'm not supposed to act like an old hen, so I manage to find rest in commending you to His keeping—in the very real sense of that word. . . .

It's Saturday night now. Just as I got to this spot in the letter, I heard what I thought sounded like my roommate coming down the street. He always wheezes on that harp when walking—as do I and Billy occasionally too. Well, it turned out to be Bill. He said he felt constrained of the Spirit to come here and talk to me. You guessed it—it was about your letter. . . . He read your letter to me, and we exercised our hearts generally about the "Renaissance.". . .

Others have come to me with such reports, and I have been tremendously helped by their frank tolerance and love. I have had to make several apologies about my overdoing this freedom on the Sneak, and kids have been most forgiving. I cannot tell you what this all means, but it is no small cause for praise on my part to our God who so works in the strangest circumstances to accomplish His will. Your prayers have done more than you now imagine. Continue for me these next two weeks—He who hears in secret will reward thee openly, my sister.

That must have felt good to hear.

The Renaissance was officially over.

I got my draft classification today—1A. They give you ten days to appeal, so I wrote asking for reconsideration. They try to sift as many COs [*conscientious objectors*] through as they can, because it's quite an ordeal to go through all the investigation. . . .

I think I told you that Mother and Dad and Jane [*his little sister*] are coming for graduation. Bert and Colleen got away about two weeks ago [*to Peru*], and Mom and Dad went to California to see them off. Mother is on crutches but is slowly losing weight and quitting work, so I feel she is on the road to recovery. . . .

You would have enjoyed the Sneak Communion. We had a huge glass flagon and an oversized loaf of bread. After a few opening remarks, we began to pray and sing familiar hymns. McCully [*Ed McCully, one of the five men later killed by the Aucas*] broke the bread and gave thanks for the cup. It took a long time for the single cup and plate to get around, so we sang as it was passed. . . . Hardly a soul that wasn't moved to worship. Oh, why cannot the Spirit lead us more often thus? How long shall we trust in man and programming to accomplish His work in men's souls? Lord, let me learn quickly.

Love, Jim

I feel sure this letter brought a smile to her face, especially because it came at a time when she was expecting another dose of welcome relief, as she'd mentioned in her diary:

MAY 27: It will surely be nice when Fay comes—supposedly on Monday.

Fay Frederickson was a friend from PBI whom she'd anticipated coming to join her. *"She rolled up here in a huge truck, in which she had begged a ride,"* my mother wrote on May 30. *"It is surely good to have someone to talk with and share the wonderful things God has been doing for me. Oh, how I pray that this trailer will be a foretaste of heaven in unity with Christ."*

Actually, she knew any "unity in Christ" would take a lot of prayer to make happen. As she'd written earlier to her mother, she expected this pairing with Fay to *"be a good test and trial of our faith, and grace! Well, we leave it in the Lord's hands. . . . Fay is a lot like me in many ways"*—primarily meaning strong-minded—*"and I can see that it would take all the grace the Lord would supply to keep us 'knit together in love.'"*

And how.

By the next day, things were already going south.

MAY 31: This a.m. Fay burst into a tirade, saying no one had ever treated her this way before and she didn't intend to allow me to. "If you can't be nice to me,

Betty, well that's just all." Oh, my heart was broken. I was stunned. Lord, take over completely.

Two days later:

JUNE 2: Command from Fay this a.m., "Betty, don't talk to me like that." I honestly have no idea when she will take what I say as an affront. Oh, Lord—I beseech Thee to make me loving and lovable.

Next day:

JUNE 3: This afternoon as we rode along, Fay began questioning whether or not the heathen were lost. I gave her a few scriptures to show that they were, and said I thought that such questions were dangerous. "Oh, fiddle!" she said, "Betty Howard, you act like I didn't have a brain in my head!" With this she went into a tirade about my attitude. We stopped and talked and prayed. O God! Give me love and grace to meet this new and very hard thing.

Part of God's answer to her prayer for "love" came by way of the mail. *"Letter from J. tonight in answer to mine of this past Tuesday. . . . J's letter such a help in light of what I have been experiencing re: Fay. He spoke of loving not to 'be a help' or 'do' anything."* More broadly, it said:

June 9

One of my Renaissance experiences was to get among kids who were on a different spiritual level than my own and to enjoy fellowship. I found a very subtle snare in doing so. I sought their fellowship in order that I might minister to them—be a help, you know, to these weaker ones. What a rebuke came when I sensed my real motive—that I might minister.

Love hacks right at this, for love refuses to parade itself. I learned to recognize no "spiritual plains," but simply to love, purely, in every group. Trying to "be a help" even has a smell of good works in it, for it is not pure. Our motive is only to *be*—do nothing, know nothing, act nothing—just to be a sinful bit of flesh, born of a Father's love.

Then you see, Beloved, there can be no defeat. . . . Where knowledge tends to swell me up, or the despair of the flesh would make me shrivel up, the love of Christ "holds me together." Any little occasion then has meaning, if only I can love while it passes. Nothing—even this three-day wait till graduation—is lost.

Oh, yes—graduation. His next letter included some apt descriptions from this event, largely in family terms.

June 16

Good to see your folks again last weekend and get in a little fellowship—particularly with your dad on Sunday afternoon. . . . I feel like your mother is disappointed in me—not that she said anything or even overtly gave sign of offense, but I sense she is not too happy that our relationship has not been more clearly defined.

She and Dave and Phil and Marg were on Willeston porch as a gang of us came in from swimming last Saturday. I was with Lyla Teasdale and (I don't know whether I read this from my own psychological set or whether it actually occurred), but I felt your mother looked hurt. She and Mother had a good talk Sunday too, but I haven't been subtle enough to worm out of Mom just what was under fire. . . .

Your mother told me a little about Fay and something of what you had written home. May God Himself be both "strength" and "song" to you, Bets. Be not afraid, and I shall pray.

SUMMER

EH (JUNE 24): Today I am faced with three of the most formidable problems that have ever come to me. All circumstances look black, all appearances seem impossible, my heart is cast down with my own sinfulness, my soul is disquieted. I fear the future, I fear what God will require of me, I wonder how He can ever begin to work through me when I am such a useless person.

I don't know specifically the "three problems" to which my mother was referring. Did they involve her future? My father? Surely the ongoing issue with Fay was one. She wrote this journal entry in Patience, having just come back from a few days at PBI where she'd gone seeking help on how to handle things—*"not to lay blame on Fay,"* of course, but to ask prayer and counsel in how to be *"better fitted"* for working through it. Returning to the trailer again, to the conflict, was certainly difficult.

One thing I do know, however. This overwhelming, all-at-once combination of problems had left her with a deep sense of loneliness: *"desperately lonely and terribly discouraged."* Loneliness was something she suffered often in life—not only here in the summer of '49 and in upcoming seasons, but certainly after my dad was killed, then later after my stepfather died. Even in her public life, when so many admired her, I remember how she could feel so very alone. She wrote in another journal, "Loneliness is a kind of death." To read the following entry from late June, we can tell she was deep in its throes.

JUNE 24: Satan is sifting me. Oh, that my faith fail not! The task at hand is a great one—I must bring the message on Sunday night—and these other three things crowd in upon my mind, as well as the consciousness of my own powerlessness in prayer and my own faithlessness. O wretched man that I am!

Lord, there it all is. I spread it before Thee, for to whom else can I go? Thou art my Father, tender, loving, ever-faithful, and all-wise. Take me just where I am, dear Lord, and lift me up. O Thou art the same; Thou art not affected by my changefulness!

I thank Thee for this from George Müller: "Therefore we should confide in Him, the unchanging one, and in our darkest moments never lose sight of the fact that He is still and ever will be the 'living' God! Be assured, if you walk with Him, and look to Him, and expect from Him, He will never fail you. One who has known the Lord for a long life write this to you for your encouragement, that He has never failed."

If discouragement ever grasps you, compelling you to think of the future as black with sadness, loneliness, and uncertainty, these are the prayers that you (and I) must lift to Almighty God—depending on His presence, His ever-loving mercy, and His promises.

My father prayed for her as she went through this tough time and as she wondered about God's plan for her. I'm sure many times she wished she could operate with the same self-assurance and courage he seemed to have . . . though it often did get him into trouble, when he spoke and acted before thinking.

Witness his letter of June 25. He was on his way west with his parents by then. They'd stopped for a week or so in Billings, Montana, where leaders from one of the local Brethren assemblies had asked his father to help calm a disturbance. The break in action gave my dad time to sit back and catch my mother up on things, since *"I cannot recall just when I last gave account of my doings,"* he said. Here is one such "doing" . . .

June 25

The night before commencement we had a mock banquet at the Lighthouse—must have been thirty or so of us. I gave a 29-cent "diamond" to [a girl she knew] and started the rumor that we were engaged. The whole thing seemed so improbable that we had a time making anyone believe it—though some were fooled, and they sang "congratulations" as we were lining up to march Monday morning.

Oh, how my mother's heart must have quaked! And no sooner had she absorbed *this* charade than he reported on another.

In Sioux City, I saw Priscilla Hoy—remember her? She told me that one of my FMF friends had told her that you and I were engaged. That bothers me, Betty, for I fear lest some should be stumbled at our rather (should I say careless?) companionship.

Pretending to be engaged to another girl, then being upset that a story was circulating saying he was engaged to my mother? No wonder she wrote in her diary:

JUNE 28: Letters from Mother, Mrs. Cunningham, Van, and Jim. All three of the first were blessed. I don't know what to think of the last. O God! Show me what to do.

Sounds like having "three problems" was just a starter.

My parents didn't write much that summer; my mother not at all. Following his letters of June 9, 16, and 25, my dad's next was from July 19—*"fourth since I wrote him,"* she said—which began with these words:

Been some time since I heard from you and got to wondering if maybe a letter had gotten lost or something. Maybe, too, thought you figured it was my turn to write. I forgot what my last postscript was. Anyhow, I want you to know that you haven't slipped from my thoughts and prayers.

There hadn't been time for her to write, or for that matter, time to be lonely. She spent her first week of July as a CSSM camp counselor, overseeing a cabin of *"eleven lively girls, ages 10–15."* She led devotions and lifeguarded by day, led special music in worship service each night. Vacation Bible School followed the next week, spilling into several weeks of heavy rains and thick mud that kept her and her bicycle mired closer to home.

But those downpours forced her to spend more time on the farm where their trailer was located, giving her a chance to see God really at work. Mr. Keller, father of the family, was an abusive, hard-drinking man, negligent toward his wife and children, when not being actively upsetting. Lots of arguing and fighting. But one night, after Mrs. Keller had threatened again to leave him, my mother and Mr. Keller talked *"for three hours."*

JULY 12: He said he is not saved. I pleaded with him to trust the Lord. Said he was too far gone to be saved. He lay down in the pasture and sobbed and sobbed. O God! O my God!

The next day she wrote:

JULY 13: Never have I been through anything like last night. I, too, cried and cried. O, the misery of this world! O that he might be saved. I have never seen a man in such agony. I just longed to put my arm around him—would that I had been a man then!

Before the summer was out, she saw him attend a closing Friday night VBS service, where his children were among those recognized. *"Mr. and Mrs. Keller both came—praise the Lord. He had tears in his eyes. The children did very well. O, may there be treasure in heaven!"* She said he stopped drinking and was *"reading his Bible incessantly. How can he help but be saved? O God! For Jesus' sake, save that man! . . . Oh, shall I meet him at Jesus' feet?"*

This encourages me, how God knows what we need. Reading back through her diary of that summer, I know how frequently she grappled with concern about her future, even to the point of doubting her readiness for the mission field.

> **JUNE 30:** It has been on my mind so often lately concerning what I should do next year. Last year I feared that I should miss God's way. This year I fear what He may ask me to do, in a sense.

> **JULY 19:** What to do next year is a problem which weighs considerably on my mind these days. As I wake up, it is my first thought. "Commit thy way . . ."

I recall, too, a sobering experience she related from late in the spring, when still at PBI:

> Tonight Mr. Maxwell asked all to stand who had never won a soul. I was among them. Oh, the shame of it! Twelve years since I was saved, not *one* soul, to my knowledge. The Lord is coming. What shall I have to offer? Shall I empty-handed be? Yes, I think I shall. Oh God, give grace to win them—how, by prayer; this summer, by contact. It was a most shameful exposure for me before my friends.

And yet here, amid all the "problems" she was facing, God was working everywhere around her and through her, saving young children through her Sunday school efforts. He even used her mere presence on this farm, where He had providentially placed her, to show what He can do through available, surrendered hearts like hers, and like yours and mine, I pray. When you hear my mother at twenty-two saying she feels "useless" and "fearful" and "ashamed," recall what she went on to become in life by God's grace and power. Think what our Father is capable of doing, encouraging you to press into Him, as she did, for His glory.

Truly, "Eye has not seen, nor ear heard, nor have entered into the heart of man the things which God has prepared for those who love Him" (1 Cor. 2:9 NKJV).

The friction between Fay and herself never really cooled, only for a day or two here and there. Yet my mother didn't hold any resentment. Not only did she forgive her but quickly repented of her own sharp words as well, asking God to help her be less judgmental and not as easily provoked. I love that she taught me this principle: once we've confessed, He cleanses us immediately and we can go on in faith, knowing our Redeemer lives for us and through us.

She heard from my dad again on August 1. He had spent the majority of his summer doing odd jobs with his father. The mission trip to British Guiana never materialized, and he'd told her *"I have had to reconcile myself to staying in the U.S. until I've proved myself in the work here. The brethren would have it no other way."* It was a waiting time for him, accentuated by his waiting to hear from her.

August 1

This July 27 letter of yours is the first I've had from you in about thirty-nine days. Forty, they tell me, is the number of testing. I'm not exactly "griped," but believe me, you sure had me wondering for a while. I have a sneaking suspicion this is another phase of your "war of nerves" to feel me out or something. You pulled a similar stunt in telling me you were beginning a correspondence with some PBI brother at the beginning of the year . . . recall? Most effective, I assure you.

Maybe, though, the waiting might soon be over.

When Mom heard you only had five weeks left in CSSM work, she renewed her vigor in pressing you an invitation to Portland when you are through. I echo an "amen" and shall pray again that the Lord will make it possible should it be found in His will.

I can only imagine the thrill she felt at even the remote possibility of seeing him soon, of visiting him in his home environment. It's interesting also to note the status of his overall plans, spoken in the next paragraph:

We have just gotten word that the blueprints are finished on the house I've been waiting to begin with Dad. I suppose I could have gone to Wycliffe—but the Lord had it in His mind that I come home, and it has indeed been His way. I could not have asked for a more restful, recuperative season than this month at home has been.

She longed to be there too, as she wrote on August 13. *"How wonderful it would be to go to Portland and visit him. In his last letter he pressed an invitation. But it is all in God's hands,"* she said, *"and He would have to work a miracle to provide the way."*

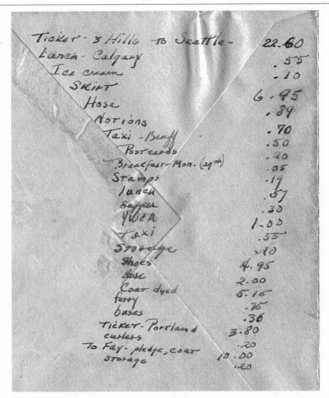

Costs for my mother's trip to Portland, written on the back
of my dad's envelope to her in Alberta.

The miracle needed to happen within two weeks.

AUGUST 15: I am completely in the dark as to what I am to do when I leave here. The Lord is able to lead me without error—only pray that I may be "in the way." In so many ways I would like to visit Portland. Bunny *[a friend from PBI]* said I might possibly ride back with her folks to Vancouver, Wash., if they bring her back to school. I hardly dare think of it. "He shall give thee the desires of thine heart." Lord, choose my desires.

AUGUST 16: Letter from Bunny saying her folks will not be driving back to Vancouver, which means I cannot go to Portland that way.

AUGUST 17: There are few things harder to bear than uncertainty—but He holds my hand, and I am certain of Him.

AUGUST 18: Mother sent me $100 with which to go to Portland. I do not at all covet this for myself, but want to spend it only for the glory of God. "Guide me, O Thou great Jehovah."

Then, this. After all she'd been through with her summer roommate, wouldn't it be a miracle for God to work out her travel plans this way?

AUGUST 19: Fay wants me to ride by bus as far as Seattle with her, spend a day or so there, and then go on to Portland. . . . It seems quite clear now that God is leading me to go. . . . I wish I would receive another invitation from Mrs. Elliot, though she has asked me recently by proxy.

AUGUST 20: Bless the Lord—received a letter from Mrs. Elliot imploring me to come, and saying how nice it would be if I could make it Labor Day weekend. That is the very time I had written to say I would come! The Lord has led so wonderfully and is working out details.

He did it! He "worked a miracle."
Less than a week later, she was on her way.

AUGUST 25: Spent the a.m. packing and cleaning up trailer. It was pathetic to see poor Mr. K. bid me goodbye. He has been kind and polite, yet he tried to apologize for anything "bad" he had said. . . . The kids all cried and cried when we left. So did I! Came to Edmonton in creamery truck. Dinner in Chinese restaurant. We are staying at Y.W.C.A.

Hitching a ride on a milk truck? Lodging in a room at the Y? How soft we've become in what we expect of our travel accommodations.
One more letter came—an excited one—from my father, for the road:

"Fantastic," as you say, is hardly the term for the Lord granting us this time—another from His bundle of Good Things which He has opened to us in Christ. Blessed be God—"Great are the works of Jehovah, sought out of all that delight in them" (Ps. 111:2).

And that is what I find myself doing during empty moments these days—seeking out His works. For I look ahead to your coming as a cup of joy tempered with trembling—not knowing what it is God does as you head for Three Hills tonight actually coming this direction. My prayers, I fear, are rather quivering, undefined surges as I entreat the Lord for guidance (and protection!) in regard to your coming—one week from tomorrow, if God's schedule is as you have suggested.

Again, prepare to be amazed at the 1949 standard for communication and travel arrangements:

When you get in Portland, have whoever is bringing you to town ship you C.O.D. to 7272 with haste. Our telephone is LI. 2104. Call if any one wants directions or if you should come via bus or train. I insist that you stay at least 2 weeks - preferably a month, as I understand you have no fall plans as yet. My family -particularly one member - is most anxious to see you.

"When you get in Portland." Excited letter from
my dad, regarding my mother's trip to see him.

I have just written a friend in Seattle to try to get a ride for you here. For, you see, you arrive the day our Labor Day conference begins in Portland, and some Seattle folk always drive down. He will contact you Friday indicating whether he has succeeded in getting a ride or not.

When you get in Portland, have whoever is bringing you to town ship you C.O.D. to 7272 with haste. *[C.O.D. is an olden mailing term, meaning "cash on delivery." 7272 was my father's shorthand for his home address.]* Our telephone is LI-2104. *[Again, an almost prehistoric language for phone exchanges.]* Call if anyone wants directions or if you should come via bus or train. I insist that you stay at least two weeks—preferably a month, as I understand you have no fall plans as yet. My family—particularly one member—is most anxious to see you. . . . "Behold, this is our God; we have waited for Him" (Isa. 25:9).

Quietly, Jim

Across the Canadian prairie she and Fay rode by bus, to the Rockies—"*I can't believe I'm here!*"—into British Columbia and on to the Frederickson house. The few days they insisted she stay with them must have seemed an eternity. She did call my dad on Wednesday morning, August 31, *"shaking all over—but had to find out if everything was OK to come. His voice sounded so deep and manly. I can hardly wait to see him."*

Two days later, on Friday evening, she was finally there.

They hadn't seen each other in almost a year.

SEPTEMBER 2: I am actually in Portland, Oregon—name that has always sent chills up my spine. Got here about 7:15. Jim met me at the depot. He has gained weight since I saw him—but, oh, it is wonderful to be with him. Family is all so nice and kind to me. Meeting tonight at Gospel Hall.

Yes, life truly orbited around their assembly gatherings and street meetings. Visiting company was expected to trail along. My father even preached at their downtown meeting that Sunday night—"*powerfully, earnestly,*" she said. She was truly getting to see him in his element. But, of course, neither could hardly wait for the one-on-one, face-to-face conversations they'd been imagining in their heads for months.

The following mixture of their journals tells of it, beginning with Labor Day:

EH (SEPTEMBER 5): After afternoon meeting, Jim took me to Mt. Tabor Park where we sat and talked for several hours. He says he still does not know whether God wants him to be married. "We rest on Thee."

JE (SEPTEMBER 6): Very intimate with Betty in speaking of our relation—Sunday on Rocky Butte, Monday on Mount Tabor. Startled to find ourselves talking about marriage so offhandedly last eve. I noticed she was pained in hearing of some of the social aspects of this spring's Renaissance. I felt sorry myself for much of it. Of the heart Jeremiah said, "Who can know it?" (17:9).

EH (SEPTEMBER 6): Haven't gotten to bed before 1 a.m. any night, so slept quite late. Helped Mrs. Elliot with washing, ate lunch, then Jim took me canoeing on Columbia River. Landed on an island, spent till dark reading over our letters of the past year. Many laughs, and explanations. Moon rose, red and full, over the perfectly still water. Wonderful time of prayer together there on the beach, for one another, others.

JE (SEPTEMBER 7): Much perplexed and vacant in soul from long conversation and some prayer with Betty last evening on the Columbia. . . . Stirred to poesy but no proper words, except to say that I wonder why God hangs onto me. . . . Oh, blessed be His name, that He leaves me not but haunts me to follow on, drawing me upward away from earth, with promises of freedom from all entanglements and bondage.

EH (SEPTEMBER 7): Talked to Mrs. Elliot quite a while this a.m. She is not too favorably impressed, I fear! Thinks I need to let myself out more—"express" myself. O Christ, be Thou my life! Jim and I walked up on Mt. Tabor and finished reading our letters. . . . Sang and played piano together this evening, then went to a little stone seat on the hillside. Had prayer together. The issue of to marry or not to marry at all . . . ?

JE (SEPTEMBER 9): Swimming yesterday with Betts. Prayer meeting last eve was warming. Betty, on reading these pages, exhorts me to confidence rather than the despairing attitude she senses is prevalent. . . . Oh, how much has been God's giving! How free and rich! But I fail to apprehend for lack of faith. Betty charges me with this daily.

EH (SEPTEMBER 9): Although it was cloudy and drizzling, we set out in faith for the Pacific Ocean! Went first to Manzanita Beach and hiked for four hours over huge rocks to Neahkahnie Head. Then drove to Short Sand and took beautiful path through fir forest to beach. Swam in ocean, ice cold. Explored rocks, found lovely sea anemones and deep cove. Seemed like the sort of thing I have dreamed of, but never imagined possible. Built a fire and watched sunset.

JE (SEPTEMBER 10): Blessed of God yesterday in fellowship with Betts at the beach. Stirred to thanksgiving for her. Heard the Lord's voice in 1 Corinthians 3 this morning. "Take heed how you build" (v. 10). God's garden takes tending that is careful; His building, work that is honorable and worthy of the Foundation.

EH (SEPTEMBER 12): One of the most wonderful days of my life! A *perfect* day. We drove to Timberline Lodge on Mt. Hood, took Timberline Trail five miles to Paradise Park—beautiful Alpine Meadow, flowers galore, crystal stream tumbling over rocks. Crossed glaciers to get there. Spent three hours reveling in scenery together. Had supper over an open fire in a lovely forest camp. Oh, it was indescribable.

And then, too soon, it was over.

EH (SEPTEMBER 13): My last day at Elliots. . . . Oh, what peace He has given us! Jim took me to get my ticket this afternoon and bought me a whole lot of fruit and turkey for sandwiches on the trip! He took me to the bus at 7:30. I cried all the way down to the station. It seems harder to leave every time.

JE (SEPTEMBER 13): She has been gone just one hour. What thunders of feeling I have known in that short time. I could not read the neon lights as I turned away from the bus, and somehow couldn't face the people as they passed me. My lip kept contorting, and I could not seem to look natural without twisting tight together both my lips. How terrible I sound sobbing. Not like myself at all, but uncontrolled grating, animal sounds—and tears that trickled over my jaw and to my throat. Leaving her is terrible.

He continued working to process his feelings for a long while afterward, writing even more about it, not only on this day but into the days that followed. Poems, hymns, tortured emotions, a day-by-day recounting of events. He hurt for her (because of the assurances he couldn't give her), just as he hurt for himself (because of his stifled desires for touch and embrace). He even began to question *"how much of my path in God's way is self-determined and how much God-determined for me."* Was all this rugged conviction about singleness, this denial of marriage, a needless restriction he was placing on himself?

I hope you'll read his own thoughts yourself from this season in his life, as found in *The Journals of Jim Elliot*. His words are poignant, powerful. But his actual letter to my mother, I publish here for the first time. It was written and mailed to her as she slowly, haphazardly journeyed home by bus via California, the American Southwest, Denver, Kansas City, the Ohio Valley, and finally into Philadelphia, more than a week after leaving Oregon.

Her mother and younger brother Thomas were there to meet her at the station. *("I hardly recognized Thomas.")* Stunning news greeted her too: *"I was electrified by news of Dave's engagement to Phyl Gibson, my last year's roommate at P.B.I.,"* a fresh happening from just that week. How exciting. *"How can it be . . ."* In addition, a letter was waiting from the head of Hampden DuBose Academy, asking her to consider coming down to teach public speaking for the year.

How exciting also, she thought, when this letter from my dad arrived for her the next morning. He must not have been able to wait before putting his thoughts and memories into words and sending them. I haven't room to reprint all of it, but will quote from it at length.

Get ready.

September 19

This hour a week ago we were driving home from the forest camp, very conscious that it was to be our last night together. Seems ages ago now, that we ate those beans from one can in the dark there. I remember sounding very absurd as we left the place, saying something about your "militant morality"—and hearing you say something about being thankful—and then the long drive in silence and tears.

"There have been some tense days since then, I want you to know," he continued. The tension had been demonstrated mostly by everyone's awkward, obvious silence. No one wanted to talk to him about her. *"Dad and I poured a concrete basement for a brother that day, and I was glad the mixer kept conversation at a minimum, as I didn't feel like talking somehow."* The tension, the avoidance, was palpable. It was killing him.

Not until everyone started talking did he realize he hadn't yet begun to feel the pain.

I was startled as I was tamping the concrete into forms to have my thoughts broken into by the brother for whom we worked, saying, "I'll bet you felt bad to have your girl (excuse the expression, I'm quoting) leave, huh?" I agreed and he went on to compare you to his wife—"different looking . . . hard to get to know . . . grows on you . . ." I know he saw you only once at the meeting, and I never even introduced him to you!

I was morbid silent around the house for three days. Couldn't get rid of the feeling that came over me listening to myself sob aloud Tuesday night after you left. I will tell you of this later. It is a little too fresh just now to discuss casually. Bothered, too, by the fact that no one had mentioned you. Mother and I had some talk Thursday afternoon. . . .

What I am going to write now, I do not know whether I should say. It seems almost like betraying my folks before an outsider, but I am going ahead—painfully for us both—trusting that this will eventually be for your good. Expect the worst.

Well might you weep in thinking of the poor impressions you make. They could not have been worse here. Mother seriously concluded that inviting you here was "a flop." Her original intention to have you when I was not here would have better suited her. Her word "obsession" comes from this feature of your visit. She thinks you should have spent more time with and shown more interest in the family and not quite so much in me. (She doesn't reckon of our slim three weeks' contact.) She thinks you uncommunicative, possessed of a "meek and quiet spirit," but a very poor maker of friends, and hence a poor prospective missionary. She cites as instances one time at the conference when you were alone and she tried to warm up a "conversation." Your retort that you didn't mind being alone "froze her inside."

Hazel Berney, Ray the giant's wife, records a similar instance when she tried to make friendly advances, and you coolly made her feel "as if she wasn't necessary." She thinks you did not enter into the home life here by way of housework and canning, and I remember one remark you made which I knew at the time would bring judgment upon you. Mom asked, "Do you sew?" Your response, "Not if I can help it—Mother has always done it." Hence you are to Mother still an immature "institution child" who sadly lacks any sense of home responsibility and who possesses little domestic adaptability. . . .

She described Dad's attitude toward you as "ferocious." He opened up Saturday as we drove to Eugene for a weekend's meetings 125 miles south of here. He described three stages in his feelings of your week's stay. (1) When he saw you first, he was abashed. "I see nothing in her that would appeal to me—no face, no form, a spindly dreamer who has cleverly set her cap for you, and you have bitten." He confesses that he wondered such things as, "Is this the product of all my prayers and labors to get him successfully through unstable youth? Is this my son's ideal?" He calls this his "feeling bad" stage, sort of remorseful that I had developed such poor tastes and been so hoodwinked. (2) His "mad stage" made him sore at me for not using my common sense in seeing right through you. (3) His "Abraham stage" . . . he heard the Lord say as He did to Abraham, "Are you willing to let all your hopes and prayers for Jim be sacrificed My way?"

After some struggle he came to the first peace he had had ever since you came. Though he can't understand our attraction for a minute, it is as a thing committed. We are "in the Lord's hands and I will not lay a finger to what He would do." He is quiet now and open. I wish I could say the same for Mom. She digs me every chance she gets to be cautious and wait—as we both will change.

Jane was looking for a spiritual whirlwind in you. She never saw you reading your Bible and taking any lead in spiritual converse. Registered effect: disappointment. . . . Ruby's was the only favorable impression: "She has lots on the ball. I admire her for not putting on a show for us." Bob: "There is no hurry. When you can't get along without her, it will be plenty of time to marry." Auntie Frost: "These quiet people feel more deeply than those of us who say so much."

I think the violent reaction of Dad and Mother springs mostly from the parent-feeling we discussed which involves pride in one's own progeny and zealous seeking for its best. I must tell you how I had to control myself from strenuously opposing their opinions. I don't know why I should have to defend you against such charges as uncommunicativeness. I have borne most of it in silence, telling only what I *know* you to be with me. I don't understand how you could have made such a universally horrible impression. Dad shook his head as he contrasted you with Bunny. I have tried to put them all in your shoes coming here, and they understood somewhat. I will not defend you further. *You,* knowing their present bias toward you, must do the rest.

One can hardly imagine a worse reception. And my dad, who also could be less than tactful in his criticism, didn't help by saying things to her, like, *"I don't write now as if they were all wrong and that you must be excused from all these charges."* Still, he was resolved in his love for her. And he hoped (and prayed) she would not consider this the end of the relationship they had begun.

Do you still believe God led you here? I do. I say without reserve or emendation. Further, I love you now by faith. What God is doing, I cannot say, but this I know: He has led us together.

> This came between sunset + moonrise— Tuesday after you left, on the side hill where we had prayer + reading.
>
> Wheels carried her into silence ~out of my reach.
> I feared lest darkness, closing round
> Might gam our souls, and we
> Lose sight of real things
> But nay, the sun that ruled our days
> Has lit The moon to rule our night.
>
> And this today— sponsored by your words in the 'ocean cave', "Pinch me."
> The bellow of the tide
> From the Blue expanding wide
> Beyond the roughness of the rocks of Falcon Head,
> Funnelled hugely, vainly tried   Which numbed us silent. We quaffed
> To rend our cavern, where it died   Each other's good
> In quiet cool of Sandy bed   But, not knowing then to breed,
> Beneath our feet.   Spoke nonsense, Laughed
>   The sea to silence'.
> We shivered as we stood   The touch of naked shoulder
> Found no words to fit the mood   As each felt His own the colder →
>
> Melted other touch things into dream
> False, every fact I told her
> As that overhanging boulder.
> All things that were did only seem
> As we knew have +
>
> — Simply, Jim

My dad's poems describing their time at the beach and then her departure.

He couldn't see all the way ahead, but he asked her to consider making a deal with him, as they grappled with the now unpleasant aftermath of these precious few days they'd enjoyed together.

> As I stood watching you weep on the bus—(forgive me for not obeying your request that I leave, but I couldn't go somehow, knowing you were still to be seen)—Teasdale's "What shall I give my love" kept sounding deep within. "How can I give her silence—lifelong?" Every time we have parted, it has been harder. I do not want to part with you on this basis again.
>
> So I have prayed, quaveringly, that the Lord would not let us see one another again without giving us some assurance of His ultimate goal in relation to us. This parting "into undefined silence" is terrible. So, though we might want to be together again this fall, I think it would be better if we prayed—"Lord, show us some word of assurance—" Oh, I can't say it. Do you understand?

Yet would anyone really expect her to go forward on such terms?

AUTUMN

Naturally, it took her a few days to give her wounded feelings time to heal.

SEPTEMBER 22: A letter came from Jim this morning, telling me of the terrible impressions I had left with his family. I could hardly believe what I read, and was utterly crushed by it. Oh, truly I am an unimprovable, helpless case. *Help,* Lord. The implication of this opposition from his folks may be greater than we realize now. And the question comes to me, "Am I standing between him and his parents? If so, have I any right to?"

SEPTEMBER 23: Why must there be these long periods of such far-distant separation? This is awful. 3,000 miles of possibility for misunderstanding. How to answer Jim's letter? I feel that his folks have been unfair in some judgments of me—and very unkind to talk to Jim as they have. Poor Jim—he has to put up with so much.

SEPTEMBER 24: Keep mulling over Jim's letter—have not answered it yet. Don't know how. He says he is praying that the Lord will give us some "word of assurance," take us from this "dwelling in silence."... Continue to enlighten us, Lord.

She finally took to writing it over the weekend then mailed it on Tuesday. Finally, too, (for us!) we reach the point where her original letters become available to us at last. No more guessing at her words or reading between the lines.

My father, when he received it, wouldn't need to guess either.

Before seeking to respond to the unfavorable reviews from her visit, she decided to begin first on a different subject entirely—something she'd discovered on the way home—*"something else that has been a burden."*

September 27

It's been a long two weeks since that Tuesday when "wheels carried her into silence . . ." for me, at any rate. And a very strange five days since the arrival of your letter. But before I dare begin on that, there is something else that has been a burden. In Pasadena I met several Wheaton kids. In the course of our reminiscences, talk of this past year and the effects of the "Renaissance" came up. Until that time I had had only my own somewhat warped view, gleaned from letters while I was thousands of miles removed from the scene, and then your own fairly logical but very honest presentation of the situation. I had heard nothing from those who "looked on." You will remember our talk that afternoon on Mt. Tabor—you said I didn't look too happy. I was imagining, then, what effect your behavior must have had on others who looked to you as an example. I found, during my visit to Pasadena, that my worst imaginations were exceeded.

I can conclude from this what I had previously feared might be true—your so-called "liberty" was nothing short of license. Now it is true that you have admitted overstepping your bounds, but there seemed to be little true repentance proportionate to the harm that was actually done. I was told that Dr. Brooks felt that you and some of the others would have much to regret if you ever looked back seriously over the year. Mr. Stafford was utterly confounded—said he had never dreamed of such things going on at Wheaton, and had certainly never seen a Sneak to compare with '49. He said that up until this year he had thought a lot of Dave Howard, but if he was going out under IVCF, they needn't expect another cent of his money. There were other things. I can't begin to list them.

But Jim, I must say these things because I feel them strongly, and am not yet at rest about your attitude toward the whole business. I thought we would get it all hashed out and over with while I was there, and I guess we did what could be done, but I didn't "look too happy," and frankly was not. To be *very* specific, for example, it confounded me how anyone who defines the significance of a kiss as you once did to me, could carry on in such an utterly frivolous vein, *joking* about it, a thing so sacred. I refer to the incident on the Sneak, of course. Jim, it doesn't hang together. You can't behave like that one minute, and turn around the next and say you love in purity. Can you? I am still not agreed that your "enlargement" or "broadening" was valid.

It seems now, after what I've heard, that you acted contrary to scriptural principles. "Hast thou faith? Have it to thyself before God," and not to the extent that you (virtually) send a dozen people to hell in order to win two for the kingdom. That is putting it strongly, but it illustrates the point. Numbers were really hurt, and stumbled. Remember, the church has the greatest influence on the world when it is the farthest removed from it. And the same applies to you individually.

Perhaps you wonder why I said none of these things before. It was only, as I said, that I did not have the complete picture before, and I hesitated to judge you or draw conclusions. Why do I write this now? It is over with and done—it cannot be recalled. But do you see the seriousness of it? Or do you feel I have made too much of it? You said that too many people had had you up on a pedestal, and you were determined to show them the truth. All right—so, whereas they thought of you as Christ-like (which I know to be a fact in some cases), you act like the devil to prove you're not so "spiritual." You proved it for sure.

Jim, my brother, (I call you that now, for it is the only basis on which I dare talk to you this way)—what think ye? Am I unfair, harsh, unduly concerned? A good deal of my thinking on the 98-hour bus trip from L.A. was occupied with this, and I seemed to have no peace, so I determined to write you of it as soon as I reached home. Little did I know then of what issues awaited me in your letter.

She now pivoted to her main reason for writing.

I fully expected that you would be hearing "the worst" of me after I left, but I did not expect a detailed account of the criticisms. Perhaps I should say of *such* criticisms, for they were not the ones I had prophesied to myself. But do not fear that you "betrayed" your folks—I sensed their feeling toward me after I had been there only a day or so. In fact, I sensed it very keenly, and was at a loss to know what to do.

Perhaps you remember my suggesting on Wednesday that I thought I should leave on Friday? You snorted and said I was staying until Tuesday or Wednesday, at least. Well, that was the reason I felt I should go, though I couldn't say anything to you about it. Your mother said several things to me at different times that left little room for speculation on my part as to how she felt. But I was not sharp enough to analyze the reasons, and your letter was full of things that amazed me. I mean, the things I expected her to criticize didn't seem to be noticed, and things I had meant entirely the other way were used against me.

For example, she wanted me to enter in more to the housework—that morning when I helped her do the laundry, she kept telling me to go out and talk to you. You were picking plums, and I wanted to stay and help her and have a chance to talk. But she pressed me, and said, "I want you to spend as much time as you can with Jimmy. You won't have much time anyway, and you kids must have a lot to talk over." So I finally went out, but found you up in a tree with your dad, so went back into the laundry, only to be reproached for not staying with you. I began to feel that she would *prefer* I didn't help her. The same feeling came over me when I went in to help Lou Berney with the dishes that Sunday. Your mother was there, and accused me of stealing her job.

Jim, I only tell you these things because I was so confused and hurt when I got your letter, and I want you to understand. Please, please don't mention them to your mom, for I don't mean them as accusations, and I do sincerely love her and did so want to please her. I do not for a minute blame her for the awful "flop" I made of my visit. The things I said in my thank-you note were perfectly honest, for she was most gracious and thoughtful of me, especially in view of how she felt about me—I don't see how she could put herself out for me as she did.

The criticisms you made of me are just. I am greatly in need of openness in meeting new friends. But, oh, Jim—if you knew the discouragement that swept over me as I realized this so poignantly at your house, for it had seemed that God had won so many battles for me on this very line this summer. And had they now all been lost? Yes, apparently. Yet He had given me such wonderful entrance into hearts and such overpowering love for the people of Patience—why did not His love have free course in Portland? This question burns in me. Only the verses you quoted in your letter bring me comfort, for I confess anger at some points, and sorrowfulness to the point of tears every time I read it over. My sorrow is more for you, Jim, than for myself. Why should this happen to you? The anger is with myself for behaving as I did, unconscious though it was; with your folks for saying such things to you.

Forgive me, I am being brutally honest, but I cannot imagine their putting you through such an ordeal. I think if my folks *hated* a person they would not say such things about him to one who loved him, supposedly. Moreover, I cannot imagine your folks talking that way about anyone. The accusations which you quoted to me are things which you said you hoped would help me in the end. Look them over, Jim. Not one is capable of being remedied. Furthermore, none of the specific examples you gave had any direct bearing on the basic problem we discussed that night on the hill. Perhaps they have in your mind, but if you could see the letter again, perhaps you'd see what I mean.

You said it is up to me to do the rest. There is nothing I can do. I have sealed my image in their minds, even if I do improve, which by the grace of God I have purposed to do. Letters would accomplish nothing now—I am the faker who writes high-sounding letters and is a different person in actuality. I don't expect your mother will be writing me anymore anyway. Gladly would I "do the rest" if there were anything I could do.

Pray for me, Jim—and continue to be devastatingly honest, even if it crushes me flatter than I am now! You are right that I cannot be excused, and the Lord alone is able to do anything with this mess. Oh what if I didn't have *Him*? "To whom, Lord, could we come save unto Thee?"

She closed with a few odds-and-ends.

As to your question about whether we dare pray for some word of assurance—it gave me joy that God had led you this way, for He had led me the same way this summer, and I have prayed to be taken from this "Silence" if it could be His will. I can see now why He could not answer this prayer yet. But I think we need not fear to pray this way, in spite of our frailty. Lean hard upon Him—He will let none of our steps slide. You ask if I understand—yes, Jim, I understand. You need explain no further.

I liked the last two lines of your hillside poem—"The sun that ruled our days has lit the moon to rule our night." You are learning the thing I have been praying for you, and for myself. The other poem was an example of the cadence of our thoughts—so much so that it came as a surprise.

Just before I got home, Dr. DuBose called me from Florida to ask me to come down to teach speech. I wrote him on Monday, saying I would be glad to fill in second semester if he wished, but that I was certain the Lord wanted me here at home for a few months. There is already so much to do, I find it hard to sit down and write letters. (It's now 12:45 a.m.) I am making a dress and shirt, believe it or not. I do sew, and enjoy it, but have done very little for some time, since mother loves to sew, and would rather I did the housework and left her free to sew. (This I was preparing to say when your mom was called to the telephone or something—I too knew it would bring judgment if I left it where it was at the time!) Also I have been assigned the job of painting the porch and a room inside; baking bread, cleaning every Wednesday and Thursday, etc., besides regular household chores. Now don't tell your mom this: I'm not trying to impress you or her or anyone else—these things simply must be done, that's all!

No doubt Dave wrote you of his engagement. Were you as floored as I was? More so, probably, for it was you who said, "Oh no, he'd never do that." Tell me what you thought when you heard. They seem supremely happy, so I am glad.

Tonight—last night now—we went to the Wheaton alumni mtg. to hear Coach Coray. Saw the movie of you and your fiancé. Coach announced afterwards that you were not engaged or going to med school. I was glad for that word.

With mixed feelings, Betty

My dad's return letter arrived about two weeks later on October 7, answering every point.

The Renaissance: Your recent concern over the Renaissance I consider neither harsh, undue, nor unfair. My private regrets are more than I care to share with you—deeper than I am able to share, I think. . . . I have confessed to God, to the senior class, to the FMFers, to you, to other individuals, and I am eased. If there is more that I must do, I stand ready for reproof. Do you expect yet more of me?

The kissing incidents: I have no sensible answer to your charge of the kissing incidents. I stood there, said and did as you have been told, entirely in the flesh. And the same "me" wrote of "purity in my love.". . . For the fact that it has blackened my conscience, hurt you, stumbled others, and brought dishonor to Christ, I now experience overwhelming sorrow. The act, the effect of it, the regret for it shall be consumed by the flashing of my Judge's eye, and I shall suffer loss. There's an end of it, and a costly one.

The family visit: In regards to Mother's inconsistencies (they are not surprising to me any longer), I think Nietzsche has well spoken: "In the love of woman, there is injustice and blindness to all that she loveth not.". . . Mother has not deep love for you [because she doesn't know you yet] and interpreted all she chose against you, unjustly and blindly. I have since shown her this privately, and she remarked, "Well, we must have her back again, I have misjudged."

Maybe, then, it wasn't so bad after all. In fact, maybe some of the rush to judgment had arisen simply from the difference in their family styles. That's a common source of friction anytime a young man and woman become prospective mates. My mother had hinted at this dynamic in her letter, when she wrote of how her own parents would never say such things about another person. My dad's parents, he said, were simply more frank and outspoken.

His October 7 letter continues:

Don't compare them with your own family. Where you or Dave would remember and be quiet, framing private opinions, Dad or Mom would blurt right out at the dinner table their feelings.

I am sorry this has prejudiced you against them—particularly because you fear lest it hurt me. None of it! I am very glad they expressed themselves—for that is all they will do. There will be no scheming, subtle tricks to prejudice me against you. They have spoken their mind and will, but should I choose to go on and marry you, they would stand by to help. Both of them have said this.

Admittedly, there's something refreshing about that kind of honesty and forthrightness. Less damage is often done by those who get it all out, all at once, rather than hide their real feelings beneath a mask of politeness and courtesy. My Elliot grandparents were more the former.

But even with the aftermath of the Portland visit dominating this letter, the most important subject remained the condition of their relationship and how they should continue it (or discontinue it) moving forward.

Uncle Dave had sent a recent letter to my dad, warning him as previously that he needed to stop writing my mother. Here is my father's report of it:

> He warned me solemnly that I will "absolutely ruin the girl if I'm not careful." He stands firm in the conviction that our correspondence is nothing but an opening for your love to flow through, which is illicit so long as I have no word from the Lord that its fruition will be marriage. He may be right, and if he is, it is your place to say so.
>
> You will remember that my word from the Lord for writing was in connection with liberty. He gave me freedom to write if I pleased—for me there is no sin in it. But in this, my liberty may have now become license in carrying things too far for you to endure, should our relation be cut off. I am ready now to renounce our correspondence if my liberty has come to its end in imposing itself upon you with harmful results. I now feel it is your place to precipitate discontinuance. You know better than David or I what our writing is doing to you.
>
> My answer from the Lord about marriage is now a decided "no" so long as present conditions prevail, with no conditions as to what might happen when and if they change. Can you afford to continue to feed a growing love in you which may be cut off without any fulfillment at some future time? One word from you will settle it. . . . My word from God for now is "Nay," and I have no right to leave you in indecision, and for now that is the oracle from the Lord. I leave you the decision of whether or not you have full liberty to write in those circumstances.

She didn't seem to like where this train of thought was going. In her response, you recognize her frustration at this strange relationship they share. (She wrote it from New York City where a family acquaintance had asked her to come substitute teach a Greek class at National Bible Institute.) Again, how were they to keep writing without expressing love, since neither of them possessed any claim upon the other?

October 14

> Your letter of the 7th came Monday. It's a toughie to answer. My first reaction as to how I would reply was a clever one, but would not have been truthful. I planned to cut out your sentence that ran thus: "Can you afford to continue to feed a growing love in you which may be cut off without any fulfillment at some future time?". . . I would have affixed the word "No" and returned the clipping with no further comment. Succinct, at any rate, huh? I can hear you guffaw.

Well, as to why it would have been "the truth, the whole truth, etc. . . ." If I have love for you, it is not a very thriving one, choked and inhibited by a multiplicity of circumstances and restrictions, and surely it finds little vent in so erratic and impassionate a correspondence. The termination of our letters will likely have little effect on either its growth or depletion.

She then took on the line from her brother's letter that categorized their so-called love and correspondence as "illicit" if no intention to marry was declared.

Consider a moment, Jim. . . . Have we not hashed this out from start to finish? Have I not told you that the whole business, for my part, has undergone exhaustive examination several times in the past six months? Would I not long since have thrown in the sponge without waiting your "permission" had I had any doubts as to its legality?

No one need worry about the courage of her convictions!

You speak of *your* liberty, *your* choices (e.g., "If I should choose to marry you . . ."), *your* decisions. Rest assured, Jim, my consent to correspond was based on the liberty the Lord gave *me*. Don't worry about whether I can "endure." This is a two-sided proposition. If you can, I can. I am not so fragile a thing as you and Dave would make out.

And I am not just sure whether your fears that I shall be hurt are fostered by a genuine tenderness and solicitude for my well-being, or are perhaps faintly tinged with the suspicion that things matter far more hugely to me than they do to you. If this latter is your thought (and I do not suggest it *accusingly*, for it may be true, I being of the "weaker sex"), I wouldn't worry my head too much about it if I were you. . . .

Funny, she broke off writing for a moment because the *Queen Mary*, she said, was steaming up in the harbor, and she *"wanted to watch her pull out."* Then she concluded:

You leave me the decision as to whether or not I have full liberty to write "under these circumstances." As far as I can see, "these circumstances" have altered not one whit from what they were when we began to write. Then why all this ado? Had I not liberty then? I have it now. Did I consent to correspond with any illusions as to the outcome? I think not. We were very clear on this point.

Therefore, for the immediate present, I am content to "endure." If you have reasons for being exercised which you have not expressed, then it is your place, not mine, to precipitate discontinuance.

Peace and safety, Betty

"Content to endure." Was the Lord giving her grace here to "endure"? I think so, although she did sound frustrated with my dad and maybe angry at his expectations of her. Yet in her diary around this time, she continued to speak of *"how I long to be with Jim sometimes,"* how *"often my first thought upon waking—yea, before waking sometimes—is of Jim."* No wonder, then, she would worry the next day after sending this letter, *"Afraid I wrote a bit harshly to Jim."*

Yes, I'd say that's the way he took it.

October 23

It is easy to misinterpret letters when one does not read them in the mental set that possessed the author when they were written. I have so misinterpreted both of those I have gotten from you since I saw you. I say "misinterpret" because I refuse to believe that you mean to sound as you carped and caviled at me, and that is what I have sensed in these. I am satisfied that your feeling toward me is the same as it was when you wrote of tender intimacies last winter, though you change your tone to fit the occasion. I should be surprised now to learn that you did not anxiously look for this letter days before it arrived, and I say this because my moods—I take it—interpret some of the things you say as carelessness toward me. Your using regular mail rather than air mail has been so taken.

Sure enough, she had made special mention in her diary of sending these letters by regular ground service, even though she noted *"he writes airmail always."* Desired effect accomplished.

Statements like "If I have a love for you, it is not a very thriving one" in your last are easily taken to mean nonchalance on your part. Your speaking of our "erratic and impassionate correspondence" makes me feel as though you were not taking me as seriously as I should like you to! . . . In short, Betts, I am persuaded that you love me, and if my saying so angers you (since you have never actually said it), well, then you had better condition yourself to my assumptions and get used to feeling "as though I had you where I want you."

After rereading what he'd just written, he tried again, a little softer this time.

What I wanted to say is that I didn't feel your last letter was long enough, gracious enough, loving enough, and some other "enough" to satisfy what I have understood to be love for me in you. Then your added suggestion that I might not really be considering "your welfare" but some notion of mine about easing you off in this re-questioning of our correspondence was unsettling. And the flat statement that you suspected in me other "unexpressed reasons" [for it] was, and is, not a little aggravating!

As a matter of fact, I think now that I wrote not for your sake nor for mine, but for Dave's. . . . What worried me was that Dave seems so sure of the dangers involved in our continued writing, that I feared he had interpreted you more wisely than I. He plagues my conscience with his words of "ruining the girl." Next time he writes, I've a notion to send him your last. I'm glad at least to have your convictions in writing.

May I ask a favor? Will you please write that brother of yours in the same vigorous tone in which you addressed me and convince him that you are tougher than he thinks? Make him understand that this is not all my decisions, my liberty, my choices, my leading. They are the Lord's leading in respect to both of us, and we have both experienced that direction. It is neither of us leading the other on, but God leading us both on. I haven't been able to convince Dave of that. I'm sure a word from you would be effective.

He also wondered if she'd be open to something else—that they should sit for and exchange new pictures of one another.

You always complain about your set of me, that I am "such a little boy" (your very words!) or that you have plenty of the back of my head, thanks to Dave. What say we get some professional proofs and exchange them for lack of something better to do for Christmas? You send yours here, I'll reciprocate, and that way we can get our own choices. Before this I have always regarded picture-giving as some form of ego-expression. In this case I argue from the standpoint of necessity.

"Necessity." He needed her.

The day this letter arrived in Moorestown was *"one of those radiant October days,"* my mother said. The days leading up to it had been less so. *"No word from Jim yet,"* she'd written on Tuesday. *"I almost hold my breath to see what he will say of my last letter. O, the uncertainty, the waiting, the wondering—it is hard, but it is God's way."* The following day, Wednesday: *"Still no word. Mrs. Elliot wrote a note simply telling all about the family. Conspicuous absence of the love and cordiality she expressed before she met me."*

Then came Thursday—*"and a wonderful letter."*

OCTOBER 27: Jim is incorrigible, bless his heart! And inimitable. Never have I been treated like this before—especially by a man! What worries me is that I seem to *thrive* on it. But I must wait a little while. O discipline—thou art a jewel, but cumbersome.

She wrote the same sentiments to him in her letter the next day, a note much more light-hearted than her previous one, full of happy, smiling personality.

October 28

Jim Elliot, you are incorrigible. That's all I can say. No man has ever treated me like this before, and I don't expect another one to. . . . I'm persuaded that you know a lot of things about me that I don't even know yet, and seem to have access to a barometer of my feelings that I've never had a glimpse at. Well, carry on, brother, it's fascinating.

And as for this picture-swap idea . . .

I had already thought of having mine made for mother, but didn't want to commit myself by letting you know, because they might turn out to look just like me, and then of course I wouldn't have sent you one! But I suppose they can't be worse than the ones you have. I would like to have one of you, though, past the age of 18—for you are now 22. I didn't forget your birthday. . . .

It is getting late—my hand is tired. So, whether this letter is "long enough," etc. or not, I must say good-night. At least it was written *soon* enough—which is more than can be said for some folk's letters! So good-night, Jim—though for you it's just 9:30 now.

Joyously, Betty

How delightful to read her jokes. I can almost hear her laughter, even as I'm writing.

But quite serious things were happening at this time as well, in terms of their thirst for following God to the foreign fields. Their friend Van (whom I've mentioned before) had recently stopped at my mother's before leaving from New York on her way to Africa. *"What a heart-gladdening thing to see her. How she refreshes my soul. . . . My, how I wish I were ready to go with her!"* In the days after Van left, my mother thought of her friend *"out on the ocean, such a new 'venture'. . . and here I 'sit'—not knowing whither or why."* Or as she'd prayed while composing her diary entry of a week or so earlier, *"You won't let me miss the sound of going in the tops of the mulberry trees, will You, Lord?"*—a reference to God's call to battle for David against the Philistines in 1 Chronicles 14:15.

Even in this most recent, upbeat letter to my dad, she had said:

I have been conscious of inward fretting over my apparent "inactivity." It gives me a dig every time someone asks, "What are you doing now?" It is not what I am doing that is nothing. But it is what God is doing, and even for that I cannot point to specific things, like Exhibit A, for questioners to gaze at in proof. I know He is working, and has purposes for which I know nothing, but it takes faith—and I've found that this means active, operative, continued faith and faithfulness.

My father knew exactly what she was feeling and talking about. *"Your comments on the present waiting period were no less applicable to you than to me. The Guiana project is slow,"* he said, mentioning that nothing would be coming of it until first of the year at the earliest. Like her, he realized that God was primarily calling him to be faithful in the now, in the waiting.

November 1

Today I went out to the Christian High School to place my application as a substitute teacher. Tonight I went to the local detention home for boys to tell a Poe story at their Halloween party. Tomorrow even, I am to help in a newly beginning craft class for unsaved kids in one of the suburban assemblies. Wednesday afternoon—children's meeting at the hall. Friday morning—chapel service for the Goodwill Industries employees. Days I spend in the books.

But according to my dad's journal, God was also beginning to reveal clearer information concerning future-tense answers as well. On October 29, he mentioned reading a letter that my Uncle Bert received six weeks earlier in Peru. As people tended to do with letters in those days, Bert had apparently forwarded it home. My parents' correspondence often included with their own letters a handful of additional cards and notes they'd received from someone else and wanted to share. This particular letter was from a Wilfred Tidmarsh, written from the jungles of east Ecuador, speaking of a need for reaching the natives in that area of the world with the gospel.

This, again, from my dad's private journal:

OCTOBER 29: On the reading of Wilfred Tidmarsh's letter to Bert written September 9, I responded to a simple urge within me to offer myself for the work there. It struck me as quite a presumptive action, and I covenanted with the Lord quietly that I would not post the letter unless I had some definite word from Him. It seems the situation he is in demands that he abandon the Indian work among the Quichuas because of his wife's illness. He had asked the Christian and Missionary Alliance to take over, but they have given no verdict as yet.

Remember, among the directives he believed he'd received from the Lord at the end of 1948:

I feel quite at ease about saying that tribes work in South American jungles is the general direction of my missionary purpose.

Was this new opening in Ecuador the door through which God would send him?

Not having the luxury of hindsight, he didn't yet know. But in seeking answers to all the year's questions, only one thing would do. As my mother said, *"The only thing that keeps me stable and settled in these days of uncertainty—yea, utter perplexity—is the absolute dependability of God's Word."* My father, of course, was on the same wavelength, challenging· himself even as he challenged her: *"Let me warn you not to neglect conscientiously directed Bible study these days."*

But what I love from watching them navigate God's answers through His Word and through prayer was that they weren't merely seeking His personal instruction in regard to *their* ways, though they desperately craved it. They were equally, if not more diligently seeking to discover only *His* ways, which would ultimately give God the glory.

I'm encouraged, for instance, reading my dad's journal entry of November 11, after he'd obviously spent much of the day in reading and study, thinking ahead:

> I see clearly now that anything—whatever it be—if it be not on the principle of grace, it is not of God. Here shall be my plea in weakness; here shall be my bold-ness in prayer; here shall be my deliverance in temptation; at last, here shall be my translation. Not of grace? Then not of God.
>
> And here, O Lord Most High, shall be Your glory and the honor of Your Son. The awakening for which I have asked, it shall come in Thy time on this principle by grace, through faith. Perfect my faith then, Lord, that I may learn to trust only in divine grace, that Thy work of holiness might soon begin in Portland.

I was all too legalistic for at least twenty years of my adult life, believing if I could just be more disciplined, God would be more pleased with me and I could climb that ladder of perfection, earning the reputation I desired. My own rules of godliness were my ideals. More than I loved Him, I loved my rules of what a devoted wife and Christian home should be. Therefore, to borrow from my father's words, I was not being "delivered in temptation," or being "bold in prayer," or understanding that His grace covered all my "pleas in weakness." Nor was I learning what my mother had told me throughout her life—how we shouldn't always be examining our own holiness but simply seeking to please Him, that it's up to *Him* to bring about change in us. As He helps us do His will, He conforms us into Christlikeness. It's all grace. It's not all about us.

Knowing the ways of God helps us know the way to go.

My parents knew this. And so while my dad was learning from the Word the deeper meanings of *grace*, my mother was learning from it as well—the deeper meanings of *love*, specifically what God was saying to her in Scripture about the way she and my dad should see and handle their uncommon friendship.

> **NOVEMBER 17:** In seeking the Lord many days and weeks for light in darkness, I believe He is beginning to give some explanation—Chambers says, "Love is spontaneous but must be maintained by discipline."

> **NOVEMBER 18:** The Lord is wonderfully opening my eyes and showing me what I believe is the explanation of my confusions and perplexities re: the course of our relationship, its changes and anomalies, nature, and degree.

This extensive few weeks of study, including deep analysis of the original Greek, resulted in an exceptionally long letter she wrote to my dad on

November 29. She began, *"'And after many days . . .' But these days have been occupied with study and thought which seemed to me necessary before I could answer yours of the tenth."* I'll let her explain, at length:

November 29

I was not a little concerned over your words, "Do you think I would dally with you if I shared any notion that you were staying with me?" I thought this over, asking myself, "Am I 'toying' with him? Has he any misconception of the nature of my feelings? Have I been fair?". . . If I were to go on now, without clarifying some things which have become clear to me in the last two weeks, I should not be fair to you.

You have been unfair to me. The question expressed in the above quotation from your last, along with numerous other broad allusions to the fact that I had never declared my "love" to you, were unfair. You have repeatedly wanted to "test" my feelings. Why? To what end? Anything but selfishness?

In other words, your love is dependent upon requital. This you will admit, I feel sure. Yet I have been content to go on, sharing *plenty* of "notions that you were toying with *me*." I need not go into all the instances which have raised serious questions. Dave tells me he is sure you are not in love. . . .

All of which brings me to the principal conclusion of my meditations of late: your feeling toward me, and mine toward you, have not been on the same basis. How to explain what I mean? Oh, Jim, this is another one of those times when I would give anything to talk instead of write. I fear that I may omit much that would convey to you my true intention.

Her study had given clarity on the different kinds of love declared in Scripture. And while she realized the Lord might one day cause theirs to be a love that would culminate in marriage, for now it was a *friendship* love. And rather than resist friendship love as insufficient or complicate it with claims and attachments, she believed they should embrace it. After all, it would hardly be a waste, she'd been learning, since *"no love in any relation of life can be at its best if this element of 'friendship love' be lacking."*

I do not wish to be unkind—last of all to you—but I cannot help but feel that you need to know more of this "friendship, which consists in loving, rather than in being loved," as friend Aristotle put it. . . .

Think back—you have spoken of the desire for possession, laying claims, etc. I was insistent that such should have no part in our relation so long as it was on this present basis. I am now more convinced than ever that a love which is pure, and of divine origin, can exist entirely without compact or condition. Yet, as you wrote once, you found joy in my letters when you wanted "to be loved."

H. C. T. says [in one of the books she'd been reading: Henry Clay Trumbull's *Friendship: The Master Passion*], "No love is more liable to misconception than a love that is without limit or claim or craving.". . . It was the love known among the

Christians of Acts 4:32—knowing no "rights." It is the love of John 3:16, poured forth freely and without return, to all the world, possession-less in a sense, until individuals become members of the family of God, when a new element enters.

The Greek word in lines eight and twelve is *philia* (friendship love); the word in line thirteen is *agape* (unconditional love).

Slowly but surely, she said, *"to return to application to our own friendship"*. . .

You will recall telling me quite candidly that you did not know a constant, "never-turning-ever-deepening flow" of love—in fact, I think you said that you were not capable of such. This I refuse to believe. You are as "capable" of it as you are of any virtue—by God's grace, by discipline, by drawing from Him the power. Whether or not you know or ever shall know such a love for me is not even a consideration at this point. My concern is that you recognize the nature and source of this love as divine. . . .

I believe the 15-week period of silence in the summer of '48 indicates that we have experienced something of true friendship as expressed above. I know I did, at any rate, and from things you said, your feelings were pretty much the same at the end of that period as at the beginning. And in many other particulars, I think there has been a mutuality of this real friendship, but I also feel that other elements have entered in. . . .

I believe that you and I, Jim, if we are to continue, must know this true friendship apart from everything else, for it is this alone which continues without consummation for it is in itself and by its very nature, a fulfillment.

For a long time, it seems to me, we have gone along—you insisting on claims and evidences, I trying to maintain a relationship that is "from feeble yearnings freed." True, there were all too many instances when I sought selfish ends. The love which is true friendship is selfless, divine. I am selfish, human. So I have fallen many times. But can you see any evidence of my goal, at least, in our past contacts?

I understand so much better that which was obscure before, and by God's grace I trust He will make of me one who is true in love, no matter to whom that love be given, and pour through me His own vast and high and holy love. If we seek now to mix the two, we place ourselves in a paradoxical position. . . .

So, to reduce the example to the degree of our relationship, I feel perfectly free to write, or not write, as I wish. It will make no difference to me whether or not you agree to the conclusions I have outlined here. You may say that you violently disagree with all I have said, or that you do not wish to continue correspondence if I am not willing to declare for you a love of the kind you want, or that you cannot continue on this basis. So far as I can see now, if I know anything of being a friend, "none of these things move me.". . . I am asking the Lord to teach me—and you—for our separate good primarily, regardless of His ends or purposes in our mutual affinities.

It was quite a treatise she'd written, both scholarly and heartfelt.

But to understand how my father reacted to it, perhaps the following insight will help. A few weeks earlier, when her previous letter had come, it didn't include a copy of one of my mother's poems he'd repeatedly requested; instead, she'd repeatedly withheld it. The piece in question was a poem she had read to him while on one of their picnic excursions in Portland during the summer, written in March 1947:

> I love not with the evanescent flame
> Of wind-touched candle,
> Or with sporadic passions
> Fostered only of the moon.
> I love with steadfast quietness of heart,
> Dynamic, strong, which plumbs an untold depth.
> I love with purest singleness of heart,
> One never-turning, ever-deepening flow
> Of warmth and power, of fathomless devotion.

After receiving (apparently) a smart-aleck reply from him, she had torn it up *right then* in his presence. But as reported in his letter of November 10, after again no poem had appeared, he took matters into his own hands.

After lunch I headed out for Mount Tabor to the place where we discussed the letters that afternoon. I had difficulty recognizing the exact spot as things are much more in a tangle since the falling of the leaves. This hindered considerably my search for those bits of paper into which you rendered the much disputed poem of March 22, 1947. I found a few pieces, some badly soaked, some only shreds, all crumpled and decomposed. You would have laughed to see me carefully inching over all that spot with the dogged determination of a paleographer, and laughed unkindly too, did you not appreciate my purpose. Well, I have succeeded by only 75%, having pieced together parts of all the lines, but completely satisfactorily only the first and last two.

Does this sound like a man who only wanted to be "friends"?

In this same letter is where he'd written the line she'd referenced: "*You insist that you are 'just Betty,' no strings, no emotion, no feeling toward me but kindly friendship, when Dave, Van, and Bunny all tell me, 'Betty really loves you.' Do you think I would dally with you if I shared any notion that you were toying with me? I hope you think better of me than that.*"

Maybe, then, she should've expected the obtuse reaction she received, even from such a well-thought-out letter. "*Very little comment on my epistle,*" she wrote in her diary a few weeks later, December 20, when his letter arrived, "*except to call it 'pretty much exalted nonsense.'*" He said he couldn't make heads or tails of it.

December 17

After two weeks of pondering your letter, I understand less of it than I did when I began. I still find myself reading two or three lines over and over, shaking my head, wondering. On Thursday I sat down with ten pages of notes to answer you, to refute and upset your new theory. After I had written four pages, I saw how impossible it was to answer, when I hardly understand what you are talking about.

She'd realized, even while she'd been awaiting word, that the waiting itself was a test of her own theories of love. "*No word from Jim for a month,*" she'd written on December 10. "*It's all right. God gives me love that asks no return—for Him, and for him.*" She'd been anticipating my dad's letter "*with fear, for the most part. I am prepared to receive a final goodbye, if that is how he takes it.*" When it came, she bravely "*spent a while with the Lord this afternoon and received peace. 'Ye will not get leave to steal quietly into heaven, in Christ's company, without a conflict and a cross.'*"

Perhaps, though, the main reason my dad wasn't inclined to worry at present about such deep issues of the heart was because of his excitement over something else that had come up.

He'd been communicating with Dr. Tidmarsh.

Since writing you, I have had detailed correspondence with two missionaries who I wrote: one, Wilfred Tidmarsh of Ecuador (whose wife was badly injured in an MAF plane tragedy [Mission Aviation Fellowship] when Nate Saint was pilot), who is having to leave an established forest work among Quichua Indians because of his wife's illness; the other, Rowland H. C. Hill of Bangalore, India. Both describe fields of tremendous interest to me, and both are quite anxious regarding my leading from the Lord.

From one standpoint, the works are almost opposite, as the Ecuadorian work is among a primitive unsettled tribe, while the India project is among high school and college age upper-crust Hindus who are studying English. Brother Hill wants to start a Bible school of some sort and is looking for someone who would qualify as a teacher of Greek, etc. . . .

Since beginning this letter, I have had one from Ecuador, asking definitely about my leading, since the work must be turned over to someone soon. I will be writing him this afternoon, but what shall I say? How is one to decide when the heart seems equally torn for both works, and one's capabilities fit either sphere? To top this, Dave wrote me asking if I could take his job with FMF next year, suggesting that it would be excellent training for the field. But what better training than the field itself?

And as to her thoughts on love, on *their* love, on whether they *had* love . . .

I think you will sense my predicament and forgive me if I sorta skip over the admittedly important, but laborious study of your friendship ideals. Further, I don't see how we could possibly come to any settlement on such a matter in letters. We should have to talk over it personally, in a situation where it is possible to retort on the spot. . . . If you read my letter to Dave, you know my sentiment about "loving in faith," and that is as far as I have come by experimental, spiritual reasoning. The degrees and qualities of that loving are variable and poor; yet they are in faith, and it is there they must grow. I don't mean that you should cut out the subject from your letters, but only hope you will understand its absence in my own.

Having read this, imagine my mother's emotions when on the Friday before Christmas, a packet arrived by mail at the house. It was the picture of himself he'd made for her.

DECEMBER 23: I went upstairs and cried.

Here's where we leave them at the end of 1949. In reading through the letters from this year, one can't help but detect a *storminess* to their relationship. My mother insisted on keeping it "just friends" because of the lack of assurance from my dad that they would ever marry. The uncertainty and heart-searching had to be painful, as they both did love each other. But my mother could not express it as romantic love, only as true friendship: a true, Christ-honoring friendship, a meeting of mind and heart. My dad, however, couldn't quite accept this. He wanted to hear from her that she desired and admired him. He hoped she could go beyond the harmony of their minds toward something deeper. But intellectually he knew. This was only his flesh talking. It's why he often confessed in his journal of how his love for God could be divided, hungry for more of my Mama's expressions toward him.

He wrote to her once more before year's end, recalling with laughter *"the vacation spent with you all there in 1947—the skating party, sledding at McHutchens, the midnight fests."* He also sent belated wishes for a happy birthday.

December 27

I forgot to mention your birthday in my last, the twenty-first if memory serves. I can't remember if we ever discussed giving gifts or not. . . . But somehow it seems such a cheap sort of a thing to do—entirely too conformist a practice to have much place in our relationship! The practice at Christmas has gotten to be such a commercialized hoax that I will be sincerely glad when all good Christians abandon it.

He closed with a prayer, asking for *"a 1950 for you that is both directed by the will of Christ and executed by His power."*
She followed with a letter written New Year's Eve.

December 31

Your letter was welcome, and I was glad you were pleased with the picture. . . . To know that you accepted [it] without derogatory remarks is enough. As for yours—I like it very much, and do not think the tinting detracts at all. The family went wild over it, but it only made me wish I could see that frank smile in flesh and blood!

Yes, we have been all through the gift business before, and I agree with your sentiments in the matter entirely. The first time was up on a grassy hill not far from the Roarin' Elgin tracks. You had thought perhaps I should be hurt if you gave me nothing for graduation. The thought had not even occurred to me. In fact, I'm sure I should have been disappointed if you had given me anything. Occasions—why must we be bound by occasion? Perhaps we have been "cradled in custom," but must we grow up in a "showcase"? Be yourself, James—as you've always been, I think—I sorta like you that way.

And *"for 1950, remember this,"* she said, quoting the ancient hymn:

The King of Love my Shepherd is
Whose goodness faileth never—
I nothing lack if I am His
And He is mine forever

The bellow of the tide
From the Blue expanding wide
Beyond the roughness of the rocks of Falcon Head,
Funneled hugely, vainly tried
To rend our cavern, where it died
In quiet cool of Sandy bed
Beneath our feet.
We shivered as we stood,
Found no words to fit the mood
Which numbed us silent. We quaffed
Each other's good
But, not knowing then to brood,
Spoke nonsense, laughed,
The touch of naked shoulder
As each felt his own the colder
Melted other touch-things into dream.
False, every fact I told her.
Lie, that overhanging boulder.
All things that *were* did only *seem*
As we knew love.

JIM ELLIOT

Lord, let this love be pure and high,
As clean and vast as Thy great sky.
O God, engulf us in the tide
Of love Inexorable—and hide
Us ever in Thy secret place
Where we, as one, may see Thy face.
Because He first loved us, we love—
So let us drink from Thine above—
And mirror, as we there abide,
The love of Jesus for His bride.

ELISABETH HOWARD

LOVE LETS GO

The year 1950 with its nice, round number, positioned squarely in the middle of the twentieth century, was enough to get my father's Brethren assembly thinking about end-times prophecy. He wrote to my mother on January 3, reporting on a recent prayer meeting discussion where another young man *"looked me straight in the eye and said, 'We are within forty years of the millennial reign of Jesus Christ, and that's a conservative estimate!' At supper, Dad said tonight, 'Children born today will see the wind-up of the age.'"*

But while any attempt at placing a date on Christ's return is certainly subject to miscalculation, the imperative of keeping a watchful mind-set is not.

> Do consider this, Bets, slowly and for several moments at a time. What is my relation—practically—to the end of the age? . . . How lost, alas, a life lived in any other light!

Maybe that's why the next day in his journal, his heart turned philosophically to the *"extremely dangerous, cumulative effects of earthly things."*

> **JANUARY 4:** One may have good reason, for example, to want a wife, and he may have one legitimately. But with a wife comes Peter's (the pumpkin eater's) proverbial dilemma—he must find a place to keep her, and most wives will not stay on such terms as Peter proposed.
>
> So a wife demands a house; a house, in turn, requires curtains, rugs, washing machines, and so on; a house with these things must soon become a home, and children are the intended outcome. The needs multiply as they are met: a car demands a garage; a garage, land; land, a garden; a garden, tools; tools need sharpening! Woe, woe, woe to the man who would live a disentangled life in my century. Second Timothy 2:4 is impossible in the United States, if one insists on a wife.
>
> I learn from this that the wisest life is the simplest one, lived in the fulfillment of only the basic requirements of life: shelter, food, covering, and a bed. And even these can become productive of other needs if one does not heed. Be on guard, my soul, of complicating your environment so that you have neither time nor room for growth!

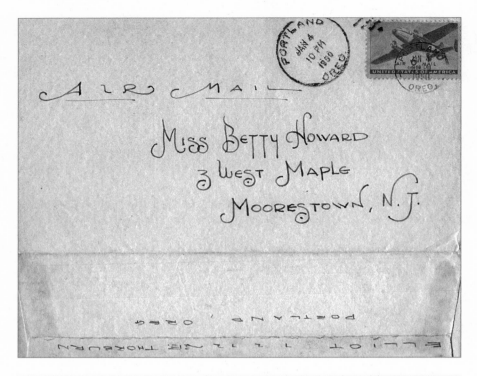

My father's precise and artistic handwriting—he loved trying different styles!

This is the typical Jim Elliot! He couldn't abide the American craving for possessions. He was right in saying they came with "dangerous, cumulative effects." How well I know it. The urge to simplify my life by getting rid of "stuff" is often inspired by memories of my childhood with the Indians, who never seemed to suffer with discontentment. We needed little, *wanted* little, being so far removed from stores or from others' homes where the finest amenities were available. My mother often echoed the same sentiment, teaching that we should hold God's gifts loosely, truly recognizing them as *gifts*, not as personal possessions to be hoarded and clung to.

But my dad wasn't referring just to material things. Despite his love for my mother, he continued to be wary of marriage, of its distractions and divided loyalties. He still felt as if marriage would only complicate his calling to the mission field, the details of which were proving complicated enough. From his current spiritual vantage point, God was speaking loudly and consistently to him about the conviction for remaining single.

> **JANUARY 7:** I cannot say what led me to read the Law of Moses yesterday, but I was strangely affected by a verse that seemed to leap out of context of itself and apply to my attitude toward marriage. I have been considerably reminded lately of the one-thousand-years-equals-one-day principle of Peter and its application to the length of human history.
>
> The third day speaks of Christ's returning to rule (see the "after two days" references in Scripture). . . . Exodus 19:15 spoke, as I said, of its own force to me, "Be ready against the third day: come not near a woman." This with Matthew 19:12 and 1 Corinthians 7 and, in type, Revelation 14:4 present to me a challenge I never heard from any pulpit.

Time was simply too short, he believed, to be weighed down with personal pleasures and entanglements, or really to plan much into the future at all.

> I must not think it strange if God takes in youth those whom I should have kept on earth till they were older. God is peopling eternity, and I must not restrict Him to old men and women.

I'm not sure of whom he was specifically writing, but he did have several "premonitions" about his own life being short, and he preferred being "burned out for God" rather than wasting his passions.

Such was his thinking at the beginning of 1950.

Now, to reset the general scene for you: My father was living in Portland, teaching at a Christian high school, leading Bible studies for teens, as well as generally helping out at home and at his father's assembly. He was often called on to preach and speak at various gatherings and ministry venues. As to his short-range plans, he did mention in his January 3 letter that he'd received acceptance into the summer Wycliffe program in Oklahoma.

> Feel as though the Lord would have me take the time there—whether I go to India or South America. The British Guiana project is dragging, so I will likely spend my spring here. Pray for more openings for the Word, will you? Oh, that God would cause His Word to "run and be glorified."

The Christian school board verified a standing offer to take two weeks' meetings in their high school. . . . I have never done any such thing and feel quite insufficient for a crowd of active minds as they will have. Pray that the Holy Spirit will do His work of lauding, lifting, and enlivening Christ before them.

My mother, meanwhile, was still at home in New Jersey—helping her parents with the cooking and cleaning, teaching Sunday school at church, and preparing to leave soon for Florida where she would be on faculty at Hampden DuBose Academy for at least the next semester. One night, after finishing a short letter to my dad, she wrote in her diary:

JANUARY 12: I think of him so much "when the dawn flames in the sky." He said he looked at Mt. Hood, in its icing of snow, and thought of me every time. I wish he could visit H.D.A., but there is no prospect of this as long as he holds to his resolution.

This "resolution," I believe, was their commitment not to see each other until the Lord confirmed in my father's mind that marriage was a clearer possibility. They prayed fervently for God's will, as evidenced in their diary and journal entries, keeping it uppermost in their minds. Their constant desire was to seek Him, wanting to ascertain the path He'd chosen for each of them.

This she clearly expressed in her letter of January 12, where she asked, *"Jim, please pray for me as I go to H.D.A. There are things involved which I cannot write, but will mean the necessity of keeping low before God."* She didn't want to sound arrogant, but the faculty thought so highly of her that she recognized ahead of time the temptation to feel *"full of herself"* as she re-entered this familiar environment. She'd learned through all of Amy Carmichael's writings (and through Scripture, of course) that she must be *"willing to be considered a nobody."*

I do not want to be cowardly, but I do ask your prayer that the Lord will perfect in me His heart's desire. I don't know what else to ask than "Thy will be done"—in me and in those at the academy.

For one thing, Jim, I think some of them have the idea that once they get me there and sink their talons into me, I will stay permanently. And if I know God's leading at all, He wants to send

She closed her letter with a sequence of biblical commands she'd discovered again recently in Psalm 37, which she'd committed to both her journal and diary a week earlier, and which would reappear in future letters.

Delight thyself . . .
Commit thy way . . .
Trust in Him . . .
Rest!

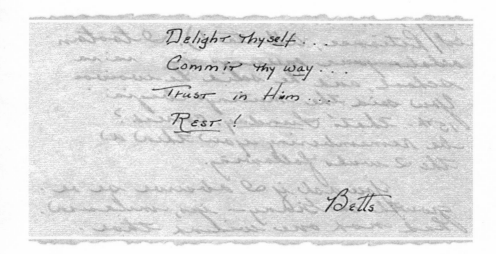

Delight thyself...
Commit thy way...
Trust in Him...
Rest!

Betts

It seemed almost like her personal charge for this year of "resolution."

And if she and my dad were truly serious about keeping themselves separated from one another, they certainly achieved it by the contrast in their living conditions as mid-January arrived—one of them in Oregon, the other in Florida.

January 19

You would not like Portland this afternoon, but you would thrill at her tomorrow morning. Last evening frozen rain lashed down the Columbia Gorge and poured a solid icy crust on drifted snow. All day today the rain has come finer—almost as a blown milk—waiting until it finds surface before freezing. Now every twig is swollen to twice its true proportions with accumulated ice.

Schools are closed; there is practically no traffic; the sky is all gray. Icicles reach wriggling from the eaves. Oddly enough, there are three or four pale robins hopping about the yard, shivering, I swear.

Tonight the temperature will fall considerably, and in the morning every telegraph line, tree limb, sign post—anything exposed—will be crackling with several times its own weight of ice upon it. And then will come what we call here the Silver Thaw. It is one of the most beautiful phenomena we know here in winters (unless it be Mt. Hood by moonlight!), and one of the most damaging as well. Dad pokes his head out the front door occasionally and casts a quizzical, apprehensive look at our sagging eaves, then turns inside shaking his head and making that little clicking noise with his tongue on his teeth.

My, his writing!

And hers!

Sunshine on the long, blue lake . . . live oaks shrouded with Spanish moss . . . throngs of azaleas, shouting with color . . . bamboo and banana leaves rustling in the warm breeze . . . palms of all varieties bowing and rattling—this is H.D.A. in January, while ice storms tear across the north!

I have just been supervising and helping with the cleaning up of some of the front lawn. It is hot in the sun, but the warm sweetness of camphor and long-needled pine is pleasant, and the lake is a cooling sight below us. I went down and hung my feet from the dock in the water, and wished I could have slid the rest of the way in!

Yet her days, she said, were busy ones. *"I have two sections daily of public speaking, and also I help with recreation, music (boys' quartet, girls' trio, glee club, as well as some individual instruction), outdoor work, being senior class sponsor, etc."*

All in all, it couldn't have been going better. My father's prayer for her, that *"all your misgivings will be melted to thanksgivings"* was truly being answered in the affirmative, she said.

The fears I had had when coming here have been dispelled, and everything is wonderful. They've given me a grand roommate—my favorite teacher when I was here as a student. We live in a picture perfect of a room: blue flowered walls, white furniture, white organdy ruffled bedspreads and curtains. Some contrast to P.B.I.! But Paul learned how to be abased, and how to abound.

She saw the faithfulness and goodness of God as she looked around. And when she looked to the distant northwest, she prayed for the faithfulness and goodness of God to cover all of my father's labors as well.

Tell me how your meetings went, Jim, the ones at the high school. Were they resumed after the storm? I did pray for you—and continue to pray that you may know God's will, that you will be filled with joy and peace, and go on to perfection.

In Him, who alone is Altogether Lovely, Betty

Yet not only were they farther apart geographically than ever, the lag between their letters would grow farther apart as well. Instead of the more customary week-to-ten-days' distance between writing, the periods of silence throughout 1950 would routinely stretch into months. They were doing what they felt sure to be God's will—pursuing Him, learning of Him, willingly surrendering themselves to be useful in His service, while ordering their feelings and desires for each other to take a back seat. *Love was letting go.* This was to be a season of following only *one* love—delighting, committing,

Ewell Hall at HDA. Home of the headmaster and headmistress, as well as a girls'
dormitory with formal entertaining rooms. My mother lived here as a teacher in 1950.

trusting, resting—submitting themselves individually to the Lord's shaping
and perfecting.

They were believing God's Word that says, "Delight thyself also in the
LORD; and he shall give thee the desires of thine heart" (Ps. 37:4). "Seek ye
first the kingdom of God, and his righteousness; and all these things shall be
added unto you" (Matt. 6:33). "This one thing I do, forgetting those things
which are behind, and reaching forth unto those things which are before,
I press toward the mark for the prize of the high calling of God in Christ
Jesus" (Phil. 3:13–14).

As my father said in a letter from early February, his last until April 1:

February 11

I have finished *Gold Cord* [an Amy Carmichael book] with threats to go at it again.
One cannot get all it's worth in a single reading. Wilfred Tidmarsh, the brother
with whom I correspond re: Indian work in Ecuador says he is an avid reader of
her works and that he constantly derives spiritual exhilaration from them. Peculiar
that such widespread blessing should come from a single life.

But God does that for those who wholly follow. It is said of Samuel that
Jehovah let not one of his words fall to the ground. What reward for the one who
listens in night seasons and requests, "Speak, Lord, Thy servant heareth."

One of my mother's diary entries from the same period yields solid evidence of this posture as well.

> **FEBRUARY 9:** In reading Luke 12:1–3, I find solemn warning against hypocrisy. All shall be revealed. Nothing shall remain uncovered. This drives me to the evermore solemn prayer, "Remove from me the way of lying: and grant me thy law graciously. I have chosen the way of truth: thy judgments have I laid before me" (Ps. 119:29–30).
>
> Yesterday I read, too, in Deut. 25—"Thou shalt have a perfect and a just weight," an exhortation to justice, fairness, impartiality, absolute truth. Lord, may Christ Himself so fill me that there may be no room for "covered things."

I'll tell you why this selection of hers means so much to me. If there was ONE thing I was certain of in my mother, it was her *truthfulness*. Many other traits, of course, were wholly admirable in her, but I loved that I could depend on her every word. I knew she meant exactly what she said, and if there was to be a consequence to any disobedience of mine, I could certainly expect it. None of that cajoling with empty threats not followed through on, which leaves children with no sense of secure boundaries or consequences for sin.

She spoke with exactness of detail and used words fittingly, so that anyone listening to her was instantly captivated. When she recounted a conversation or described a person with her keen observational power, I could picture them perfectly. She also spoke with authority on the Scriptures because she not only spent time in God's Word but lived it out.

Now she did enjoy "having the floor." I smile to see her confessing in her journal that she oughtn't wish to sound so dogmatic or authoritative, that she needed a more listening heart, because I clearly recall her confessing these same things to me. She could be cut to the quick at times by her own insensitivity toward others who were speaking to her, and she wanted to become more gracious to those who didn't have their words or facts straight.

But, oh, the habit of *correction*—of correcting others! I'm afraid I inherited it, too, and I am frequently ashamed of myself for practicing it. She wrote in a couple of her books about her realization as she grew older in Christ, that she didn't need to have the last word on everything and didn't need to always be straightening people out. But I so appreciated her honest appraisal and her clear thinking on just about everything! The truth of the Bible and her experiences of God's faithfulness to her were the high marks of her speaking, and were also indicative of her private practice at home.

"Absolute truth?" Yes, indeed.

I feel similarly drawn to what she wrote in these next two entries:

> **FEBRUARY 16:** "The Lord is the strength of my life." Ps. 27:1. This morning I was on the verge of discouragement because of the instability and sinfulness of my

heart. The future seemed to be dark before me, and the past loomed heavy in my sight. There is no strength in me. I am the weakest of the weak. The Lord, then, in gracious revelation, gave this verse: "The Lord is the strength of my life." Here is rest and victory, peace of heart and confidence of mind.

MARCH 3: "The beloved of the Lord shall dwell in safety by Him, and the Lord shall cover him all day long, and he shall dwell between His shoulders." Deut. 33:12. Oh, the joy, first of all in simply *being* "the beloved of the Lord," then in the assurance of dwelling *safely by Him*. Analogous to the sense of security in being close to one whom one loves, I feel this rest and peace in being "by Him," secure from the multitude of confusions which Satan has tried to hurl at me. The words "all the day long"—that means all *this* day—moment by moment. Not just from now till 11 a.m. but to the rising of the stars. Could there be any place of greater quietness and love than "between His shoulders"? I thank Thee, dearest Lord, for this verse today.

These two pieces typify her life story. She walked carefully with the Lord, needing His strength and peace continually. When I was a child, she gave me that same security in her own love. She always pointed out to me how much the Lord loves us, that we have no reason to fear anything. Whenever I would grow discouraged, she reminded me that He would be my helper and that I could depend on Him completely for everything I needed. Even years earlier in the jungle, she never gave me any reason to be fearful. Because of her confidence, I was rarely concerned about the very real dangers around us.

Obviously she'd been cultivating her trust in His love and protection long before.

Finally in March, she wrote to my dad again.

March 10

Your letter of a month ago has sat on my desk, amid stacks of papers that need grading, and yearbook material, and declamations. Finally, a moment (which is likely to be broken) has come when I could try to answer.

I wonder if you are still teaching at the Christian school . . .

Yes, he was. In fact, *"they want me to teach for a year in the high school,"* he'd recently written in his journal, and *"the board wants me to decide soon about what I am to be doing in the fall."* My mother's brother Dave also was eagerly recruiting him as a speaker and conference leader with the Inter-Varsity ministry organization.

FEBRUARY 18: O God, so many turns, so many ways, so many pits! Help me, Lord, to see all Thy way for me—and to do it without consideration of any man. If I refuse Inter-Varsity work, I offend Dave; refuse the school board and offend them; go to India and discourage Brother Tidmarsh in Ecuador. How am I to know, my Father? It looks like I must make a decision soon, but I can make no decision unless I hear Thee speak, O Lord. Be not silent unto me.

The kind of work my uncle Dave was proposing drew my father, of course. He was certainly skilled at exhorting students and young people to take seriously the mandate of Christ on their souls and futures. But *"this leaping from place to place, here a night, there a day, has been shown in the summer of 1948 to be ineffective, lacking the substantial quality of settled building. My exercise* [a word he often used, meaning striving in prayer, searching God's mind] *seems to be undergoing crucial fires just now."*

> **MARCH 6:** I sensed afresh last evening the truth of Paul's word, "How shall they preach, except they be sent?" O God, here I am, *send* me. Let me not miss my path in running ahead. Send me, oh, *send* me afield!

My mother, too, equally desirous of the foreign fields, continued faithfully in what she was sure would be her *"temporary work."* But God was working in her heart, graciously allowing her not to rest too much in that contented place which might give way to complacency. Closing her March 10 letter, she said:

> Such love He has given me for these students, along with joy and peace in this temporary work, is something I had not thought possible.
> The Lord has opened to me new avenues of love in the past few years—so different in scope, but so illuminating of the love of God! Truly, it "hath neither brim nor bottom." And, lest discouragement come in measuring my portion of the fruits of the Spirit, I simply think of this: All that I ought to be, Christ is. And Christ liveth in me. Enough? It is enough.

Amen.

"There are times," she wrote in her diary, *"when I should like to tell someone about Jim. Not a soul here knows anything about it, and I would dare not let Mrs. DuBose know."* But though far from home, and though far from certain about where her life was ultimately headed, she rested in the knowledge that God was there, that she was surrendered to His will, and . . . well, her words still say it best: *"It is enough."*

If only other people would stay out of her personal business . . .

"Your letter was full of joy and blessedness," my father wrote on April 1, yet it had arrived in Oregon not long after her brother had been there visiting. Despite being engaged and busy and moving ahead with his life, Uncle Dave continued to feel responsible for coming to my mother's defense against what he considered my father's almost toying with her emotions.

April 1

Dave stirred me up again to reconsider our relationship, and I had come to agree with him. But it seemed like re-digging old graves to begin. Somehow it does not seem that I must explain myself to you again.

Dave and I are both in agreement that if you are "clutching at any straw" (as he puts it, referring to an unsurrendered hope for marriage), and that straw is our correspondence, it must be dropped pronto. Dave feels still that it is so; that you are fooling yourself into thinking that you have no expectation, but that your actions deny it. These actions to which he refers are the weeping episodes you undergo upon receipt of my letters—evidence, says he, that you are deceiving yourself. . . .

Betts, if this is so, and it represents in you an attitude which defines our relationship more deeply than the family one we know in Christ, I must hear of it and take action. (Dave says if anything is going to happen, I must be the one to do it, since you cannot tell your own heart.) You cannot be any more to me now than a beloved sister. Anything beyond that . . . must culminate in marriage, and for that I have neither word nor prospect of word.

myself to you again. Dave and I are both in agreement that if you are "clutching at any straw" (as he puts it, referring to an unsorrendered hope for marraige) and that the straw is our correspondence, it must be dropped pronto. Dave feels still that it is so; that you are fooling yourself into thinking that you have no expectation, but that your actions deny it. These actions to which he refers are the weeping episodes upon you undergo upon receipt of my letters, evidence, says he, that you are deceiving yourself. I had not heard of them and may not judge, but he verifies it by both your Mother's and Mrs. Cunningham's sentiments in the matter.

From later comments, which we'll soon see, as well as earlier ones we've already seen, I don't think she felt any need for this rehashing of terms. She knew where things stood in their relationship, and she knew her own heart and mind better than anyone else could know it. I can imagine a frustrated sigh escaping her lips as she read this admonition from him, where he said:

> If you are in any way unsettled, deferred from thoughts which would exalt Christ, shaken with underground expectations of any sort by the reading of my letters, then my letters shall come no more.

Okay. If that's how it needed to be, she wouldn't send a reply explaining her side of the issue again. She'd already done as much—to her satisfaction. The best use of his time, she believed, was to continue the waiting and struggle in trying to hear from God, which he said he was already doing.

> I have been under deep exercise re: the field again, yet have no leading from God. Who can search the wonders of His wisdom; who can follow Him in His ways toward His children? But surely Light shall arise in darkness for them who fear His name. In His Word is my trust.

Yes, as hers would continually be too.

SPRING AND SUMMER

Still, the specific way forward in my father's missionary calling was no more exact to him as springtime arrived, and the approaching warmth hinted at the nearness of decisions needing to made for the summer.

> **APRIL 19:** In seeking a promise of God's acceptance of my trust in Him for guidance in the next one and a half months, I got this encouragement from Isaiah 42:16—"I will bring the blind by a way that they know not; in paths that they know not I will lead them; I will make darkness light before them, and crooked places straight. These things I will do, and I will not forsake them."

I then picture him sitting back from his Bible, perhaps smiling to himself, before writing this priceless prayer and takeaway:

> I fulfill the qualifications for once, Lord. Most surely I am blind.

Yes, even blindness, he was learning, was not the same as having no direction. As he wrote in his journal the following day, *"I asked earnestly last night for some token of guidance to be shown me today concerning my going to Wycliffe. I got none."* And yet . . .

APRIL 20: I see that God is going to give me specific leading, not when I ask for it, but when I need it, and not until.

What God *was* giving him, however, were some overall principles to establish within himself as he looked beyond Wycliffe, beyond the summer, looking more broadly toward where the Lord was ultimately leading him. Among the main ones were these:

One, remember always that God has taught you the importance of a *building* ministry. Staying in one group for some period of time, stressing emphases consistently, is the best way to accomplish lasting work for God.

Two, do not put yourself in a position to any man or group so that *they*, and not you, direct policies which you know must be decided on the individual's exercise before God. Never let any organization dictate the will of God.

Later that day, a third principle seemed to coalesce in his mind as coming from the Lord—not quite so general in nature as the first two, but more directed at my father personally.

Three, whenever the choice is between the doing of spiritual work (whatever sort) and a secular job (again, of whatever sort)—the choice for me must be the former, regardless of financial conditions.

Therefore, with this guideline in hand, he felt assured of at least one specific ramification:

Turned down Vancouver school board's offer to complete the school year as a seventh and eighth-grade teacher. Found some difficulty in discerning the Lord's will, but believe He has guided. It is easy to be swayed by minor (or even major) points when one comes to making decisions if one cannot hark to *principles* of guidance.

By summer, he was certain. The path that God had painted for him through these principles and through the Word was leading him to Wycliffe. And if he would diligently obey what he felt in his spirit to be God's will—as well as the teachings of Scripture he *knew* to be God's will—he was certain of staying precisely where the Lord could keep speaking to him and using him.

JUNE 2: Impressed with Ephesians 5:17—"understanding what the will of the Lord is," and Romans 12:2—"proving what is the . . . will of God." Every moment I may be conscious and rejoice in the knowledge of God's will. Obedience to every command puts me on that track and keeps me there.

Decisions, of course, must be made. But as in railroad, so in life. A block signal—a crisis—is lighted only where there is special need. I may not always be in sight of a "go" light, but sticking to the tracks will take me where the next one is.

Understanding the will of the Lord is believing Him, that He will in all situations where I have obeyed make that way His own way, effectual for eternity.

How marvelous, though, when God's ways that are "effectual for eternity" are able to be enjoyed in the moment as well. This is what happened when, on July 1, my parents' journeys brought them together again, in Wheaton, at the event of my Uncle Dave's wedding to my mother's old PBI roommate, Phyl Gibson ("Gibby").

They weren't together for long. Only a couple of days. And obviously the wedding festivities occupied most of their time, preventing them from any prolonged, private conversations, such as the ones they'd been able to share in Portland the previous summer. But being around each other was precious just the same. *"Saw Betty again with joy and refreshment,"* he remarked in his journal on July 1. *"I am most grateful to Thee for her, Lord Jesus."* His comments were almost as brief as their visit.

The lengthier account came from my mother's letter to him, written from the quiet of her family's home in Moorestown and sent to him in Oklahoma.

July 8

Little did I dream when I wrote last that I would see you before I wrote again! I had no idea, of course, that there would be such a long interval, but furthermore I surely never expected to see you at the wedding, since you had told me in February that you were going to Wycliffe. But once again the Lord's direction was unmistakable.

Last night I was reading Psalm 71, and it seemed so appropriate for several things God had been showing me. Jim, I wish I could tell you how wondrously the Lord has given me an absolute rest and confidence in Himself. Though He has not shown the next step, I find it impossible to "take thought for the morrow" or to be anxious. This, to me, is miraculous. . . . Does verse 7 bring comfort to your soul as it does to mine, Jim?!

Her whole letter, which wasn't long, indicates a maturity that exceeded even the highly mature character already present in earlier letters. This one is confident, focused, noticeably exalted, reflective of the comment my father made a day after seeing her—*"The Lord is at work in her."* Rather than bemoaning the shortness of their visit or gushing with emotional reaction to it, she was far more interested in celebrating what God was accomplishing in her heart.

The last time she'd heard from him, you may recall, had been the letter from April in which he'd felt need to affirm the uncommitted, nonbinding status of their relationship. But spring had been incredibly busy at HDA, and she'd never found the time (or had the desire) to respond to it.

"It's a bit late to answer your letter of April 1," she said, *"but I have it before me now, and it blessed me and riled me as I reread it."* She'd been

"blessed" by its reporting of God's favor on his preaching and the effects the Lord was producing in people's souls as a result. She was "riled," however, by the rather demeaning insistence that her heart needed constant petting and coddling. After all . . .

"*Well, we've discussed that,*" she curtly said. "*Let people think we are nuts. We have trusted and, I think, been obedient.*" She hoped to be over and done with all this tiptoeing around her feelings.

Though no one could seem to understand why they weren't getting engaged and making plans to go to the mission field ᐧgether—or, if not, why they weren't just leaving each other alone—she knew she'd put God first and knew my father was attempting to do the same thing (maybe with a little more frustration than she). And as long as God's will was uppermost in each of their hearts, they were under no obligation to explain themselves to anyone or give out all the details of their prayer life and relationship dynamics. "Let people think we are nuts," then—while she and my dad went on alone, seeking to expand God's kingdom by being His witnesses, to the ends of the earth.

This was what "defined their relationship," if such definitions were even necessary. There was simply so much more than themselves to be thinking about, as my mother said. . .

> My—as I write, there are so many things that crowd my mind which I wish we had talked about. But what are two brief evenings? I do praise God for them, though. I think I was conscious of a happier fellowship than ever before on Saturday evening.

Isn't that beautiful to hear? After everything they'd been through? Love had let go. And God had given them a friendship even more special in return.

My father answered her letter quickly, grateful as well "*for the time together two weeks ago. I hardly remember two lines of conversational sequence from that Saturday night, but am impressed with a most pleasurable sensation on recalling it.*"

(Some of this "pleasurable sensation," to be frank, may have come from the transporting scent of her perfume emanating from the envelope as he opened it. "*The Tweed was delicious,*" he said in signing off. "*More?*")

But more importantly, he was writing to share with her a monumental development in his calling to the mission field. [Note, in the following excerpt, "Bill" is Bill Cathers; "Bob" is Bob Weeber, a roommate at Wycliffe.]

July 16

> I must tell you now of the ten-day period Bill and Bob and I spent praying about the abandoned station *[Shandia]* in Eastern Ecuador among the Quichua Indians. On the fourth of July, we were at dinner when a brother from the area began casually discussing the work. We were so impressed that we came up to

the room to pray and covenant for ten days of separately seeking God's mind about our going there.

He was really getting serious about Ecuador and the Shandia location. But beyond this agreement to keep praying, he and his friends sensed nothing more definite that night. The only connection they'd become aware of, beside the leading they'd felt at the dinner table, was that *"unbeknownst to each other"* the previous fall, both Bill and my father had communicated with Dr. Tidmarsh about the possibilities of coming there to continue his work.

"Well, to keep the story on this page," he said in his letter to my mother, *"we met yesterday morning"*—Day Ten. But in his journal from a few days earlier, he went into more detail about what all had happened between the Lord and him, just prior to that morning meeting.

> **JULY 14:** I was reading casually in Exodus 23 when verses 20 and 21 came out vividly: "Behold, I send an angel before thee, to keep thee by the way, and to bring thee into the place which I have prepared. Take heed before him. . . ."
>
> Coming as it did (plainly out of context) with such preceding feelings and such simple believing for some promise, I take this as leading from God that I should write Tidmarsh telling him that I should come to Ecuador in the will of God.

Bob, he said, had no such leading, but Bill did. *"So, in the will of God, it is destination: Shandia from now on."* None of it was the result of any *"thinking visions,"* but simply a *"quiet confidence that a door is open which no man can shut."*

> Gird me on, fearless in battle,
> Draw me up tight to Thy side,
> I would drink blood as true metal;
> I would with warriors ride . . .

tell him we were on our way there. So, under God it is destination : _Shandia_ from now on. No thrilling visions, but a quiet confidence that a door is open which no man can shut.

I have written the elders in Portland; Bill, those in Wheaton. We have asked either counsel or commendation for the fall. Letters are on the way to Tidmarsh. My confidence verse which came Friday is Exodus 23:20 "Behold I send an angel before thee, to keep thee in the way and to bring thee into the place which I have prepared."

Have you ever thought of taking the missionary med course at BIOLA?

The Tweed was delicious. More?
   Gird me on, Fearless in Battle,
   Draw me up tight to Thy side,
   I would drink blood as true metal
   I would with warriors ride...
                                    Jim

"*Shandia* from now on." July 16, 1950.

He had faithfully waited.
And God had faithfully answered.
The Lord had chosen for him—Ecuador.
My mother was exultant at the news. Writing in her diary:

JULY 20: Bless God—He has answered many prayers for J. that he would be guided as to a mission field. Had a letter from him saying that he and Bill Cathers are setting their faces toward Ecuador, to a place among the Quichua Indians which has had to be abandoned. They have written the elders of Portland and Wheaton, respectively asking counsel or commendation for the coming fall. How very glad I am to hear this. "God is faithful."

Again, two days later, still beaming with spiritual excitement:

JULY 22: The more I think of the decision Jim has made, the gladder I am. The Lord keeps His word without fail, though we wait what sometimes seems a long while.

Through it all, of course, through all the praying and waiting, she remained very much in love with him. But she had given him up to God and was truly thankful for how the Lord had led him so specifically toward a mission focus.

As for herself, she'd received no such clear direction toward the mission field as of yet. But despite what she considered to be areas in her life still in need of sanctification—*"a tendency toward too much casualness,"* for example, *"and a sort of off-hand attitude"*—she maintained absolute confidence in God's love and His working in her heart. He had led her *"into such a new sense of His nearness and restfulness and intimacy with Him."* Oh, that he would lead her toward an even *"greater reverence for Thee, my dear Father, and a deeper thankfulness that I know Thee as Lord and Master."* Her spirit was willing. Willing to wait.

As always, though, it wouldn't be easy. Waiting rarely is. Back home in Moorestown as the fall drew near, she often wondered what my father was out there doing, knowing he'd set his sights fully on South America.

AUGUST 26: No word from Jim since July 19. I suppose Wycliffe is over now. Wonder where he is, what the advice of the Portland elders was?

What she couldn't really know, until his next letter arrived, was that my father—even with Ecuador so richly on his mind—was often wondering about her too.

August 31

Your name has come to mind much lately, and I have asked God to strengthen you and demonstrate His leading plainly to you this fall. I presume you are back at Birdsong now, or at least will best be reached there. I have wondered if the Lord has given further guidance about working in Philly and perhaps becoming acquainted in some assembly there. That seemed best to me last time we talked, but perhaps His ways of unfolding secrets have led to something better.

Yes, "to something better"—to be revealed through the Lord's "ways of unfolding secrets." I'm sure she thrilled at knowing my dad was praying along these lines for her, just as she'd been faithfully doing and would continue to do for him. Nothing in this world, nothing in this life—nothing, absolutely nothing at all—can ever be "something better" than that.

AUTUMN

September came, dawning upon my father at the conclusion of ten weeks of language study. Yet even so, *"Bill and I felt that the pillar-cloud was not lifting for us, so we are staying on,"* he'd said in that August 31 letter he'd written to her. *"There is abundant opportunity to minister in the area— high school kids in Norman, needy country folk all around, welcome in the Oklahoma City assembly, and when school starts, work on the University campus."* Their plan in the interim was to find paying work as odd-job handymen while simultaneously seeking the Lord for openings through which to pursue their true mission, their first love: evangelizing the lost and boldly discipling the believers.

It was a good way of staying busy through an unavoidable holding pattern.

> Bill has not yet received word from the brethren in Wheaton re: commendation, though he wrote weeks ago. They may refuse to commend him on the basis of not knowing him well enough. We rest in the Lord as to the outcome of this exercise.
>
> Yet on the plus side . . .
>
> The brethren in Portland wrote a very encouraging letter of commendation for me, and seem quite happy about letting me go. All are agreed that we should go out together. Brother Tidmarsh was expecting to go on furlough this November, but he is holding up his plans if we can get there soon so that he can introduce us to the work.

Apparently then, even in waiting, things were picking up speed. *"If it is God's mind,"* he said, *"we will leave as soon as we have gotten passports and seen home once more."* To this end, there were a number of related matters to handle, other official documents to be pulled together, as well as *"some supplies to be collected."* But nothing major. Nothing extraordinary. In fact, (naturally, he couldn't keep himself from saying it)—

> . . . nothing like most married couples require.

There it is again—the missionary's freedom of being unencumbered by marriage. Sounds like those three resolutions he'd made at the end of 1948 were each coming together in real life: (1) tribes work in South America, (2) a summer at Wycliffe, and now (3) *"jungle work, single."* How else, unless he were unmarried, could he be seeking passage to Ecuador by *"working on a deal which would take us there as crew members on a banana boat"*?

To be single at this key moment in his life meant that no matter how dangerous the challenge or how daring the cost, he need not worry about anyone's safety or well-being other than his own—which meant, for him, since he was willing to do absolutely anything in pursuit of proclaiming the gospel, he was free to sail ahead with no worries in the least.

No wonder his fearless example has inspired so many people's zeal for taking Christ to the nations.

Yet as genuinely thankful as my mother felt when hearing of these exciting activities in my father's life, I'm sure all the breathless updates left her at least a little bit envious, as well as lonesome for his company—someone with whom she shared equal dedication to the gospel commission.

She'd once pondered to herself, in daydreaming about the foreign-land work she longed to do, *"Is this 'love of adventure' a mere desire to do something hard? Is it wrong?"* No, it wasn't wrong. But like everything in God's kingdom, it must be done in His strength, in His time, and in response to His guiding hand—the result of waiting, resting, and trusting. Yet to the patient, watchful follower of Christ, it can still be a time of blessedness, even against the cries of comparison.

SEPTEMBER 4: The past weeks have been an almost agony of waiting—wondering what the Lord would have me do this winter. And the waiting has not been without its manifold temptations of doubt and discouragement.

But it is in times like these when our dear Father speaks to the heart most blessedly, giving reassurance and new promises, and almost fondling His child with an "excess of love."

Oh, the joy which has come in knowing that I am one with Christ . . . oh, the marvelous, unspeakable interchange of joy—He my joy, I His joy—He my satisfaction, I His satisfaction. For I am accepted in the Beloved. Right now I am as fit to stand in His eternal light as I shall ever be, for I wear the *perfect* robe of Christ's righteousness. I am *in Christ*—may He be seen in me.

Her next journal entry on the subject, though lengthy, is worth reprinting in its entirety. Perhaps you're in one of those places where these insights of hers will speak with perfectly timed wisdom in your life.

SEPTEMBER 7: For some, the steps which are "ordered by the Lord" are illuminated with such a bright light that they are visible to others. There seems to be a great and wonderful series of "miracles," "surprises," "open doors," "coincidences"—one thing after another in rapid and thrilling sequence. Those who look on say, "That man is truly led by God." And indeed, that man truly is.

But, "He calleth His own sheep by name, and leadeth them out." So His merciful and miraculous leading is individual—"Thou (singular) shalt remember all the way which the Lord thy God led thee." The temptation is great to imitate or to expect the same manner of guidance which God has given another. "What is that to Thee; follow thou Me." His Word abounds in examples of His separate leading of His sheep.

For me, He has not chosen to give signs which may be shown to others. He has not led in any spectacular way, or by steps which could be proved to another. Rather, my Father has quietly opened the way, often after much "sitting still" on the part of His daughter; repeated disappointments; "hope deferred"; and finally, a revealing of some plan which does not at all fit my expectations.

But, oh, His thoughts are not my thoughts! And He knows the thoughts which He thinks toward me—they are "of peace, and not of evil." And in the meantime, while I am waiting, watching, praying, He gives quietness and peace. He will never suffer me to be tempted above that I am able. (And it is He, not I, who knows what I am able!) "So I go on, not knowing—I would not if I might. I'd rather walk in the dark with God than go alone in the light."

Over and over, I am impressed with the importance of walking alone with Him, following Him regardless of all else, not concerning myself with the paths where He is leading others. "Thou will show *me* the path of life." "He shall direct *thy* paths." Amen, Lord.

Summing up, she then sealed all these thoughts about God's all-wise, individual thoughts toward His children in a fitting, closing prayer.

I accept Thy way for me as good, acceptable, and perfect. Thou knowest every thought and desire of my heart. They are not hid from Thee. And Thou well knowest that my ways have not been Thine—my plans not what Thou hadst so wisely planned. So once again I acknowledge that "so foolish was I, and ignorant . . . as a beast before Thee . . . nevertheless, I am continually with Thee: Thou hast holden me by my right hand. Thou shalt guide me with Thy counsel and afterward receive me to glory. . . . My flesh and my heart faileth, but God is the strength of my heart and my portion forever."

I praise Thee and thank Thee, blessed Lord, my Father. Thou hast done all things well.

Though she was such a young woman when she wrote of it here (only twenty-three), this practice of being alone with God—waiting, trusting, being assured of His Shepherd heart toward her—was her lifelong journey. People often said of her, "She seems so serene and peaceful." But only through the sincere reading of Scripture and continually giving her heart in trust to God was she able to maintain that peace, even as she entered into dementia in the early 2000s. She truly lived out the deep, hard beauty of these words she wrote, bearing witness, like she said, that He does "all things well."

My father also, during this time of active waiting, was learning from the Lord some of those maxims for which he's become most remembered:

September 24

1. Answer to the Rudder, or answer to the rocks.
2. Wherever you are, be *all* there. Live to the hilt every situation you believe to be the will of God.
3. Determination, not desire, determines destiny.

And this one:

SEPTEMBER 25: He who maketh Ease his god, Sufficiency his altar, Pleasure his priest, and Time his offering knows not what man is born for.

He was trusting, as Psalm 31:15 says, that "my times are in thy hands." Or as Psalm 139:16—"In thy book they were all written, even the days that were ordained for me." These were *"ordained days"* then, he called them . . .

. . . whether spent in waiting, working, or whatever. We have asked guidance, been obedient where we understood what was to be done, and now wait word for the next step.

Meanwhile, no letters passed between them until my mother wrote on October 2, saying her brother Phil had received *"a card from Bill, and I think he said you two would not be able to go out to the field for a year or so. I didn't know whether this applied only to Bill or to you also,"* but . . . either way, the letter she wrote him at this juncture was both charge and blessing.

October 2

Jim, you and I have had so much of the Word, with so much of the fellowship with those who know Christ, and so much knowledge—oh, that we might *know Him,* the Altogether Lovely, that His life might literally be manifest in us. . . .

I realize afresh how desperately little of Christ others may at present see in me, but truly I have learned to love and adore Him as I never did before. This of course makes me the more earnestly desirous that the inward peace and joy, which are of His Spirit, may be daily, hourly manifest, that my life may be hid with Christ in God.

And surely, if I ask this of my Father for myself, can I not also ask that you, in preparation for His special work for you in Ecuador, may become truly *Christlike?*

I have prayed fervently that you might know the Shepherd's voice, and no other. I trust that you will let nothing deceive you in the details of your going out—not common sense, experience, advice, ambition for souls rather than adoration for Christ, or any other voice than that of the living God, who *will not* suffer His faithfulness to fail.

All the things God had been showing her and doing within her this year—all the things she herself would want to be told if she were the one who was currently in my father's shoes—she shared them now in ink through this letter.

But as she reread the previous paragraph—the one counseling him to trust none but "the Shepherd's voice," being careful not to get ahead of God in "your going out"—a thought occurred to her. He might misconstrue the motive behind her words. *"You may think I am concerned for selfish reasons. I am quite sure nothing of that nature enters in. In fact, I was disappointed to hear that your going would be delayed."*

Yet perhaps the fact that she even caught herself and questioned how her words would be received is telling on its own. I'd say she couldn't completely escape the disappointment any person would feel, conflicted over her desire for someone—a desire which now seemed more unlikely than ever of leading where she once had dared to imagine. As recently as ten days earlier, she'd written in her diary, *"Dreamed last night that I was with J. again. I miss him beyond words."*

But here was the truth, as plainly as she could say it:

You are to me, now, only a brother. I understand what you have felt in calling me "sister," and the freedom with which you associate with other girls. I have been, in part, blinded by feeling. I trust it shall no longer be so.

She closed, simply and inclusively:

Say hello to brother Bill for me. May the Lord strengthen each of you with might by His Spirit and cause you to know Christ as you had not dreamed it possible to know Him. For who that knows Him can help loving Him?

[Signed] Your sister, for we are "builded together for an habitation of God through the Spirit,"

Betty

Being "just a sister" to my father was now her aim, though her feelings did still rise up in hope of some future day when she could be more assured of God's leading them together. Certainly for now, though, she did not want to interfere in his desire to go to Ecuador. And I believe she did not . . . even though my father, perhaps reading between the lines, picked up on whatever traces of loss and heartbreak she was possibly feeling. I think you'll spot him doing it in his next letter, mailed a month later from the home of a former Wheaton friend, Ed McCully, in Milwaukee, Wisconsin.

Ed McCully with my father. They were best friends at Wheaton and beyond.

This letter requires a bit of setup. He'd received word near the end of September that Ed was considering quitting school and beginning to look *"for open doors for a sold-out life."* He was speeding up his interest in leaving for the mission field. *"How I praised God to hear!"* my father wrote in his journal at the time, *"even wept as I read of the Lord's dealings"* with his old friend.

> I wonder if he may not be the man God would send with Bill and me to Ecuador. I have prayed for one more for the work, and perhaps God will answer thus. Grateful if so, Lord, very grateful.

Several weeks later, as new developments arose in their timeline, my dad had felt *"constrained to go to Milwaukee to seek Ed McCully, much the same as Barnabas went to Tarsus to seek Saul long ago."* He elaborated on the current status of their mission plans in his note to my mother.

November 4

A letter came from Tidmarsh this week informing us of his intended departure for England in November and his projected return to the States next spring. If he goes to Ecuador in the fall of '51, as is now planned, Bill and I will probably return then with him.

He followed this update with a second wave of news, intimating how it related to him and my mother.

Bill writes that he intends to marry as soon as Irene graduates from nurse's training—September 6, 1951—and that they will go to the field together. I do not share his liberty in this for adjustment reasons, but will let God lead. My personal exercise over the entire marriage problem remains fixed as it was at the IVCF-FMF convention in the winter of '48–'49. You will recall my letter from there.

(She certainly would.)

Now back to the part where he reacted directly to what she'd written in October. He began this paragraph of his letter with rather ominous sounding words. They were surely sparked by the disruption he felt was being created by the change in Bill's marriage plans. Imagine my mother's thoughts when she read *this*:

You are still a problem for me.

What did *that* mean? The "problem," I think, is that when he finally locked in on the coordinates for his missionary pursuit, he slammed the door for good on marriage. He'd mentally moved on, I believe. And I think when he read my mother's attempts in her letter at explaining what she meant, he saw someone trying too hard to keep her feelings from showing through. She hadn't given him all the way up, he thought. And though he didn't really want to slow down in the midst of his gung-ho efforts toward Ecuador to do it, he again felt the unwanted pressure to apologize for ever starting something with her that the Lord was refusing to let him finish.

He did it rather awkwardly this time.

My fluctuating and forgetful affections cause me often to wonder if I have ever loved at all. But the boldness with which I have stirred up affection in you shames me now to silence, and I could wish for your sake something had come of it sooner. This is not to reopen old sores. I am delighted at your remark re: the predominance of *family* feeling between us, as brother and sister, for it is all I can appeal to now for a basis of fellowship. But it is sufficient.

Translation: When you said, "You are to me now only a brother," I hope you meant it.

And I believe she did, especially judging by her initial reaction voiced in her next letter, sent two weeks later. She opened with a few select Scripture verses she'd recently encountered. *("Read these words several times, Jim—I wonder what words stand out especially for you?")* She poked fun at him for writing so seldom. *("Thanks for breaking down and letting me know where you were!")* She challenged him to go easy on Ed, not to exert his own will upon him. *("I trust that you are trusting the Lord to lead Ed, and not putting undue pressure on him to do what seems good in your eyes.")*

In other words, she was writing the way an older sister in the Lord might write a younger brother.

November 19

And, oh, I do entreat you to really rest with regard to our relationship. You say, "You are still a problem to me." Let it not be so. *I* am in the Will; *you* are in the Will. Therefore, there is no problem. Tomorrow does not concern us. It is our Father's.

You speak of "forgetful affections." If this is what created the "problem" or any confusion of mind, cease wondering. Are we not creatures of time and space? Are we created constant by Nature? No—whatever there is of steadfastness in us is Christ Himself. It is not for us to strive to control and steady ourselves. It is for us to commit our poor beings to Him who is all steadfastness and truth and love. Then let Him do with us today as He wishes—perhaps as yesterday we should never have anticipated He would do. . . .

She returned then to a theme carried over from earlier in the year.

So "delight . . . commit . . . rest." It is the only way. I have prayed, when thinking of you, the psalmist's prayer: "Let not them that wait on thee be ashamed because of me." Have no care for me, Jim. He alone is enough. And He has never failed us yet. "Lacked ye anything?" And they said, "Nothing."

I rejoice, oh, I rejoice—and you do the same. I do not like to think of you troubled about all that has gone before in these two and a half years. You know that there is no need for any feeling of strain between us.

In closing, she joked again about the work he said he'd been doing while staying with the McCullys—painting their house.

Should you happen to be any farther east in your "missionary journey," there is always welcome for you here—in fact, I'm doing some painting, so any willing workman would be more than welcome! . . .

Say hello to Ed, if you happen to be there or to your Auntie Eileen [in Chicago] if you are there when you receive this. Trust our Thanksgiving will be one of thanksgiving.

Gratefully, Betty

See, I think she'd truly let go—out of a sisterly love for him, out of a childlike love for Christ.

His final letter of 1950 came from Huntington, Indiana, home of Bill Cathers's parents. He was redeeming the time by leading a number of families in Bible study on basic tenets of the faith as well as robust discussions on the more controversial theological topics of the day. He'd been there since a few days before Thanksgiving, and it was now nearly Christmas.

December 19

Last week Ed and I met in Chicago for a spying out of a little town (5–6,000) in southern Illinois called Chester. The prospects in radio and in literature distribution seem now so bright that we feel it to be of God to go there, facing a pioneer situation together and trusting God for that demonstration of His power that Paul knew in the early days. . . . After the first of the year, we will return there, and then I shall be better able to describe the work for your prayers.

Billy may be home next week for a few days. We have heard recently that he ponders marriage early—perhaps by March. Tidmarsh is furloughing in England now, and will return in the spring for U.S. preaching, intending to return to Ecuador in the fall, God willing, and we with him.

Those were the high points of his latest news. But the best, most satisfying piece of news seemed to be what God had done in their relationship through this year, spent all but two days apart. I think he finally believed her, that she wasn't covering up or pretending. They were discovering the real joy of just being themselves, the result of being fully His.

Somehow I have a new rest in thinking of you now. Far from troubling me, thoughts of you bring thankfulness for the steadfastness Christ has wrought in you. I trust you, in a way I cannot explain. Not in the sense that we usually use that word between man and woman, as if you would be faithful to me. (That now has no place in our thinking.) But in the sense that I have no fear of offending you. I trust your understanding of me—an understanding forged in the furnace of distance and long silences. The trial of separation has made us one in a way the pleasure of association could never have done.

So we end the year of 1950 in their writings with both of them deeply committed to God's work and His plan for each of them. Even if it meant no further reunions, they were willing to give those up, if only that Christ be magnified even more. My mother captured both their feelings well, I think, in the following journal entry on her birthday.

DECEMBER 21: For twenty-four years the Lord has guided and preserved me, taught me and loved me (yea, He has loved me from before the foundation of the world), been merciful and gracious, and in thousands of ways shown His lovingkindness. What shall I render unto the Lord for all His benefits to me? There is nothing, nothing which I can give, save the very life He died to redeem, and in this life He designs to dwell! . . .

Lord, I do once more acknowledge, with all my heart, that I am Thine. No claim have I upon this life—past, present, or future. I am all, all Thine own. . . . Therefore, O dear Lord and Master, Redeemer, Lover, Friend, Beloved—do Thou work out Thine entire will in my life henceforth at any cost, in the time that is left for me on this earth. How short that may be, I do not know at all.

But I trust Thee.

I set my love upon thee, Child,
I knew thee far away
I wept to see thee wandering, wild,
I yearned 'til thou didst pray.
One of a hateful rebel band,
Strong in thy lust for sin,
A furtive, fitful, fiery soul,
I loved: I called thee in,
Stripped thee of thy grimy pride,
Laid bare thy secret want,
Poor vagabond of empty ways
I sent my Spirit to haunt.
Now, desert son, the choice is thine;
So let us drink from Thine above—
The love of Jesus for His bride.

JIM ELLIOT

Kiss me, heavenly Lover, in the morning.
Be Thou the first to sweeten
This whole day's speech with that warm, honeyed touch
Of Thy caress.
And tenderly, while yet each eye lies unawaked,
Come lightly and impart to them
For day's long hour a heavenly set
To see all things as through a lover's eyes,
By soft caresses from the lips of Him
Who lives in Paradise.
Kiss me, Christ of beauty, here alone
The two of us, while dawn
Steals down the slopes and
Wakens day's bright eye to smile on me.
Let not its luring draw me from the sense
That I belong to One
Whose first embrace full ravishes,
Who has kissed the son.

JIM ELLIOT

LOVE'S LONGING

My father's prose was as poetic as his poems. I find myself rejoicing with him in this next selection from mid-January 1951, where he celebrates the view of evening light and the sense of God's surrounding presence and beauty. I share that same amazement when awed by the glory and splendor of creation, but I don't have his ability to express it.

> All day the sun dropped hints of spring, and at dusk, returning from the shop, I exulted in the distinct wall of purple—the Ozark foothills—close guarded by the unblinking Venus. The night spread black and blossomed brilliantly with stars.
>
> I walked out to the hill just now. It is exalting, delicious. To stand embraced by the shadows of a friendly tree with the wind tugging at your coattail and the heavens hailing your heart, to gaze and glory and to give oneself again to God, what more could a man ask? Oh, the fullness, pleasure, sheer excitement of knowing God on earth. I care not if I never raise my voice again for Him, if only I may love Him, please Him.

But the way he closed this excerpt takes me even deeper into the praise of our Creator.

> Mayhap, in mercy, He shall give me a host of children that I may lead through the vast star fields to explore His delicacies whose fingers' ends set them to burning. But if not, if only I may see Him, smell His garments, and smile into my Lover's eyes, ah, then, not stars, nor children, shall matter—only Himself.

God gave him only one child—me—and yet gave my husband and me eight children, with a little one already in heaven, named Joy, whom I'm hoping he's met. Each of them knows God as the Lover of their souls, the Giver of all good things. They are, like all children, one of God's blessings as a heritage, and are part of Jim Elliot's heritage as well.

But of course he couldn't know all this yet in 1951. Nor could he know, except in his keen mind's eye, the many challenges and adventures awaiting him hundreds of miles nearer the earth's equator in South America, where he so wished to be. His being a missionary, for now, looked more like laboring for Jesus in the small Mississippi River town of Chester on the Illinois-Missouri border, fifty miles southeast of St. Louis.

January 11

Ed and I bought a '38 Chevy and came here after New Years. We have a $40 per month, two-room efficiency (whatever *that* may mean) apartment. I am cook. We could use anything any normal young couple of bachelors would find helpful by way of household hints. We have taken a job selling loaders to feed mills—so far no sales. If worst comes to worst, I may have to get to painting again.

Today we contacted the radio station owner, and tomorrow we will meet him to sign a contract D.V. *[Deo volente: "God willing"]* We will have a fifteen-minute program on Friday morning and a half-hour program on Sunday afternoon.

It wasn't going to be easy, as he went on to observe in this same January letter.

These things I write for your prayers. Ed and I are enjoying the work here, although adjustment to small-town thinking is different from what I supposed. There is nothing of any account for God in town—much formalism and joining of churches, but no life in its fullness, richness, depth, and reality as we have found it in Christ. It is as in the days of Samuel—the word of the Lord is rare, precious. Pray that it might run in us and be glorified.

Ed has enjoyed a brief introduction to our dear A.C. It is amazing how many I have found who light up and thrill at "Make Me Thy Fuel" or "Hast Thou No Scar?" Bless God for the sweet gift to His church.

Nearly midnight. Good night, Betts—

Jim

But as the month wore on, he and Ed were running on empty. A week later, he wrote in his journal:

JANUARY 18: No sales or income thus far, just draining resources, and those will not last more than another week. I have had hopes of laying by some money for the field, but selling is not going to be able to do that at our present rate. Desired to share in the work of financing the radio here and other evangelical efforts otherwise, but God has hemmed me in to nothing, that I may have nothing, do nothing, want nothing, save Himself.

His wanting to be "nothing" reminds me of Paul, who said he counted "all things but loss for the excellency of the knowledge of Christ Jesus my Lord" (Phil. 3:8).

He wrote this poem also in January:

Jesus, Thou art now my end;
Thou my starting, too, hast been,
Oh, be Thou my present friend,
I would walk and on Thee lean.

My mother, meanwhile, still at home, was tutoring two high school girls privately, leading children's Sunday school and afternoon Bible clubs, and also working part-time on the sales floor of a women's department store in Philadelphia. Though it wasn't exactly where she saw herself headed—still eager for the self-sacrifice of foreign missions—she received these current tasks as blessed opportunities from God's hand. She'd written the previous fall:

> The Lord, true to His Word, has guided me once more, when every possibility which I could see failed. It is when we cannot conjecture as to what He will do, that He most thrillingly exposes His plan—exceeding abundantly! Not that that which I can demonstrate to others, of His leading, is so unusual. But the soul knows. The apparent disappointments are His new opportunities to love us and hold us by the right hand.

She feared this picture *"might turn out to look just like me, and then of course I wouldn't have sent you one!"*

Having finally filled the pages of her little five-year diary, she turned now to keeping *"a series of notes, perhaps as a journal, that I may record only those days or thoughts which appear worthy of remembrances."* Among the first of the year was this one:

JANUARY 19: Since I last wrote, I have read the biography of Frances Ridley Havergal. It did what other Christian biographies have done—deepened my hunger for knowing Christ in His fullness, for living wholly "unto Him who died for us." I am impressed, always, upon reading of someone who lived a holy life, with the reflection, "What would be written of me, were I to die today?"

God alone knows how very, very little I know of *true* holiness, Christlikeness, and Calvary love. My closest friends know that there is very little that could be truthfully said of my "Christian character." But, oh, let me *cease* from myself, to behold the beauty of the Lord, to inquire in the tabernacle. For Christ is my righteousness. *He* is my joy, my peace, my salvation. He is forever, unchangeably, and *altogether lovely.* Praise Him! I will trust Him with my whole heart. He will lead me, by His Spirit, into all truth. He will do whatever His lovingkindness dictates.

From this humble, spiritually attuned heart, she composed her first letter of the year to my father. It contained, once again, a sisterly tone and message.

At last I have returned to the actual realization that you are still a person, and not just a Letter-Every-Month. Do you know the feeling? Especially when it goes way beyond a month, as it so often does nowadays, it is hard to keep fresh the memory of the real *person*.

As before, she seemed to catch herself at this point, adding, *"I find this to be true with anyone—not just with you, Jim!"* I think she didn't want to give a wistful impression, as though longing for him, but wanted simply to say . . .

How very good it is to hear from you. The Lord has answered prayer, and led you forth by the *right* way. (Is it not wonderful to know that whatever other adjectives may be applied to our appointed path, this one invariably fits perfectly, for we are in His hands, whose ways are forever *right!*). And I am thankful.

She wrote freely, flowingly. She picked up a train of thought he'd begun in his previous letter, concerning the importance of seeking the Word of God rather than the word of man. *"I think now we, you and I, are beginning to reckon this paramount,"* she said, commenting that it was another one of those areas where they were feeling drawn toward the same spiritual emphasis at the same specific time.

She made further observations on current events, particularly the rather apocalyptic feel of the escalating war in Korea, following so soon on the heels of World War II. My dad was a declared 4E draft classification—conscientious objector, on religious grounds—which left him unclear on what the Selective Service would demand of him. As he described it, *"Waiting is living these days."*

She also said she was *"glad that you felt at rest concerning me, Jim,"* referring to what he'd written in December about his comfortable, trusting feelings toward her. One can tell from her letter that she was mainly just enjoying talking with him, sad only that she felt *"straitened by the use of words—further by the condensing of them to fit a little 2 x 4 letter!"*

But there will come a time when you and I will have no need of words—for I believe that in Paradise we shall express exactly what we feel, effortlessly and perfectly. How could words do that? Well, it's fun to try, anyway. And it is always good to share what we are able to share.

One thing about his current situation, however, was truly arousing her curiosity.

I have been wondering especially how the radio work is going. What a difficult thing this must be—to keep always in mind, when there is no visible audience, that "the kingdom of God is not in word, but in power" (1 Cor. 4:20).

This radio ministry was a puzzle to both my parents. It was such a new, untried medium for religious broadcasting. Who was your audience? How could you know who was listening? What would cause those who were already believers to make time for tuning in? And who of the non-churched would care to listen or feel led to respond by mail? Interesting to read her quizzical comment in hindsight now, aware of how her own radio ministry would occupy a treasured fifteen minutes of each weekday for thousands of *Gateway to Joy* listeners throughout twelve flourishing years—and still be airing currently on Bible Broadcasting Network stations.

"Teach the believers, Darling." It was the last thing my father said to her, as he left on the plane with Nate Saint for the beach where he would be killed. When she'd asked, "What shall I do if you don't come back?" he answered, "Teach the believers, Darling, teach the believers." Yes, and she's doing it yet today!

(Speaking of her curiosity, she also mentioned in this letter *"a perfectly maddening taste for the study of nuclear physics, stimulated by a friend of ours who is a Ph.D., and who has shown me around his lab at Rutgers University. I spent last weekend with him and his wife."* A month later, she'd be talking about a free clinic she visited in the inner city, sponsored by the Christian Medical Society. *"If I had had the managing of my life,"* she said, *"I should most certainly have been a doctor."* She was just eagerly curious by nature, about everything. And she'd love knowing her youngest grandchild, Sarah, is currently in medical school.)

But nothing captured her attention more completely than both the present and eternal reality of life with God. Writing in her journal, she said:

FEBRUARY 11: So long as we are in the flesh, I think we shall never be loosed from the things of time. Of course we shall not. Else how should we learn to be "overcomers." This thought came to mind as I came to my room to seek the Lord's face, and, upon seating myself at my desk, found myself reading over one of J's letters—from 1948, at that! Ah, joy in its purest form shall never be found there. Fellowship with Christ alone rests the heart, cools earthly desire, "satisfieth the longing soul."

Watching these thoughts crystallize in her mind, as she continued letting go of my father's affections, stirs in me the memory of my own "falling in love" as a teenager. I recall her telling me how feelings come and go, that I was probably too young to be absolutely sure this was the person I would marry, and that I needed to trust in God for His appointment and timing.

But of course, I thought I knew His mind already. I knew God had brought the two of us together. Here was a guy with whom I enjoyed a lot of laughter and who I thought was just plain fun. I was certain he must be the right one. But her wise counsel proved true. I saw this young man in a new light once we entered the same college. I realized I hadn't thought seriously enough about what it meant to wait and trust the Lord to lead me toward the husband He'd chosen for me.

Reading her thoughts on the page now, from this distance, I see a young woman who'd been in the furnace of waiting much longer than I ever thought could be possible. Yes, she lived with questions; yes, she felt her longings. But her sincere desire was to go only where the Lord wanted, and only to marry if He had chosen someone for her.

Finishing the thought, she quoted a stanza from the hymn "My Faith Looks Up to Thee":

> O may my love for Thee
> Pure, warm, and changeless be,
> A living fire.

Her love for God, made possible by His unchanging love for her, was the only reason for waiting and trusting. It remains our only reason, too. The silence of waiting is the crucible of our faith.

And in February 1951, the crucible was as active in Chester, Illinois, as in Moorestown, New Jersey. My father's next letter:

February 22

Things are not any easier here. Discouragement has hemmed us sharply this past week, for although we have known no lack in the outward things, there has been a strong sense of not having possessed boldly as we should have. Ed grows depressed more easily than I, and the scarcity of blessing hereabouts has not been easy to take. He said yesterday, "Brother, everything I do here is putting out the fleece; if souls aren't saved and this isn't my calling, I see no point in putting my life into it." I couldn't find words somehow, and there was a long silence after.

The radio work, a joy in itself, has yielded only one card of encouragement, and that from believers. We have asked, and are asking, for a witness that will divide the whole city on the TRUE ISSUE. But as yet, there is no sign. . . .

There is a certain despairful loneliness snooping about these days, and I can almost hear the streets and building bristling with the note that haunted David—"Where is thy God?" I don't mean to sound dismal, but there is a certain bleakness about a place like this where no liberating truth is being sounded out. The "synagogues" are full, but still hollow with unreality. Oh, Bett, if earth in its brighter shades be so drear, what must its denser ones be? Thank God for that sense of "looking for a city which has foundations," which prevails when one sees the basis of these.

As if the lean ministry times weren't wearying enough, he was finding the business world *"a crude one, almost animal in certain aspects, and powerfully affecting to a newcomer, as I regard myself. The very principle of making money by selling things at a profit is distasteful at times, yet it seems to be my job for now."*

One way he sought to combat the tug of both discouragement and tent-making duties was by treading fearlessly into the slums one Monday night to declare the gospel.

Not easy, but comforting to be among those blessed poor—with Jesus in a sense that we are not when among the self-sufficient. We must go again soon. It makes one scornful of vanity and not much I love with life—especially this life of banks and bills and rates and percentages.

In addition, desperate for some way of sharing Jesus effectively, they'd gotten access to a little storefront space along the river.

We hope to use it for children's meetings, but it must have some work done on it first. It has fallen into a terrible state, and will probably take some time to recondition. There are many of the little "raggedies" about, who will be our first fruits in Chester, we trust.

My dad wasn't giving up, obviously. But he was uncharacteristically low. He mentioned Ed's parents passing through for a day or two. They'd been an encouragement, he said. But as he meekly admitted in the next breath, *"Almost anyone from outside would be now."*

Integrity, simplicity have been our guides under God and are now our defense before Him. This Jericho must fall or I shall be unable to go on in the path of faith. Pray for us, as Jesus for Peter, that our faith fail not.

What I see next is a marker, a turning point in the development of my parents' story. He'd never been the one in real need of encouragement. Even during his "Renaissance," when my mother had challenged him roundly, both in print and in person, he took it, dealt with it, and moved on to the next thing. He didn't let it slow him down much. But the wheels were really grinding at this point. His faith, though still incredibly strong, was being put to an extreme test. Some of the doubts which Ed had expressed out loud were now showing up more regularly in my father's journal, in my father's voice.

FEBRUARY 24: Was much cast down in spirit last evening. Ed and I have been here in Chester six weeks, with so little evident blessing from God.

MARCH 5: Evening. Too weak even to demonstrate weakness. Have come to such a state that I must desire to desire! The tears of my heart are frozen in the cold of my intellect.

MARCH 17: Sterile days. The past few days have been very trying and difficult. . . . Have had thirty-two nights of "Youth Rallies" in Sparta with fifty to sixty-five out in the public school gymnasium. There is little interest, and very few young people are reached in this way. . . .

There has been a sense of discouragement and doubt come over me through this. I prayed, simply, earnestly, believingly, insofar as I knew how, and did not receive what I asked for, namely, 150 people and six conversions. I know all the old reasons for not being heard and getting better answers and so on, but all that does not solve this difficulty.

Up until now, in all his correspondence with my mother, he'd often been the strong one who felt called upon to rally her spirit, exhorting her to sail forward on the winds of kingdom ideals—*with* him or *without* him. But now, as a true sister, my mother was the one who really stepped up, delivering just the right balance of encouragement and coaching. Seeing him in this state, I think she understood him better than ever before. She knew what he truly needed from her. And because the Lord had met her so richly in recent days, she wanted my father drinking from the same well of divine sufficiency that she, too, had been surviving on.

She didn't stop until she'd written *"one paragraph of three pages! I feel that I could write a book, just about now. Forgive me."* (For our sake, I'll insert a few paragraph breaks so we won't tire at a word of it!)

March 15

It was not hard to detect the discouragement in your last letter—it seemed to drag each word back. In a letter from your mother, she says she sensed the same in your letters home. *[Yes, at my father's prompting, she'd begun writing to my grandmother again, with better results this time!]*

Jim, dear brother, it is just here that the nature of your consecration—which is the same as saying the nature of your love to God—is tested. The decisions which are made in "green pastures" are tested (a good word, isn't it? Think of the test tubes in a lab, etc.) in the "valley of the shadow," for it is here that He is most vitally with us, if I may use the expression, although He is forever equally "with us," since He tabernacles *within* us.

You say, "This Jericho must fall or I shall be unable to go on in the path of faith." Surely you were not really thinking when you made that statement. The very principle of faith precludes any and all necessity of dependency upon *anything* but God Himself. . . . Do you love God for Himself alone? Or do you love Him for His gifts, His conscious presence, His love to you, His evident blessing upon what you do, etc.?

This next part could hardly be in greater contrast to the spiritual expectations of most people in our day, and needs to be clearly expressed and communicated for this reason alone, if for no other.

Jim, I truly believe there comes a time in the progress of the soul who truly desires to be comfortable to Christ's image, when God strips him *not only* of earthly props in the form of friends, possessions, talents, or whatever he may have *outside of God*—but also a time when the all-wise, all-loving Father strips that soul of even His own conscious and evident blessings and gifts. (These

> March 15, 1951
> Moorestown
>
> It was not hard to detect the discouragement in your last letter—it seemed to drag each word back. In a letter from your mother, she says she sensed the same in your letters home. Jim, dear brother, it is just *here* that that the nature of your consecration—which is the same as saying the nature of your *love* to God—is tested. The decisions which are made in "green pastures" are tested (a good word, isn't it? Think of the test tubes in a lab, etc.) in the "valley of the shadow"—for it is here that He is most vitally with us, if I may use the expression, although He is forever equally "with us," since The Tabernacle within us! You say "This Jericho must fall or I shall be unable to go on in the path of faith." Surely you were not really thinking when you made that statement. The very principle of faith precludes any and all necessity of dependency upon *anything* but God Himself. It has He has left us, in

may include an infinite variety of forms—joy, a sense of His nearness, conscious grace in prayer, fruits which may be seen or definitively enumerated, etc. etc.) This process, however devastating it may seem, must be recognized as another further *providence*. Another gracious answer to our sincere cry of *faith*, "Thy will be done.". . .

When we ask in the most entire honesty of our hearts to be made like Christ, we ask usually with certain more or less vague ideas as to just what that means. But Christ takes us at His word—indeed, why shouldn't He, for it is He that inspired that very prayer in our hearts—and does exceeding abundantly above all that we asked or thought. He purposes holiness—nothing less—in His child. So He sets about to produce just that in us, by His own methods. . . .

It is the duty of the Christian to receive. He receives the initial step of salvation, which of course includes the scriptural truth of immediate sanctification, but he also receives just as truly thereafter each new step in his progress of conformity to Christ. It is wonderful to know that it is not only required that we love God with a pure heart, but is also possible. The soul who loves God only for Himself, apart from His gifts, knows indescribable peace.

She closed with an uplifting spirit, sharing in his struggle.

The Lord has been so merciful in leading me, in teaching me to trust in a way I never dreamed possible. I want you to trust Him wholly, Jim, for the accomplishment of His will in you there in Chester. He will be glorified—only believe.

I am trusting for you and Ed. Perhaps the Lord does not purpose that you should ever see "results"—(oh, earthy word! not in Scripture!)—in order that you may the more clearly see Him, who is "before all things." So long as the *object* of your faith does not fail, *your* faith need not fail. If that object, however, is the visible gifts of God, it may fail. If the object is God Himself, it will never fail!

I thank God for your friendship, and I praise Him over and over for the way in which He has directed our paths and our relationship. I can't get over how wise and loving and merciful and Father-like He has been!

Because of Him, Betty

I love reading that again. Closing my eyes, I can picture her lips forming every syllable. And from the sound of it, my father received it with equal, and humble, appreciation.

April 16

Your last letter was like Paul's to the Corinthians, at once rebuking and comforting, and I am grateful for it.

He then summarized her points in the language of his own translation.

This trial of faith, a courtroom drama constantly in session for believers, is more precious than gold, Peter says. It has been that here. Faith has been under fire—I think its Source is Christ—and it has been strengthened and proved precious. New problems have arisen and combined with some unsettled ones sufficiently to dishearten me, but God is faithful and the prayers of His Son effectual when He prays that my faith fails not.

Yet even with the ongoing challenges, he had a good many intriguing news items to report. *"This letter has been congealed up in the barrel of my pen for some weeks,"* he declared. His writing sometimes astounds me with its wild creativity in images and metaphors. I love it!

First item: Wedding Bells?

Ed has had two long jaunts up Michigan way to see Marilou Holboth, youth and music director for Robert Savage's Baptist church. Just between you and me, Betts, don't be too surprised to hear about old Ed giving a ring soon. It isn't official yet, but this Moody grad has sure been piling the letters into Box 242 at least one per day! He is "worse" than I've ever seen him.

Second item: Tidmarsh?

Word that Dr. Tidmarsh and wife are arriving in New York this week. They were to have left England the eleventh. I have been hoping you might have an opportunity to meet them, but have only now gotten any idea of where you could contact them. . . . I feel sure you would be stimulated by getting in touch with them. You will meet them before I do, if you see them now, and I have not told them anything about you, but your contacting them now may be helpful in future reference.

"Future reference"? Was this a hint at an unspoken prayer request? Or was it merely unintended foreshadowing?

Third item: Ecuador? Soon?

I filed my passport for Ecuador last week. The brother I think I mentioned in my letters to you from Wycliffe, Dave Cooper, was drowned three weeks ago. . . . He went out for a late afternoon swim in the ocean and never returned . . . . His work and vision for the unreached, smaller tribes of Ecuador has got to be carried on. I have given myself to the Lord for it, if He wills.

But as of yet, he still didn't know what the upcoming months (or years?) truly held.

Everybody is considering July marriages, but no one has given public notice. Bill C., Bob W., and Ed Mc. are all sorta working on me to stay in the Midwest until then, but I don't let it out until I can give official dates. I had hoped to be home by July, but don't know what the next few weeks will decide.

He was starting to feel conspicuous in his singleness—brought on, of course, by the hard line he'd drawn for himself in college, which he steadfastly maintained until he was almost twenty-five. But now, through continual contact with his best friends who were getting married or engaged, he was feeling the brunt of his own choice.

Perhaps that's why he sealed this letter with a closing he hadn't used in a long time.

Love, Jim

I think he just couldn't help himself in his impulsiveness. It's something we've rarely seen, and won't see a lot again in their yet-unclaimed future. But . . .

"Love, Jim."

I'm sure she instantly noticed it.

And I'm sure it brought a mixture of agony, hope, and consternation to my dear mother.

SPRING AND SUMMER

Mid-year brought more specific direction from God, bringing much encouragement as she waited for a clear leading on her mission purpose. The balance of the year would provide even more.

> **MAY 2:** New guidance from my Shepherd—praise to Him. Miss Haines called last night to ask me to be pianist again for the Inter-Varsity conference at Keswick [a nearby retreat center] in June. Although this gives light for just one week of the summer, it is *light!* And I need know only one step. How many times since college graduation God has seen fit to teach me this.
>
> Furthermore, I have been offered the job of pianist at the Hepzibah Heights Conference in the Berkshires of Massachusetts for July and August. Of God's will in this I am not yet sure. He will show me.

I seize this opportunity to speak of my mother's love for music—not only for music, but for all kinds of art. She knew that God was the Creator of all beauty, and so she admired those extensions of His creation in classic art and music, often wishing she were more skilled in all of them.

But "skilled" she was, both on the piano and in singing. She had a clear soprano voice, and she taught me to sing from the time I was tiny. Being put to bed while she recited prayers and sang the great hymns she wanted me to learn was a true joy, and was instrumental in laying for me, early on, a foundation for my faith. As she often said to thousands, much of the theology she learned in life came from the hundreds of hymns her family sang as she grew up.

She knew also, however, the need for being very careful with the praise she received from others for her talents. From a journal entry back in the winter (again, following a day at Keswick), she'd written:

> Oh, sometimes I wonder if I should not abstain from singing altogether until I know that Christ alone is my motive. Truly I do desire that my voice, as well as my life and will, be wholly given to His praise. But the flesh is ever with me—it manifests itself in the most singular forms at times. I discover that self-effacement, springing wholly from selfish motives, taints my very highest aspirations to act of

God's glory. So I am driven once again out of myself, for I am all unprofitable. . . . I am but a branch, and without Thee can do nothing.

A good word for all who excel at the creative arts.

My dad wrote from Chester on May 12, sounding more encouraged than he'd previously been. In fact, my mother had mentioned that even his April letter had been *"brighter than the preceding one, and I was glad for that."* Not only had he been able to schedule his first face-to-face visit with Dr. Tidmarsh in Wheaton for the following Monday, but he and Ed McCully were finalizing preparations for a tent-meeting campaign they planned to conduct in the coming weeks. Getting the gospel out was such a passion to him.

May 12

The Lord heard us for a tent this week, and we will begin meetings May 19, Saturday, just one week from today. Please pray for us, Betts. I will be doing most of the preaching, and these every-night meetings are sapping to spiritual potency, especially when half the day is spent selling. We had fair interest in the High School rallies two weeks ago—but mostly "churched" people. Praying for an awakening among the business people and factory class.

He also described in more detail the work they were doing among the kids along the riverfront—their "River Rat" Sunday school, for which they'd coined the term "Club 66." (My mother, when hearing only the name, had quipped, *"What on earth is 'Club 66'? Sounds like a nightclub, but I don't think you and Ed are running one of those yet."* Although, she added, *"It would take more than that to surprise me by now."*)

The "66" is for the number of books in the Bible, and also the number of points required for a first-class member. We have a steady gang of thirty "trustys" every Lord's Day morning. . . . It's the most encouraging thing here. Pray for several junior high kids who show definite interest and some understanding.

Their tent meeting would eventually run through the middle of June. As with all ministry efforts, it was *"impossible to register the good that God has done in Chester,"* he said. But at least *"I can see several reasons for coming now that I did not see in January. Surely the Lord has led,"* despite *"nothing 'big' or extraordinary"* taking place.

Or maybe it had. Bill Cathers had come during the last week of May, staying to preach for a couple of days at their tent revival.

MAY 23: Enjoyed fellowship with Ed and him together for the first time. Believe now that God is going to lead us into work together in Ecuador, and trust His grace to knit us and make us compatible. The Lord has answered, rather is answering, my prayer of August 9, 1950, for another man.

Father, preserve Ed and Marilou; preserve Bill and Irene; preserve me and prepare us all for Thy work in Ecuador. Many, many thanks for our leading to this moment. Lead on, O King Eternal.

Truly my parents' sense of waiting and watching and seeking the Lord's will is exemplary to anyone who's searching for what God desires for them, no matter one's age or place in life. My mother, of course, like my dad, was just as eagerly yet patiently seeking direction. She'd accepted a speaking engagement at a women's missionary gathering in Philadelphia, with high hopes that it might shed light on her future.

MAY 22: I had felt all winter that perhaps God would open up a way for me to get to the field through someone at the conference, but He was pleased to keep the "cloud resting above the tabernacle." It has not yet moved on.

Then, hearing of Sir John Anthony Clark's desire to meet me, I was once again elated, thinking that he might be God's channel this time. He is a veteran of many years of missionary work in the Congo, and has done much translation work. . . . Had a lovely talk with Mr. Clark, but still felt no constraint toward any definite place.

God has his reasons for this withholding of much sought light, and I trust Him absolutely. Having asked repeatedly that He would reveal any sin or failure which might be hindering His revelation of the way, I have trusted Him to do this. Nothing, so far as I know, is between my soul and my Master, so I rest in the peace that goes beyond.

She seemed to have an unusual ability to make her mind *rest* and *wait*— though she also said many times to her audiences that she was a "first-class worrier." Thus she had that battle to fight, knowing how God commands us not to worry. Our natural tendency is to figure everything out, thinking God has given us a capable enough brain to do that. But as she often said to me, "It's a matter of the WILL; you make a CHOICE"—emphasizing the words "will" and "choice" strongly—"not to worry or fret." We must choose to obey, period.

Oh, for such steely devotion and courage.

Oh, to be dependent on Christ alone for our peacefulness.

She wrote my father only once more before spring melted into summer, finding time to write while she was away in Florida for her younger sister's graduation from HDA. *"As I write the date [May 31], I remember three years ago. It all seems very remote and detached from my present surroundings."* This whole visit, really, had struck her as being a surprising strain on her emotions, which she'd tried expressing in her journal a few days earlier.

MAY 28: HDA is to me the scene of the highest delights emotionally, sensuously. It is also the scene of agonizing conflicts of spirit, devastating fears. It is the scene of tenderest love for young people put to my charge during the short teaching days. It is now a place of indescribable longings and loneliness, in a sense. I do not exactly know why.

But she stowed away these private episodes of conflict, greeting my father with mostly cheery highlights and takeaways from her trip:

"Don't get too organized, brother!"

May 31

In many ways I wish you could have been here for the commencement. I find that my attitude toward the school is very different from what it was seven years ago. I should like to know your reaction. I know many things about it which you would not like. I also know things about *you* which *they* would not like. So it is perhaps well that you could not have been here.

She also couldn't suppress a "big sister" laugh at hearing of his multitasking efforts, from tent preaching to children's outreach to Bible study leading and beyond.

You sound like a regular Y.F.C. leader now—conferences, retreats, schedules, etc. etc. Don't get too organized, brother!

But within a few weeks, she too would be in organizer mode herself, wrangling a tent full of little boys at Pioneer Camp in Port Sydney, Ontario.

I had the "privilege" (?) of going to this camp for two weeks when I was ten. I'd never been away from my mother for that long, and was never so homesick in my life. I'm sure I was surrounded by much beauty and spiritual teaching there, but the only things I really remember well were the ice-cold lake water, flunking the swimming test, flunking the canoe test, and singing

"We gather together to ask the Lord's blessing" before every meal. The only good part was my counselor, a sweet girl named Trish. I remember her comforting words more than her instruction.

According to my mother's report, both in her journal as well as in a single letter to my father on July 29, the place didn't sound a whole lot different in 1951. But for about six weeks, she said, while trusting God to *"lead me to the field in His own time,"* this campground became her mission field—*"His chosen sphere for me."*

My dad, meanwhile, had headed home, following Bill and Irene's wedding in Wichita, Kansas, as well as Ed and Marilou's in Pontiac, Michigan. (*"Yours truly feels more conspicuous by the hour!"* he wrote.) But even returning home did little to put him at ease. Among his journal postings from those days was one that said:

> **JULY 12:** Lack funds in hand to buy equipment now. Folks are not wholeheartedly for my going to Ecuador. Want me to be a preacher in the States, I fear, or else to join Bert in Peru.

He didn't surface again on my mother's visible radar until a letter he wrote from Washington State arrived while she vacationed with her family at their annual summer retreat in the White Mountains of northern New Hampshire. He wrote it with apologies for *"this wretched ball-point,"* remarking how he hadn't remembered to fill his fountain pen when he'd left home for their own family vacation.

August 21

> You'll be at Gale Cottage by now with the Pioneer Camp experience a remembered blessing. I rather envied your time there, for though Nature sings loudly out here, it takes solitude to hear her, and I've had little enough of that since coming home. . . .
>
> We came to this little cabin for a couple of days. . . . Up here there is a long peninsula with twelve miles of wide beach, good clam beds, and not a break of river mouth or mountain head shouldering the sea in the entire length. The drive is exalting to the spirit, but not so breathtaking as the more rugged Oregon coast. I never think of that without recalling Short Sand Beach with you. I haven't been there since, and don't know if I would want to go now—alone.

My first thought on reading this selection is imagining them together on the Oregon shore line two years earlier, pointing out sea anemones to one another or the way the water flowed over the rocks. She often did the same with me, always exclaiming about the details and designs of creation.

My second thought is the rather noticeable longing in that final line (final word, really) of the paragraph: *". . . don't know if I would want to go now—alone."*

Maybe it came from twice recently having to stand up for his friends on their wedding days. Maybe it came from feeling not quite as at home around his family and in his old familiar haunts as he'd once been so easily accustomed. Maybe it was the same gnawing of loneliness my mother had admitted to feeling as if out of nowhere on her brief visit to HDA, a loneliness that now clawed at him the same way on the opposite corner of the country.

Or maybe it was because, with his sailing date tentatively scheduled for December 1—departing *"probably from Los Angeles,"* he said—he'd already drawn a circle around one particular piece of business he needed to handle before departing for South America. *"First, I'm coming East."*

Bill and I are scheduled for a meeting in the Jersey-New York area from September 21–October 12. Some ministry, some missionary, but mostly to get acquainted with the believers. I have a few days open in a rugged schedule and would certainly like to see you if the Lord would have it. Will you be at Birdsong?

My father and Pete Fleming, on the right.

He'd mentioned this prospect, somewhat offhand, in his previous letter two months ago (June 27), in discussing the potential plans for his embarkation.

There is a very strong possibility that I may be leaving from New York, and I am tentatively planning to spend a couple of weeks in the metropolitan area around October 1. This brings hopes that I may see you again, if you are to be at home. . . . I will make sure of a visit if you are there.

But who could know? His plans were constantly up in the air. Had she considered his visit likely, I think she would have written about it, whether excitedly or nervously—certainly prayerfully—which she did within hours of this more definite pronouncement in August. *"Word came yesterday from two very different (significantly different) sources,"* she wrote almost immediately in her journal.

She'd hinted at the first in her entry from a week prior, while still in New Hampshire.

AUGUST 19: The Lord seems to have been directing my thoughts to Dr. Northcote Dick's work in the Solomon Islands. I saw him a few weeks ago when I was over at Campus-in-the-Woods, and he was very encouraging. I have written to ask for his literature, and am asking God to open or close this door, as He sees fit.

The requested packet of information, detailing the work and opportunities for service among the South Seas Evangelical Mission, apparently arrived in the same day's post as my father's letter, which accounted for the second "word," for she added, *"Jim also wrote, saying that he is coming east on September 21."* What did it mean, these two things converging on her, all at once?

AUGUST 26: "Trust in *the Lord* with all thine heart, and lean not unto *thine own* understanding. In all thy ways acknowledge Him, and He shall direct thy paths." This I believe. How very thankful I am that I am not my own. Since I am the Lord's, He will show me the way. I know that I could never make the very weighty decisions which face me now. If the Lord directs me to the S.S.E.M., it means utter renouncement, and for this He alone is sufficient.

"Utter renouncement." What heavy words. Though she'd long known this day was coming, she sensed now the finality of not sharing life with my dad. It was a window she'd already turned away from, allowing it to close, though imagining there might yet be a chance it could somehow open once more. The choices before her now, however, made "utter renouncement" nearly inevitable. Even so, her faith triumphed over her wishes and feelings.

The struggles my parents experienced in their relationship were heartrending and intense. The shadow of that cross knifing between them— the symbol of their own death to self—had been enormously difficult, a consternation. But as my father, too, had done, she was willing to say, *"My life is Yours, dear Lord, do with it whatever You want."*

She'd known of Amy Carmichael's leaving her dear family for the rest of her life by going overseas. She also remembered having met Betty Scott Stam, only to hear a few years later how she and her husband were beheaded in China. Each of these examples and many others were all pointers to her, declaring the high risk of following the truth, the high cost of discipleship.

She didn't write my father back immediately. In fact, she wasn't thinking so much about the thrill of seeing him but the torture of knowing she'd soon be saying goodbye to him—again.

AUGUST 27: Last night I was beginning to dread already the parting which must come when J. leaves. There have been four goodbyes so far—each one very difficult; but this, it seems, must be the last. I thought to myself that I could not go through another—better not to see him again than to meet only in part. But how foolish of me to expect grace in advance!

The sorrow of saying goodbye to one so dearly loved, when she was more sure now than ever that no future marriage was coming, would have been beyond heartbreaking if she hadn't possessed such serious, intimate fellowship with God. I sincerely think there are *very few* people who could willingly submit to what she was preparing to do, knowing that one word from her lips could perhaps enable her to avoid the forever-ness of it. Countless people through the years have admired my parents' courage to go stoically on, past what human will or choosing would ever do. Count me, their daughter, as one who highly admires them as well, for so willingly casting all their care and each other on the Lord.

As the summer of 1951 ended, with each day swirling down a funnel toward September 21 and my father's visit, my mother more often took to paper, her thoughts too heavy and substantive to keep inside.

In one journal posting she wrote:

SEPTEMBER 9: Today I have asked again that the Lord will keep me from mistakes in discerning His will. O, it is so possible to be badly misled by one's own whims, but I will not fear even this, for has He not promised, "I will instruct thee and teach thee in the way which thou shalt go; I will guide thee with mine eye.". . .

O Lord, if Thy presence go not with me, carry me not up hence. For I have asked of Thee, and I cling to Thine assurance of guidance. Let me not go down to the South Seas (Egypt) and trust in Dr. Dick or anyone else, who, if I place faith in him instead of Thee, would even be a Pharaoh to me.

In another:

SEPTEMBER 10: There are things in my heart tonight hardly understood even by myself—fears, doubts, wanderings, huge questions. And, instead of fretting myself about them, or seeking anxiously for an immediate resolution of these things, I simply abandon them to Him who is perfect in knowledge. O, I trust Him—how wonderful it is, simply to trust.

But despite these rather daily entries on the private page, she apparently didn't quite know how to respond to my father directly about his impending visit. In fact, by the time he left home on his long journey by rail across the country, no letter had come from her. Nothing. No word. I can imagine him rolling along, mile by mile, jotting notes to himself about the various plans he needed to implement upon reaching the East Coast—places to go, people to meet, topics for his various speaking engagements. Time would be short. He'd need to make the most of it.

Yet perhaps he occasionally looked up from his writing, staring out the window as the blurred scenery rushed past, wondering—why her silence? What did it mean? Had he pushed the brother-sister relationship too aggressively? Had he distanced her heart from him by being so vocal in his independence, so determined not to need her? If he indeed had allowed himself to daydream about rekindling their closeness on this trip—and I don't know if that's true—I wonder how much any disappointment was weighing on him as he traveled eastward, and how much it may have competed against the focus he was trying to maintain.

I do know, when he'd made it as far as his aunt's house in the Chicago suburbs, my mother's latest letter—which had barely missed him in Portland—had been forwarded ahead, and he *"read it with joy,"* admitting to being *"a little concerned not hearing from you before I left home and wondered if I should make bold to visit Birdsong without an invitation."*

Her letter, finally in hand, made clear he was welcome. It was brief, saying she was glad to hear he was coming, hoping his days weren't completely booked.

Much to say—but why write when we can talk?!

Yes, *"there is much to speak of,"* he agreed, in the letter he dashed off to her from Chicago on September 13, which she hurried to answer in a flash so he'd receive her reply before he moved on.

September 15

Your letter came this morning, and it surely seems strange to be answering it the same day, now that we have accustomed ourselves to intervals of weeks! . . .

You say you plan to leave there Wednesday, which means that unless you are walking, it shouldn't take more than thirty hours at the most. So—why don't you come straight to Philadelphia by bus, arriving probably Thursday evening. I could meet you there, you could stay here that night, and then we could drive up to Plainfield in time for your meeting Friday evening. (It is about sixty miles, I think.) Even if you don't get to Philadelphia until Friday a.m., it would be easier to meet you there than very late Friday night. Mother says the car won't be needed here at home that day. If this plan is OK, please wire me as to the time of your arrival.

She went on to add that Bill and Irene were welcome to stay as well, if the two of them were coming. Her brother Phil, she said, was also looking forward to the visit. Everybody was really excited that Jim Elliot was going to be back at the Howard household again, like that Christmas of '47.

And so am I.

Betty

AUTUMN

With this surprise visit upon them, I thought it worth taking a moment to reconnect the small bits of time they'd actually spent together since the spring of 1948. Those three final weeks of my mother's senior year (when they first realized just how mutual were their feelings for each other) were the lengthiest amount of time they had spent together, though it was punctuated by final exams and graduation exercises. She then saw him for a couple of days in September of that year, you might remember, stopping through Wheaton on her way to PBI in Canada. They enjoyed the week at his home in Portland near the end of the following summer (1949). And they were able to steal one or two private chats when family and friendship obligations brought them together at my Uncle Dave's wedding in July 1950.

It all added up to barely a month—four weeks and a few days—covering a total range of almost three and a half years. From these scarce but sacred moments of face-to-face exposure came all the intensity of this story and their relationship.

Certainly they wished it had been more. Or, seeing how they'd resigned themselves to being only close friends, they might have wished it had been *less,* that it had all gone unspoken, rather than occupy so much of their attention and energy through the years. But if that had been the case, this autumn of 1951 would never have happened. And as the following letters and journals attest, neither of them (and none of us) would want to have missed it.

I said earlier I wasn't sure if my father carried many romantic hopes for his journey east. But I'm going to say now—I think he did. Otherwise, I have little explanation for the suddenness of his first recorded words after seeing her again.

SEPTEMBER 20: Arrived in Moorestown, New Jersey. Came to settled rest about Betty. I love her. The problem from now on is not "whom should I marry?" but "should I marry?"

This didn't mean, of course, that his renewed sense of love and attraction made life any less complicated.

Nearer to her now than ever, yet more confident still that God is leading me away from her, to Ecuador with Pete, and she to the South Seas.

("Pete," by the way, was Pete Fleming, an old friend traveling with him on this tour of speaking engagements and relationship building, who would later be among the five missionaries killed.)

I'm probably less sure of my *mother's* hopes for this visit, borne out by my dad saying that what passed between them as they talked in the *"fields behind Birdsong"* on Saturday was *"terribly upsetting to her."* Probably "overwhelming" would have been a better word. It was only "upsetting" as to how it affected their lives going forward. In any event she, as was he, was struck with the significance of what it all meant and what she was feeling. I'll let her words take it from here . . .

SEPTEMBER 21: We took a walk, and talked of many things, our relationship included. The Lord has tested us sorely, and I do pray and trust that "when He hath tried us, we shall come forth as gold."

I suppose there is no greater issue in the life of a young person than that of love. But Jim and I have long since settled it, that we are wholly at His disposal, at any cost, now and forever.

Jim says he loves me. There is no question in my heart anymore—I love him. I love him as I never thought I could love anyone. The thought of going on without him almost chills me.

Even so . . .

Jim is sure that God wants him on the field as a single man. May the God of all grace grant to him the great grace that will be needed, the strength to withstand the temptations which abound in such a stronghold of Satan.

> I bring a prayer that God will bless and keep you
> Thro' every moment with its joy or tears.
> I pray His arms may tenderly enfold You,
> To guide you, dearest, thro' the changing years.

Such an experience serves to wean our hearts from earth. We are pilgrims and strangers, and life is but a short journey Home. What will it be to be with Him who is our Well-beloved, the fairest of ten thousand? If it were not for the hope of His coming—the Daybreak when all shadows will flee away—one could not go on. But I love Him, trust Him, and praise Him, and ask only that I may know that I do His blessed will. Nothing else matters.

After the things that have been shown me in the past two days, I make bold to pray—"Father, if it be possible . . . Nevertheless, not my will but Thine be done." And I ask, too, that my will be one with His. . . .

I want to walk humbly and quietly with my Master, sensitive only to His wishes, not fluttering and eager with my own. The child that wholly trusts the lovingkindness of his Father watches expectantly for His next move, willing to wait until it is made clear, not jumping and skipping fitfully along in front of Him, afraid He will miss something if the child does not keep his eyes open. "My soul, wait thou only upon God, for my expectation is from Him."

All this happened, as she said, in only two days. But thankfully, their time together didn't so quickly conclude. He cycled back to her house whenever free of his other responsibilities. These opportunities for ongoing conversation led them to some monumental decisions—made not rashly, of course, even though made in quick succession. As we know, these decisions were the result of long testing as to the purity of their motives and the proven devotion of their surrender. And with each one—as often accompanies the favor of God's guidance—came an almost tangible sense of His peace.

SEPTEMBER 29: My heart is at peace, more than I have known, concerning Jim. I love him with all my heart, and it seems that God has once more guided us each aright.

Last night we spoke of the possibility of engagement before his going to the field, but it is not yet the Lord's time. Each of us feels, in our heart of hearts, that God will eventually lead us together—an amazing thing in itself, that we should feel this way and be free to speak of it to one another—but as yet it seems best for Jim to go entirely unattached, so that he can apply himself wholly to the task of orientation on the field.

In her scrapbook, my mother wrote, *"Just friends."*
New Jersey visit, Fall 1951.

"The possibility of engagement." The belief that "God will eventually lead us together." These were important developments. *"Furthermore,"* she added:

> God's will for me seems to be directed toward some Latin field. He alone knows how desperately I want to do only His will, so I know He will not suffer me to make a mistake in this.

This was huge obviously, since her latest leaning had been toward the South Pacific, though she was yet unclear about it.

But not even these mutual places of agreement comprised the sum total of what God was doing to astound her. There was also this: *"Jim's parents came down today for the weekend—another interesting circumstance, that they should be here just now."* (They'd dropped off their youngest child, Jane, at Wheaton and then worked an extended eastward swing into the trip.) *"Their attitude toward me seems to be one of friendliness, contrary to that which I sensed while visiting in their home."* What a change this represented which, based on that critical letter from two years ago, no one could've seen coming.

Only God could orchestrate all these events, she thought. And watching Him at work brought to her an almost indescribable relief . . . about everything.

> At long last, I feel an easiness, a rest, about our situation which is new to me. Last night, in our time alone together, there was a new sense of liberty and release from vague doubtings and fears. I can look back over the years of our relationship, and see such very marked development. In mind and spirit now, we are one.

Yes, finally, "we are one." My dear mother could now understand and believe that although my father still needed to go on singly to Ecuador, God in His kindness had brought them together again at this time with the added hope that He might bring them to marriage eventually. She was at rest—a depth of rest that belied all worry and fear—and could wait with patience until the exact time when perhaps they could be *more* "one" with each other. As she wrote to my dad in a quick note on September 30, mailed to catch up with him in New York where he'd be spending the week, she said:

> Know this—that I am at rest, as I know you are—in the revealed will of God in this regard. He has given light in the darkness. "Wilt thou love Me, trust Me, praise Me?" Yea, Lord—forever.

> *Saturday night —*
>
> *Jim, I have just read Vine's chapter on marriage. My heart responds **wholly**. I thank God for the grace of continuance, the steadfastness of purpose which He has wrought in you by Jesus Christ. Know this — that I am at rest, as I know you are — in the revealed will of God in this regard. He has given light in darkness. "Wilt love Me, trust Me, praise Me?" Yea, Lord — forever.*
>
> *EH*

He quickly answered back, affirmatively.

October 2

The will of God is sweet tonight, altogether "good and acceptable and perfect." The considerate love of the Lord Jesus for us seems such a kind thing now. I know it has always been so, but somehow I didn't see how wise it was when it didn't seem kind. . . . Remind me of this when I cannot regard His love as considerate sometime.

He then shared a story—one which my mother included in her biography of my father's life—but remains so poignant that I can't help but reprint it.

Stayed overnight with a brother in Queens who raises chrysanthemums for a hobby. He was telling me they don't bloom until every other flower is gone or going with the frost. I suspected that the frost might be what brought them to bloom, but he said, "No, it's the longer nights." He described a process of shrouding them before sunset and leaving them covered till after dawn to hasten their bloom. I really never realized the point of Rutherford: "But flowers need the darkness"—not just for rest evidently, but for blossoming. Need I allegorize?

No, his insight was perfect. Both of them saw the hand of the Lord in bringing them together, even as He had kept them apart during "the longer nights." In time they would observe many more signs of their Shepherd's leading and lovingkindness. They knew that the same Creator who makes chrysanthemums bloom in the dark would guide them as He does for all His children, through sunless days.

Like right now, my mother must have been thinking. If God was truly fitting her for a Latin American destination, *"I am perplexed,"* she said, *"as to what my next step should be."*

OCTOBER 2: Should I write Dorothy Jones, a girl who intends to go to Ecuador and needs a single woman to go with her? Should I go to New York and visit the Voices from the Vineyard office? Should I take steps toward getting to some Spanish-speaking country immediately, in order to begin working on Spanish?

My father was free with advice:

There are several things to keep in mind re: preparation for Ecuador. (1) Spanish, by whatever means. (2) Teacher's certificate, very valuable if attainable. (3) Medical training.

Yes, much to contemplate and prioritize, but only one place to start—in prayer. She closed her journal entry of October 2 with the words, *"Lord, these questions are all known to Thee. Do Thou give Thine answer. 'I would not take a single step apart from Thee.' And, Lord, keep me ever in utter dependence on Thee."* Then, as she occasionally did in her journal, she punctuated this next fragment of hymn lyric in print, rather than cursive, as well as in bold, repeated pen strokes, *"Hold o'er my being **Absolute Sway**,"* which truly reflected her heart—and my dad's—who encouraged her by saying, *"The Lord will not let you make any mistakes."*

But oh, how beautifully He did let them have this time to themselves— such savored moments throughout what amounted to five light-filled weeks.

Their next encounter included a bit of unexpected drama. My mother rode with her brother Phil and his wife, Margaret, to Hackensack, New Jersey, to hear my dad speak. But . . .

OCTOBER 12: Rain and heavy traffic delayed us, so that we were unable to reach there until the meeting was all over. We had a message delivered to Jim at the hall by the police, to tell him we were coming, and he should wait!

It was so good to be with him again. On Monday we had the whole day together—the first time since he's been east. We went to Oswego Lake, then down to the shore, then to Keswick, where we ate a picnic supper as the sun set by the lake.

Two weeks later, rather than unexpected drama, it was unmitigated delight.

OCTOBER 25: We have had four perfect days together. He and Pete Fleming, the fellow with whom he is going to Ecuador, Phil, Margaret, and I left New York City on Sunday night, after Jim and Pete's meetings, and travelled all night, arriving [at their vacation home in Franconia] around 9:00 a.m. It was surely cold, and the cottage was all boarded up and very bleak.

But to be here with Jim—it was beyond imagination. Monday afternoon we all climbed Bald Mountain and then hiked down over Artists' Bluff. Tuesday we hiked through the Flume, and then up to Lonesome Lake. Wednesday, a gray day, we took the Ammonoosuc Trail up to Lake-of-the-Clouds on Mt. Washington. The enjoyment of nature—all the loveliness our Father has made with His hands—is doubly rich sharing with Jim. Our minds run quite in similar patterns—complementing each other, dovetailing and meeting.

Last night he took me to Littleton, where we ate dinner at Thayer's Hotel, then drove up to the "Noth" *[the way New Englanders pronounce it]* where we sat in the car by Echo Lake, in a howling rain and windstorm. Just to be with him is peace, peace.

The thing that comes to me, time after time, is that each heavenly truth has its earthly counterpart, and human love reflects so much of divine love, of course, since it is of God. "He that dwelleth in love dwelleth in God." It is truly wonderful—and our dear heavenly Father has planned so perfectly, so lovingly, for us.

"There are three things," said the writer of Proverbs 30, "which are too wonderful for me, four which I do not understand: the way of an eagle in the sky, the way of a serpent on a rock, the way of a ship in the middle of the sea, and the way of a man with a maid" (Prov. 30:18–19 NASB). Genuine, pure love between a man and a woman, especially when each person seeks the others' best, is truly an amazing gift from God. Only He could have thought of it! *"And He has given us this love,"* my mother said personally of she and my dad—a love which bore such similarity to God's own love for them.

Our love is *His* love, manifested in us toward each other. Our passions and natural affections are awakened, vivified, channeled by the love of God.

"God is love." And for five autumn weeks in the Northeast, having had the privilege of spending at least some of that time together, their love filled them with a new wonder, awareness, and assurance.

The next day it filled them with something else. With longing.

OCTOBER 26: Alone. The word never held so much meaning. Jim has gone—and with him my very soul and heart. . . . As I look over this five weeks since Jim came east, I stand awed and amazed. What hath God wrought? True, we have loved for three years—nearly four. But never has there been any prospect of marriage, and consequently our relationship has been cautious and limited in expression.

Now it seems that God intends for us to marry, [but] we cannot enter into a formal engagement because of the uncertainty regarding the demands of jungle life. We know not how long the work may require of single men. Pete and Jim are ready for whatever the Lord indicates. . . .

But, oh, my flesh and my heart faileth! I feel absolutely empty, hollow, aching with loneliness. I want Jim. I love him strongly, deeply, powerfully. He is my life.

"Devotedly, Mother." Note to Mama from her mother, my Grandmother Howard (Katherine Gillingham Howard). She was sad for them at my father's leaving.

My father, clattering away from her on a bumpy railroad car—enough that he apologized for the shaky handwriting—was equally as undone.

October 29

All the while I have been unable to think for five minutes without being interrupted by thoughts of you. Your face did die with consciousness as I went off to sleep, then rose as I woke. Images, attitudes, phrases, looks, embraces hailed me from out of the past few weeks, and I nearly succumbed to think that it is not to be again for years, perhaps. All day Saturday there was that pressure at my chest that made me look away to the sky and exhale in a sigh, signifying I don't know what.

I am nearer tears this morning than I have been all weekend. Remembrance of what you said about missing me on waking came as dawn broke this morning, and I thought of you with your slender, white, and empty arms there in a warm bed . . .

This may be a phase—the sort of thing Pete wished me a speedy recovery from. I hope in a way that it is, but as yet it intensifies and shows no signs of let up. There is no need to analyze. I love you, Betty, and I feel it keenly this morning.

But what sounded like a wrap-up of his thoughts led only to more memories, recalling their last sighting of each other.

I will not forget your clear, wide eyes vanishing at the station on Saturday. The unfeeling lackey who tugged me back on the platform and shouted, "Watch out for the stairs," and slammed the cover, cut me out of a pleasure, that of seeing your eyes grow smaller and smaller until they disappeared. I had no tears. After a few minutes of strained silence, we began a slow conversation, and Pete soon had me talked out of tears.

"*Yes,*" she wrote in response, recalling the precise moment:

October 31

I was sorry, too, to see you jerked out of sight so abruptly on Saturday. I stood there until the last car had rounded the curve, then came to find myself completely alone on the platform, with gates closed and every human soul vanished! But I, too, was amazingly kept from tears just then. I am glad. It was not until I came to my room alone, after lunch, that I could let go.

Jim, I still stand amazed at the wonder of it all—the Lord's perfect planning for us, bringing you here just at this particular juncture when I had no idea where to turn (or, I should say, when any further delay would have precipitated my going on out to the South Seas). He knew all the thoughts, intents, and needs of our hearts and met every one.

And the exceeding abundantly (no, the train isn't rocking—it's only my heart) was the trip to Franconia. "O God of stars and flowers, forgive our blindness; no dream of night had dared what Thou hast wrought." Let us not cease to wonder at the wondrous things our God does. Let us forever hold the glad surprise of children.

And for tomorrow—for those "years" of which you speak, of which I cannot think with equanimity—it is just one day of separation at a time. The Lord has been with me this day, and with you. He has sustained and guided the same as He has ever done. And should He never see fit to bring us together, we are His; we are still loved by Him. "He will bear." Grace for tomorrow is never given today. Remember the manna? Neither is grace for imaginations ever given.

She closed with a line from Whittier's "The Eternal Goodness."

> And so, beside the silent sea I wait the muffled oar
> No harm from Him can come to me on ocean or on shore.
> I know not where His islands lift their fronded palms in air;
> I only know I cannot drift beyond His love and care.

Oh, it was wonderful, Jim . . . just being with you. I thank my God upon *every remembrance.*

Gratefully, Betty

I still marvel at how little physical touch they'd actually experienced. All they'd allowed themselves were a few embraces, hand holding, possibly a kiss on the cheek. But how important to learn from my amazing parents that their absolute priority remained the love of God, dependence on God, and continual prayer for His leading.

A person may ask, "Is God enough for me, to satisfy all my longings, even if I've not been given the romance I've dreamed of? Will He help me through those 'long nights' of loneliness? Will He stay my desires when He hasn't clearly shown His blessing on the relationship?" My parents' experience would say, definitely, He is worth waiting on! Their four-plus years of waiting produced such a weight of godliness in them. It built into their character those things necessary for being content with God alone: a determination to love Him first, as well as using that time of waiting to know Him in deep intimacy.

And they would need it all, because in many ways the true test of their faith had only begun.

November 3

Although I cannot mail this until Monday, I feel that I want to talk with you, Jim, and so there is no better time to write. . . . It is just one week today (forgive me, I'm sounding "sickly sentimental!") since we said goodbye. How well I know that "pressure" of which you speak, which causes one to look off to the far horizon and sigh. How many such sighs have been drawn from me this past week—and a long week it has been, believe me.

For you, I imagine time is flying, with all your traveling, meetings, contacts, etc. I have discovered a subtle thing in myself this week—I find that I welcome *any* activity, any social engagement, any place to go, not for the thing itself, but merely from an impatient, undisciplined desire to *kill time*. This bespeaks a soul not wholly at rest in the Lord.

"Oh, Time! Time!" I think to myself—"Begone! Let's just skip over the next few years, any old way, slipshod, carelessly, but quickly!" Yet gently, quietly, the Shepherd leads me beside still waters, makes me to *lie down*. And the lovely old words of Psalm 33 come to me:

> Our soul (note the plural adjective, singular noun) waiteth for the Lord:
> He is our help and shield. For our heart (again) shall rejoice in Him,
> because we have trusted in His holy name. Let Thy mercy, O Lord, be
> upon us, according as we hope in Thee.

And He is answering—He is teaching me to rest in His everlasting arms, unconscious of all besides Himself and His happy will.

And Jim, this too had its counterpart. When I remember those evenings by the fire in Franconia, or above New York's light and bustle, or just here at home—I am almost faint with tenderness.

"Almost faint." Perhaps he was feeling the same way.

Actually, what was making *him* feel faint was that her letters were not reaching him along the road. My mother suspected it, and grieved her carelessness. *"Yesterday I took my train case back to have it initialed. The sales slip I turned in with it was evidently the scrap of paper on which I'd written your Oklahoma City address. I'm sorry, Jim—I did want this to reach you this weekend."*

But it didn't. None of them did.

November 5

I was disappointed at finding no letter from you in Oklahoma City. When nothing was waiting at Sparta, I felt sure there would be word from you Saturday at Jones. We hustled through some real scenery in fall tones to get to Oklahoma City, and then—no word.

Pete had one waiting from Olive. It was hard to choke back disappointment and to smile. Funny how little accusations against you would be met in my mind immediately by apologies and explanations.

It was worse to have to leave there this morning before mail time. Even went to the PO to try and intercept something—but the carrier had already gone out. It means another whole week with no word, Betty, and I make no bones about it—it isn't easy! . . .

Tomorrow, Pete and I will be heading to Carlsbad Caverns, the folks trailing a little later in the day. El Paso tomorrow night. Then Phoenix, then LA and, I trust, word from you! Two weeks! Two weeks of silence after those close, oh-so-close days in Franconia!

Another trial to my patience occurred yesterday as I was rewinding my camera. I thought I had the film all ready to take out, so I opened the back—only to find the winder stuck and a half dozen pictures desensitized. And nearly all of them of you. I don't know which ones yet, of course—but it sure made me bite my lip.

Pete just remarked that he felt powerless these days. So do I. It's mostly the pace—not time for concentrated prayer and waiting on God. Pray that we might not waste these contacts on this account. It's hard to be alert to the mind of God when you're dull and sleepy. And that's what we've been since Washington, D.C. That's what's the matter now.

I wish I were better able to compose a letter to the woman I think so highly of. Anyhow—all this for tonight.

Jim

Poor man! No letters, no pictures, no time for rest or unhurried prayer. Among his few consolations was an offhand encounter with a young woman in OKC—a *"red-haired pianist"* who *"remembered you"*—from college, I assume, or from her summer in Oklahoma.

Without any prompting she volunteered, "Oh, she's tall and graceful. I always admired her—the way she handled herself." She thinks you must be pretty smart to have hooked me—everybody seems to have the impression I was sorta impregnable. I find it a stunning way to open conversation among the old friends—just to start off, "I've found the girl I'm going to marry." Causes quite a stir, if I do say so myself.

Yes, she was sure it did. But despite the warmth she felt in knowing how he felt about her, and despite the thrill of hearing such joy in his voice when he thought of her, she could probably have gone a while without hearing of it. Word of his sharing so freely with others about their relationship came during the same week she'd been praying the following words: *"If, in Thine own perfect time, Thou seest best to bring Jim and me together, to work for Thee as man and wife, prepare us for such event. But ever let us fix our minds and hearts upon Thyself."* Hear the total surrender? The lack of any presumption?

So while she answered his letter with much less verve than, say, her response to his Renaissance, she gently let him know he was pushing the boundaries again.

November 13

Another thing I feel I must speak of—you go about telling your friends, "I've found the girl I'm going to marry." This, you know as well as I do, is not strictly true in the sense others will understand it. I would not dream of saying that to my friends. So—until it is mutual, until such time as the Lord may make it clear that we are to marry, please, Jim, for my sake, if for no other reason, don't spread this around.

To me, nothing is more obnoxious than rumors, and undoubtedly rumors are flying. "They're engaged." "Oh, no, it's some odd arrangement—not exactly engaged." "Yes, but they might as well be," etc. etc. Then, if we ever *are* actually engaged, all the joy is taken out of announcing it, for everyone's reaction is, "About time!" "I thought they were engaged long ago." Do you understand, Jim? I hope you will.

Call it silly if you will, but to me, these things are high and holy, not to be lightly spoken of, and as yet, so far as our relationship is concerned, it is not ours to banter about, but His entirely, in His hands, until He may see fit to give us to each other. Then, and only then, may we feel free to speak of it to *anyone*, without fear of equivocation.

My father was a little too free and impulsive with his tongue, and he repented quite often of it in his journals. My mother, by contrast, was very strict with herself and chose her words carefully, thinking through the possible ways they could be misconstrued. She did not want the relationship talked about because they were not yet completely given to each other. She felt that the claim they might want to have on one another was still in the mysterious future of God's plan. Talking about it, in her view, confirmed it in other people's minds and cheapened what they'd committed to prayer.

I admire both of their personalities. I admire my father's fearlessness, how he wasn't afraid of the spin other people might put on his words. But I also admire her plea that he not speak of her as being "the girl I'm going to marry." Her falling in love with the man whom God had appointed for her was something she considered a "high and holy" matter, something to be kept sacred by keeping it to themselves.

I do understand my father's eagerness to talk. I'm afraid I inherited more of his spontaneity and quickness to tell—the easy gab—rather than the commitment to keep things secret and hidden until such time as the Lord is ready to reveal His answers. But how few women today have such control over their tongues or emotions, as my mother did, pondering holy things in their hearts without blabbing about them, without telling "three hundred of their closest friends." We over-share today, more than people need to know, not discerning those things we should rightly regard as precious and holy before God.

To my father's credit, he received her gentle rebuke with mostly humble contrition and consideration.

November 19

Really, Betts, I'm sorry if I've begun rumors by careless talk. I don't really feel that I've been flippant or undue in speaking of our relationship. Still, I've been known to be unwise. I want you to get the full benefit of announcing an engagement. And those I've spoken to, I have cautioned for your sake. Dave will tell you that I asked him to keep it quiet on this very count, and I've tried to be consistent with the same note to all. What's been done, you'll have to charge up to blunder and commit to God.

This was simply a man in love, caught up in love's excitement—surprising even himself with the new *"constancy"* in his love, something he'd once thought himself incapable of feeling, much less giving. As he said in a letter he wrote to her a week or so earlier:

November 10

It's a good thing, this loving you—a good, strong, bracing thing—the very thing our God would be apt to do for me prior to my going out. . . .

Anywhere I desire you. *Always* I want you with me. Is it walking in the morning, long before dawn? Then I hear you breathe somewhere close to my face, coming fast and noisy, then quickly indrawn and let out slowly. Is it watching scenery—the trees of Texas which have no trunks but grow like branches right from the ground—the frightening depths and fantasy of Carlsbad—the savagely twisted skeletons of dead trees on Grand Canyon rim—I want to point them all out to you and describe them. Every place is evaluated by its suitability to a honeymoon situation. . . .

Woke early again this morning and shared my devotional with dreams of you. It bothers me somewhat that you are on my mind when I ought to be praying, and it's a discipline not to indulge overmuch in remembering. Not that I feel a conflict—I am assured that loving you is part of my life now, important as eating, and God knows I need it.

Being in love, he said to her in another letter, was like "rediscovering" the whole world around him.

November 17

Loving has let me in on a whole new area of poetry. Since high school days I have regarded love lyrics with some disdain, and that's why I say rediscovery. I learned them academically, now empathetically. Strange how universal love is—I can pick something from nearly every piece and say, "That belongs to us."

Especially did I thrill to "First Time He Kissed Me" *[a sonnet by Elizabeth Barrett Browning]*. It linked itself immediately with our ride to Franconia that Sunday night. Will I forget how, feigning sleepiness, I crowded you against the clothing hung against the door—how your body stiffened as my hand made its way to being received by your fingers—how the whole of you slackened and how my fingers were pressed to your lips? Will I forget? Not soon. Excuse this indulgence.

I thank my God. Life has been made so much more the fuller for His giving me you. I was recounting today as we rolled the last three hundred miles up from Klamath Falls, how rich, how full (I can't find a better word!) He has made life for me. Sea-like, but having no ebb, no, not at my fingertips. Nature, body, soul, friendship, family—all full for me, and then, what many have not the capacity to enjoy. "And He said, 'Lacked ye anything?' They said, 'Nothing.' Part of me was lacking until this now—oh, I needed you, neither of us knew how sorely! And even now, though I don't have you in the fullest sense, still I do—in a sense I will not when we have known each other.

I'm glad that last is still ahead. Glad I'm not jaded by nights in bed with you. . . . I'm glad I still can't quite keep my hands off you—still must be warned not to "mess you up." I have you now unravished, and that is just how I need you now. The schoolboy in me still wonders and is awkward. Experience has not taken the edge off. We will, I suppose, get used to each other, the feel and smell and look of one another, but I am glad it is not so now. As never felt before, I feel now that I must keep myself for you. God knows it is a stay to purity, and He knows how many shakings to purity are ahead. . . .

I wish I could touch your cheek with my own to say goodbye again. But it is not for now. I am glad it was for once, and shall be again, God leading.

Your Jim

This is true love. In high honor. How it makes the heart beat faster to hear it expressed in such strong, innocent purity. And how glad I am that they remained pure as a testimony to Christ's power and the Spirit's control over their relationship. Some of these restrictions annoyed him, for obvious reasons, and she too wanted to give in to physical desire. But they knew they each belonged to God alone, that they could give only a portion of their hearts to the other for now, until the time He planned for them to be married. The verse they later chose for their wedding day (Isa. 25:9) was speaking to them already. "Lo, this is our God; we have waited for Him."

The fall of '51 was still their waiting time.

By Thanksgiving they were each at home, celebrating with family and guests, thinking longingly of one another, and thinking with renewed clarity on the future.

November 22

Pete just passed through en route to Seattle. I met him at the bus depot and took him some baggage we brought up in the car. Word from Tidmarsh says that a minister of government who is favorable to us must leave his post December 7, and that our entry permits must go through him. . . . So now we await word on a sailing date in January. The Lord has a certain slow dignity about His movings which constantly shames my fretting unbelief. He will take us to Ecuador in His own schedule, and it will be neither late nor early, regardless of what we hope or plan. . . .

I didn't intend to write news. This was intended to be a release-chat with you; I probably won't mail it until I hear of your affairs. I needed to get some idea at least of being in contact with you this morning, and writing is a help.

I needed you yesterday—wanted you more than for days I have wanted you. The sighs were coming again—the little noiseless cries I feel inside when everything and everybody seems so unrelated to you—nobody to talk to about you, nothing that brings strong recollection in the whole context.

My Kodachromes [an early brand of Kodak camera film] are little comfort. The one Pete took of us at the shore, he moved, and though it looks like fair composition, it's hopelessly blurred. The one of you at Great Bay lying on the sand, you have your eyes shut. The other, with you standing in the little sandspit with the salt flats behind, is over-exposed. I abuse myself mercilessly for not taking more pictures of you. Incidentally, I have nothing suitable to carry with me for demonstration and remembrance. Maybe your mother would show mercy and take some shots of you in that green suit—the one you wore when I saw you last. . . .

Let me tell you honestly, Betty, I love the look of you. My favorite of you now is a wallet-size of a Tower shot [the Wheaton College yearbook]. You are in a dark suit and have a white flounce at the neck and look straight at me. The larger one in '49 looks off to the side.

I wonder if you were conscious of averting your eyes in many of those Franconia passions when I looked straight into them. One time in particular I remember you rolled your head clear away to look into the fire when I wanted to face you. Please don't feel that way. I like the look of you! I'm glad that I love more in you than looks, so that if I went stone blind I would still have love. But your looks are not disconnected from it.

Love you for love's sake only? Not exactly. For love's sake, yes, but for dozens of other things too, and not the least of which is every dear remembrance of your face. The grace of your forehead, the clearness of your eyes. "But, oh, that carven mouth with all its intensity of longing."

Ever, Jim

I don't think he knew what to make of himself these days. Brash and bold for Ecuador, yet weak in the knees for my mother. *How had this happened?* he wondered candidly in his journal. *To me? Jim Elliot?*

NOVEMBER 20: Frightens me to think of finally leaping over all the old barriers I've raised against marriage. Is it to be, after all, the conventional life of rugs and appliances and babies? Is Paul's example of single intensity beyond me? Am I at last not one of those who make themselves eunuchs for the kingdom's sake?

I feel no bitterness, but a sense of regret at losing all the good liberties God has allowed me until now, should I make the promise. No settlement in my mind one way or another, though I feel strongly that for my own stability, for Betty's ease, and for most folks' tongues, I should buy a ring.

Lord, which way? "Thou hast heard the desire of the meek: Thou wilt prepare the heart" (Ps. 10:17). What shall I say to all the liberty I've been given to preach adherence to Pauline method—even to single men working in the field, and illustrating it from Pete's intention and my own? Rather, what will men think who have heard me say, "I go single, in the will of God," when, if I were really engaged, my plans would be otherwise?

Well, it is in God's hands. He gave direction to speak that way. And after all, an engaged man *is* still single, but purposing to be married. And Paul would have me free of care. Did he ever love a woman?

Or ever lust for a woman? Let's not pretend that my father was above the temptation. Yet in response to it, he did what all godly men (and women) must do when accosted by strong, unholy thoughts. He called them out, considered it war, and made his impassioned pleas that God would be His strength to endure.

NOVEMBER 21: My God in heaven, how am I made! Oh, that I had never tasted woman at all, that thirst for her should not be so intense now, remembering. It is not good that man should be alone—not this man, anyhow.

Frightfully depressed this whole day, a sense of inner wrong from defeated thinking from lust which warred against the soul. A day when things did not go well—all things seemed to betray me, and nothing satisfied—a day in the presence of demons, crafty, cruel demons who fight under camouflage. God deliver! Oh, take me to Thy ways of escape.

Much of this—the intensity of it at least—was new to him. With my mother featuring more prominently than ever in his future, the approaching unknowns had become freshly hard to contemplate.

NOVEMBER 23: I feel now as though it may mean five years of single life yet—these next five resilient years, years when I will most want her, most need her, and better be able to satisfy her. These years I see in the plan now must be spent alone. . . . Perhaps I'm wrong in planning in terms of years, but a man can't feel the "lustihood of his young powers" swell and surge inside him and not be affected by restraining them. It may be that He hasn't planned to make us wait five years, but it certainly looks from here that it can't be any less.

DECEMBER 6: What will it be like in Ecuador? God, make me to forget! I remember too keenly to endure much retrospect. Passion, bordering on frenzy, grips me at times—not always, thank heaven, but often enough to make any denial of her for the work's sake a very real, poignant thing.

In this just now I feel more than anywhere the Lord Jesus' requirement, "Except a man forsake . . ." Well, thank God for the privilege of giving aught up for His sake. But I know from this present sense of need that I cannot do so forever. Or, perhaps, if He requires that, He will teach me disciplines of desire, something I am not now acquainted with.

Yet when buffeted by conflicted feelings—by struggles within himself as well as expectations placed upon him by others—he returned as always to the sure Word of God.

NOVEMBER 29: My refuge is in Jehovah, whom I have asked to preserve me. For now and always, "He is the portion of my inheritance and of my cup; Thou maintainest my lot.". . . My going to Ecuador is God's counsel, as is my leaving Betty, as is my refusal to be counseled by all who insist I should stay and stir up the believers in the U.S. And how do I know it is His counsel? "Yea, my heart instructeth me in the night seasons." Oh, how good, for I have known that—my heart speaking to me for God! . . .

And so I sense that I may share the Christ's words, "I have set Jehovah always before me; He is at my right hand, I shall not be moved" (Acts 2:25). Not moved? With all the awful pressure of inward desire to move me to lust? Not moved. With all demonic hatred to move me to fear and doubt? Not moved.

"Not moved." And my mother, with her face equally set on following God going forward, would not be moved either. She courageously entered the next open door He presented to her in preparation for going to Latin America—doing short-term work with a Spanish assembly in New York City.

My father had made the connection—Luis Montalvo, a Spanish brother who was a leader among the Brethren there. *"They have an apartment ready for me,"* my mother wrote on November 25, *"and Mr. Montalvo is going to teach me Spanish"* while she worked in their ministry office, known as Voices from the Vineyard.

Within a week after Thanksgiving, she was situated for this new chapter in life.

NOVEMBER 28: Imagine me—living in a tenement in Brooklyn! More fun! But here I am in bed alone in a little flat in the Spanish section. The Lord is here, and I am happy. Mother brought me over, and we spent last night with Anne at Shelton. The memories there simply tore me to pieces. Oh, how I miss J! We had such a *perfect* three days together (oh, that word—*together*) there, and I kept seeing him in "all the old familiar places.". . .

Tonight I went to Montalvo's for dinner (rice, beans, chicken soup, corn, and some sort of chicken boiled in a kind of tomato mixture—everything vaguely flavored with garlic!). And then to the Baptist Temple for prayer meeting.

O Lord—a new phase of my life. Have absolute control. I have prayed, "If Thy presence go not up with me, carry me not up hence." But Thou hast carried me here, so I know Thou art with me. Let me not miss a single lesson or blessing Thou hast for me here.

The first lesson was loneliness. And culture shock.

NOVEMBER 29: Lonely. What do missionaries do who go to a foreign field alone? Here I have friends nearby, but feel so very much alone. The atmosphere here is not conducive to bright spirits. I have been cold ever since I got here, with the exception of a few minutes in a hot bath (heated water on the stove) this afternoon. Now I have on my winter coat and feel okay, except for cold feet.

The place is so filthy too. I have tried to clean up, but got only so far as the kitchen and the bathtub. Had a Spanish lesson this a.m. with a Mr. Johnson, formerly of Venezuela, who was staying with Don Luis. Had lunch there—cooked by Don Luis—and washed up the messy dishes. Came home and studied a little. Very little. I haven't the heart to apply myself. O Lord—be not far from me. Make haste to help me.

My father's letters to her became true lifelines. She described her hunger for them in this early December letter she wrote from Brooklyn.

December 5

Few of your letters have been so eagerly torn open as was your last, Jim. I was working in the Voices office when Don Luis called wondering where I was and telling me there was a letter for me which had been there since Friday. (It was Monday afternoon, and I had been away all weekend.) So I had the rest of the afternoon to wait, then the long, dark ride on subway and elevated, then I had to rush to a meeting without a chance to call at Montalvo's first. Finally I got it, and my hopes were fulfilled—it was yours.

Well, seated alone in my little living room, I gave myself to your letter. I was with you once more, at peace, conscious of your love, the utter wonder of it all. I do not deny that I am sometimes lonely here, surrounded entirely by foreigners, with not even a tree to relieve the oppression of filthy walls. But the Lord has given many kinds of balm, not the least of which is your love, which seems to me now so matured and established.

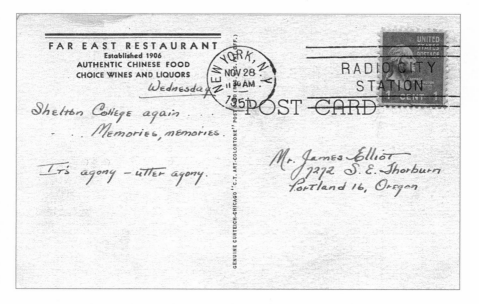

As my mother ate in this restaurant, she remembered their *"perfect three days"*
together at Shelton College, a Bible institute in New York City.

Indeed, his love had become so. It had grown deeper and more unselfish, if that's possible when one desires another so much, as these two did. Even his tone of voice had changed. At the beginning of their correspondence, he generally wrote with exhortation and rebuking. He spoke to her more as he spoke to all at Wheaton, where he was known for sternly challenging others to stay the course and seek first the kingdom, to leave behind the worldly pursuits of natural man. But now his words were tender and loving. Gracefully expressed. Where he once had scoffed at her "militant morality," he now thanked her for *"refraining from intimacies you have wisely withheld from me."* Where he once had felt honor bound to specify his parents' initial criticisms on her character and appearance, he now felt ashamed at how unkind he'd been in passing along their views so heartlessly.

November 28

Got to browsing old letters again for a few minutes today. Yours of the fall of '49—particularly that one written after you were here—seem so far away. What a heartless letter mine must have been, describing the folk's reaction to you! I really wonder at myself being able to write so. I think I could not bring myself to do it now, even if occasion demanded. . . .

Know this, Betty, that my longing for you is begetting a tenderness that makes me think I could never be unkind to you or speak sharply. Hearing the petty bickering of married folks annoys me, and I wonder if they can know what I know now of tenderness. Remind me of this in years to come (if they are granted us) and remember that you have been loved with a love that is all softness by . . .

Jim

Almost doesn't sound like the same man, does it?
Nor did the place where she was reading his letter feel like home.

December 5

A far cry from Birdsong, this. . . . The apartment is about five blocks from Montalvo's, sandwiched in between the Rheingold Breweries and the Hungarian Pickle Works! All around are typical East Side tenements, with their rusted fire escapes, broken stone steps, bedding drooling from the windowsills, etc. This building is no exception. The smell of boiled cabbage, garlic, rusted steam pipes, and crumbling plaster greets me each time I labor up the five flights of dank stairway . . . utterly removed from anything I have ever known.

The sights and sounds made thoughts of him all the sweeter.

I dreamed the other night that you came east again for some business matter before sailing. And I guess I dream of you every night. But when I awake, it is rather like the end of a roll of movie film when it starts flapping, and one catches instantaneous glimpses of a picture here and there in the sputtering grayness. So now—I go gladly to bed, for I may dream again.

Note their context and mind-set as 1951 draws toward a close. My mother was adjusting to a whole new set of living conditions, amid the complex challenges of trying to learn and master a different language. My father was barely a month away from his sailing date, hustling to make preparations while dealing with the permanence of leaving home, this time for good.

Naturally, with this setting as backdrop, the interplay of their letters became all the more serious, hungry, and heartfelt.

JE (DECEMBER 7): Tomorrow your last letter will be two weeks old. I can almost quote it. Every day since Saturday, I've been of no use at all between 10:00 and 11:30 a.m., the hour of the mail's arrival, usually. And every day, the big stack of mail—checked through, twice—with no signs of the fine-scripted envelope that means so much to me now.

EH (DECEMBER 9): There is always a special thrill in the unexpected (e.g., the time you called from NY just because you were "hungry"—or the one time I was alone in the kitchen at Franconia and you came around the porch in the dark). Your letter of November 28 (and other dates subsequent) was one of those. I mailed a letter to you on Thursday.

JE: There was a time when I could pass off not hearing by saying to myself, "Forget it, you can get along, you don't need word." That's no solace now. I feel that I *do* need word, that somehow I *can't* get along. Before it would have been possible to harden my thoughts and go on. Now that's impossible. Even if I want to be tough, there's a tenderness.

EH: I opened your letter on the subway going into NY. In spite of the sad, stupid, hard, or blank faces around me, and the roar and swaying of the train, I was once more carried away, out of myself, and I felt that I was with you. . . . And where do you suppose I emerged from the subway? 59th Street, Columbus Circle. It was almost too much for me. I walked down 8th Avenue, remembering that Thursday morning breakfast in Hotel Park Sheraton, Central Park, Columbus Circle.

JE: Your copy of AC's poem was fitting: "But from thy brier shall bloom a rose that is for others.". . . I am asking that it will be so for you there, Betty, amid the cabbage smell and the crumbling plaster and all. It would drive me mad thinking of you alone there, dreaming about me in the darkness, did I not know that roses bloomed on briers.

EH: It never ceases to amaze me, the incompleteness I feel—I, who was of all women most independent and proud of it! I wanted you beside me, your strong arm to hold, just to feel your sleeve, and know that you were *there!*

JE: I dreamed about you last night. Coming home last evening and reading your letter before I slept was like coming home to you, almost. You came to me in bed, serious and shivering. I made you laugh and warmed you with my body. Such things are seldom, and I enjoyed it because it seemed good and right, and not much like a dream. Your letter did it, your talk of holding my arm and of being cold there in Apartment 15. . . . I wish I could be there to share your "little stew" and fill your evenings—sharing other things. . . .

All this week I've been thinking of reasons for loving you, and the Lord has counseled me. I like to remember that He gave you to me. You are His own gift, granted in mercy and in all the wisdom of His choosing. Given, not deserved, scarcely asked for, never merited, but given in grace, without my hardly lifting a finger even to "woo" you. Without my knowing what I needed or even that I needed. He selected you for me and gave.

This, among many other thoughts, has strengthened me in love, for, as nearly always, I see it illustrating the truth concerning Christ and the church. Does not He enjoy speaking to His Father about those that were *given to Him* in John 17? And this is motive for His prayer and concern. The Church was a bestowal upon Christ directly from God. Does it seem too strong to say that you have been such to me? No. May our love be all that Eternity makes it to mean.

EH: Oh, may God grant that the bond which is even now so pure and strong may be tempered to an even greater purity and strength by His living grace. Let us never resign ourselves to the trivialities of the commonplace. Familiarity need never breed contempt. Deeper, fuller union with Christ only augments our wonder and adoration. So let it be.

Goodnight, Jim, dear friend

I often hearken back to her telling me of their love, their delight, and the consuming fire of longing, and I am forever grateful for this perfect plan of a romance which God created. How much sweeter hearing her say the same things in real time, as their love was happening.

DECEMBER 14: A letter came from J. this morning with a fine picture of him. Funny—others think of him as handsome. I only know it is the face I *love*, the dear features that haunt every dream of every night. Dear man! Tender, strong, kind—can it be that his love is really for me? We are Thine, O Lord and Master—forever, only Thine.

But as Christmas came, the "longing" part was what she felt more strongly than anything else.

DECEMBER 23: The whole family is at home now—for the first time (at Christmas) since 1947—and in '47, there was one other here with us. *Jim.* The rest of the family is basking in its utter completeness. I, for the first time in just this way, feel my incompleteness. . . .

This morning as we gathered in the living room for family worship, I was so overwhelmed with longing for J.—tears came. He had sent the family some lovely Oregon evergreens and holly. They were all about us to remind me of him. And I thought of how he had told me once that he knew, oh, how well he knew what it was to see others about him happy in marriage, and to long for me.

I suppose, really, that I am writing this journal, in some sense, for him. At least that is the way it seems now. It has not been conscious, but perhaps I am recording some of the things I wish I could say in my letters to him, but cannot. Why can I not say them in letters? Because we are not engaged (I'm not sure if this is true—that is, I'm not sure it is all the reason, or the *real* reason), and I shall never feel that I can fully express myself to him until (or unless—Lord, grant that in Thy will it may be "until") we are engaged.

But I love him now—I love him. And it is strong, constant, and pure. Therefore it is of God. Love is of God. (I should say, "It is of God, and therefore it is strong, constant, pure.)

I cannot say these things to anyone. So I feel that I must write. Oh, I wonder how long it will be before I can say them, release them—to him? Beloved man, dear Jim.

Sight and hearing.
These two be in God
Not like in man.
We hear what's heard;
He lists where hearing is not,
Views where eye
In all her pilgrimages long
And probings sharp
Has not yet guessed
That being is.

JIM ELLIOT

LOVE WAITS (AGAIN)

EH (JANUARY 2), NEW YORK: Alone once more, in my little apartment. It is dreary with rain outdoors, and I feel how sad this world really is. Truly a vale of tears, with nothing but meeting and parting and much sorrow and suffering. I think of dear Mother at home, alone now after a happy Christmas with all the family. As I look forward to my departure for the field, it is very hard to think of what it will mean to her. The Lord alone can sustain us. . . .

This being alone is an awful thing to me. I do not know why. It was the same when I spent three weeks alone in a trailer in Alberta. There is an overwhelming sense of uselessness, and a pall of darkness that seems to "veil His lovely face."

Just now I read in Psalm 90:15, "Make us glad according to the days wherein Thou hast afflicted us." I have asked the Father for His joy and peace. Just now I feel very close to tears. There is that tightness in my throat, and I feel that if I try to speak, I shall cry.

I know that in reading over this entry later on, I shall say, "What a way to begin a new year." But I am honest, and after all, what is one day above another? Time means nothing to God. He is with me "all the days."

My desire for 1952, the prayer of my heart—oneness with the Lord.

She would not dissolve into that "vale of tears" the way she'd seen others do. She often used that same expression with me—not "dissolving into a vale of tears"—when I experienced hurt and disappointment growing up, because as she helped me see, it wouldn't do any good! If my faith was deeply affirmed and taught by the Scriptures, I could be assured the Lord was in charge, He was with me, and nothing could separate me from His love. And she could say it with such confidence because she had so often put it into practice after reading His Word.

I'm sure she faced this difficult beginning of the year with her usual stoicism and desire to do only what pleased God, not herself. Yes, waiting on His timing and direction, as she was currently doing, is probably the hardest thing He asks of a true disciple. But as 1952 dawned, despite not knowing what her departure for the field would look like, she knew His Word would hold true, and she would accept it, whatever it meant.

This was the year in which being a missionary would become more than a mere concept to her and my father. Being a missionary would now become a living reality. What would it mean for them? How would it change them?

In late December, she had lamented in her journal from this same, lonely New York apartment . . .

> I have been here three weeks today—and have visited not one family with the gospel. My conscience (I guess it is my conscience) condemns me constantly. Somehow I cannot bring myself to do it.
>
> I am afraid, for one thing. Of what, I hardly know. Is this direct, deliberate disobedience? Am I defeated, Lord?—undertake! Show me what to do. Give me power or love, or both, or whatever it is I need. I know that to do anything in my own strength, even if it salves my conscience because I'm "doing something for the Lord," is worse than useless. And here I am, a prospective MISSIONARY.

The truth, as she'd written to my father between Christmas and the new year:

> I think often we "prospective missionaries" get a false idea that somehow everything is going to be different on the "field," including ourselves. Not so. Granted, there will be much that is different in our environment, many adjustments necessary. Let us not minimize these. But on the other hand, it is the same Presence and Power that accompanies and indwells us, the same necessity for drawing from the Source.
>
> And as old Pike used to say, "You're STUCK with yourself." It is the same "sad, sweet, stinking self" that we shall have to deal with. And the more trying the circumstances, the sadder, the sweeter, the more stinking that self! . . . Oh, Jim, what a tremendously serious thing—this missionary business.

Simply the mechanics of it, if nothing else. The logistics of it; the decisions to be made. Traveling by air or by sea? Leaving from what city? The shots, the permits, the paperwork. And what to take? What kind of clothes? What kind of cooking equipment? And books? And bedding? And everything!

That's what my father was finalizing right at this moment, engrossed in his last-minute packing.

January 15

> Your letter came a week ago today, and I have only had time to look at it three times. I opened it with the end of the paint brush with which I was lettering my name and destination on my packing barrels. . . . Wednesday, more packing. Thursday, all the stuff has to be taken to the dock and billed for leaving. I ended up with two steel barrels (best way to pack anything), two wooden crates, two footlockers, and a wardrobe trunk—seven pieces—1,400 pounds. I hope you will do better. Pete only had 900 pounds. I had most of the heavy stuff—slides and recorder, tubs and guns, pots and kettles and dishes.

Quite a challenge. But of all the needed preparations, none was more valuable (they knew) than hearing from the Lord, staying spiritually sensitive, remaining deeply in prayer.

As evidence of my father's devotion to prayer, be inspired by this snatch from the same January 15 letter written from Oakland, California, where he and Pete were continuing to speak and raise pledges of support, right up to departure time.

My father in Oakland, California, waiting and praying to sail to Ecuador.

I find no time at all for closet prayer. We haven't a room of our own here, and I miss the sense of "bowing my knees," as Paul says. Praying while seated does not lend the effect that kneeling has, and I cannot be comfortable kneeling in the living room where we sleep. Privacy before the God who "sees in secret" is an integral part of true prayer, and one hates to be obvious in asking for privacy somehow. God knows and hears. But I miss a certain effect, with others walking about. What will Shandia be with the curious eyes of Quichua boys?

When was the last time any of us took our private praying so seriously? But just as the Lord met my father in prayer, He also answered my mother's prayers for direction and leading. God's timely preparation was proving more than adequate—and, as you'll see, more revealing of her future than she could yet know. The following is from her journal:

JANUARY 18: Last Friday I spent the day with Doreen Clifford, British missionary returning to the western jungle of Ecuador for the second time. It was very profitable to talk with her and get some idea of conditions there. She gave me much practical advice on what to expect and necessary equipment.

But more than that—she told me of the burden she has for the yet untouched Auca tribe of Indians on the Napo River. Humanly, it would be impossible for women to do such work. Men have tried, and been killed. But she believes the Lord has given her this concern for *some* purpose—if only to *pray*. Or perhaps she might be a stepping stone for someone else to go in. She said she felt she should work with someone else if God leads her into the field, and asked me to pray about whether He might want me to go with her.

I feel that I can record this in my journal, for I am asking God's direction about it. But I would hardly dare mention it to others. It would seem so fantastic and visionary. And I have no idea what it involves. I have not had experience of *any* kind in Ecuador, let alone such a seemingly hopeless task. I do not want to be an upstart. "Fools rush in . . ." *God,* and God alone, must guide. . . .

But over six years ago, when I asked His will for my life pursuit, I felt that He wanted me in pioneer work, especially with a view to linguistic work. If this is a glimpse of His ultimate purpose for me, I am glad. But I must walk softly. And I must be very sure of every step. Sometimes I think we are more concerned with what is commonly called prudence than we are to "go in and possess the land." May God give to me the spirit that led Jesus to Jerusalem, for "as the Master, shall the servant be."

The weeks ahead would yield greater clarity, of course. But as God would have it, her experience of discerning and applying His will (as with most of us) would come about through long days of staying diligent, staying teachable. And in her case, staying lonely.

My longing for J. does not abate. It is a hunger that causes my whole being to cry out in anguish. Oh, I am weary, so weary of being alone. How often I say in my heart, involuntarily it seems, "Lord Jesus, how long?"

I'm sure hearing word from my dad by letter was somewhat helpful, while it lasted. He was leaving soon, and she knew it. But judging from the three letters he wrote during the last week of January, the loneliness was as deeply felt on his side of the continent.

January 25

It seems like a long, long time since I've been with you, and even the memory, though happy, is fleeting and unreal. . . . Your last letter which awaited me here (for which I was thankful) was moving to me. It made me wish I could be with you just once more before leaving, to hold you close and soak your warmth up into me. Aunt Mabel suggested you fly out here (with what, I don't know), and I have toyed with the idea, but feel now it would not be good. I dare not get the taste for you again, Lisa *[a newer nickname he'd been calling her]*—never, until it can be completely fulfilled. Even if you should come to Ecuador and we were in a certain proximity in Quito, we must guard ourselves from much loving.

They would. And they did. And my mother would do most of the guarding.

But this will be more clearly seen there, and we can decide then. God help us to "look not back." I know it will be easier for me than for you, a woman left with no promises, and hoping toward God in a man so volatile as I. Hope thou in God, for we shall yet praise Him, who is the "help of my countenance." I'm needing a help for my countenance these days, and I know you will need the same. . . .

I think it is part of God's reason for bringing us together, our mutual need, and I see only good in stating it and realizing God's purposes before one another. You say I can "take it or leave it" *[referring to something she'd written, saying she felt at home by his side]*. I take it. All of it. And I hope my side will one day be as home to you, your solace and haven. It's what my side was made for.

But before he left, he wondered something. Would she be open to a phone call?

If you're of a young enough age, you won't relate to what the planning for this event entailed. These were pre-cellphone days, obviously. But not only that, she didn't have a landline in her apartment. And she wasn't at her family's home with a familiar number. Nor could she alert him fast enough by mail with a time and telephone number where he could reach her.

The only solution was what now seems an archaic one. He phoned her parents by way of a "person-to-person" call. This was a commonly employed safeguard against racking up long-distance charges. If the person you were trying to reach wasn't home, no minutes would be billed even if someone picked up. The one who answered heard the operator say who was calling, and for whom, and could then relay information back through the operator to the caller (who could hear all this), telling what time the person would be back or where he or she could be currently located. That's how my dad learned what number to dial in New York.

Not the first night, however, my mother said.

FEBRUARY 2: Spent an agonizing night waiting for his call here at Shelton College, only to find a telegram from him in Brooklyn when I got home. He said he would call on Friday. . . . So last night, following a meeting in Newark, I came to Shelton and stayed in Phil's room *[her eldest brother]*, since he and Margaret had gone home for the weekend.

At long last, the call came through.

"I talked with Jim at about 11:45," she recorded in her journal. *("I've no idea what it must have cost,"* she later said—*"nine minutes!") "His voice— so clear, so loved, but so far away. I felt so cut off from him. But we were happy in this brief form of contact."*

> He told me he loves me, and asked if I loved him. I said that I could hardly help myself. Oh, how I long for the day when I can *volunteer* my love to him, freely and unfettered by present limitations.

Because, truly, she loved him more than words could say, even if she'd felt the permission to say them.

> **FEBRUARY 4:** O, that I could tell him of my love. I feel that I cannot let go until we become engaged. Then, then I shall tell him all that I can find words to express. And there is so much—stored up during these nearly four years! . . . I never dreamed it possible so to love. I love him with all my being—strongly, passionately, tenderly, as only one can love who has had it tried in fire and water.

And on this day—February 4, 1952—though delayed by a couple of weeks for various reasons, their love was being tried on the waters of the Pacific Ocean.

Pete Fleming and my father, ready at the dock.

> Wire just came from Jim that he is sailing at noon today. It is now 4 p.m., which means he has been on the sea for an hour. . . . Now that he is no longer even in the same country, I feel more cut off than ever. The "sword-cut" *[an Amy Carmichael term]* is not a myth. The Lord is "touched with the feeling." It is comfort.

As a way of staying present with him, my mother sent him letters in advance to be opened on certain days of his voyage. She knew he might not receive any more of her letters than those he'd received in Los Angeles before he boarded. *"Very sweet of you to think of that, Betts,"* he said. *"If my wanting you increases in the next two weeks as it has in the past one, I'll be needing a little touch from you about then."* She had a keen sense about the joy of surprises, and often planned them for me as well, which always gave me hopeful anticipation in the waiting. I'm sure her postdated letters delighted my dad on ship.

Do not open till 4th day at sea

Feb. 1952

Not yet — wait till 6th day and prepare for shock

Examples of the envelope inscriptions my mother wrote on
a series of notes she sent along with him, to open during his voyage.

His published journals are already rich in details of his journey on board the *Santa Juana*. I'll only summarize by saying that the freighter held twelve passengers, as well as the ship's captain and crew. Meals and accommodations were first-class, like nothing to which he was accustomed, and he expressed his awe of it. The ease of travel and the delicious food (which they ate at the same time as the captain and crew, in the same dining room) made Pete and him feel spoiled, knowing how austere and simple their life would be in the jungle. But they knew beyond doubt their only motive for going was to point the Indians to Christ, so they received this brief time of luxury as a gift from their gracious Father. My dad reveled in watching the ocean and the night sky, experiencing the incomparable quiet (unlike the bustle of modern cruise ships, with too many activities planned to allow time for even reading a book on deck), and anticipating the longed-for arrival in Ecuador.

But back in Brooklyn, in my mother's lonely walk-up, there wasn't much new to see or to feel. Yet God was there, and in His presence came encouragement.

> **FEBRUARY 12:** Oh, it is one thing to declare, in giving a brave testimony, that there is no such thing as sacrifice, in the light of eternity and its rewards, but it is quite another to believe, in my heart of hearts, that it is not sacrifice. For there is constant longing, longing for Jim—for his presence, the comfort of his arms, the strength of his body, the love of his heart.
>
> This afternoon, in one of those "upward glancings of an eye," accompanied by a sigh, directed Godward, I found myself asking for a child—for a little boy of my own—that I might learn of him and give him back to God. I am past twenty-five. I read the other day in an obstetrics book that the best time for a woman to bear children is between 20–25. That prime of life is gone for me.
>
> *It is lost,* I said to myself this morning. "Lost?" said the Father. "Yes, lost," said I. "But I thought you had given *Me* those years?" "Yes, Lord, I did. They were Thine." "Then they are not lost. They are kept in the heavenly storehouse. Someday thou shalt see the glory. Thou canst not see it now—thou seest only the apparent loss on earth. Thine eyes are blinded with fruitless longing. Look away to My eternal purposes."
>
> So, Lord—I look. I thank Thee for the word of assurance. "Give the world joy, but patience to the saints."

Isn't it true, we never know the "eternal purposes" God has in store, no matter how certain we feel of what's over and done with. He even knew of her need for a daughter, not a son. She often told me of her gratitude that God gave her a daughter, believing a girl was easier to raise without a father than a son would have been. And speaking of "patience," she would need lots of it as she continued the work of seeking support for her upcoming missionary undertakings. From two of her February letters:

February 12

I am wearied-wearied of meetings, teas, contacts, letter-writing. And this after so short a time! I don't know how you stood it for at least five months straight. Last night, Plainfield; tonight, Palisades Park; tomorrow, Jersey City; Thursday, White Plains. I don't know how I'll live through it much longer. And these women are the eatingest crowd—they feel they must serve tea and cake at every meeting. It seems so useless to me. One has plenty of opportunity to become acquainted without eating all the time. If only the money spent on needless food—

I am not complaining. The Lord is sweet to me just now, and He has given great cause for thankfulness. The truths concerning Himself which He is unfolding seem to be opening a whole new realm to me—chiefly along the line of His Fatherhood and my sonship. The book of John is tremendous on this truth.

Your letter from Mexico came Monday. . . . It is good to hear that your trip has been enjoyable so far. You didn't say whether or not you'd been sick! That might help keep your weight down. You must be positively blubbery by now. Horrors. (I am the same charming crowbar.)

Thank you for describing your stateroom. It is those little things that help me picture you in your surroundings—and I want to be able to picture you. But *who* uses the Avon cologne? The very idea is revolting to me. It goes along with suede shoes and greased pompadours. Let me know when you start polishing your nails.

Your exhortations on accepting what is, and not longing for what is *not*, were helpful to me. There is no possible comfort to assuage the "fury of desire" of which you speak—and which I too experience—except for the constant "looking away to Jesus, who for the joy". . . the recognition of that eternal weight of glory, which surely is stored in the heavenly garners in mammoth proportion to every earthly "sacrifice." But there are times when the short-range view makes it seem a very real sacrifice.

February 21

You and Pete must be having the time of your young lives. My, what a contrast your situation is to mine! And by the time you receive this, things will be even more interesting, I imagine. I have to remind myself now and again that I am writing to a foreign missionary. You are actually "on the field" (what a strange terminology—how did we get it?) and in the place of God's choice for your life. It is a milestone, indeed. But it is no different, I suppose, than any other place. You have the same Lord. (I'm not giving a homily—only putting down the thoughts that come as I try to imagine your setup.)

The other day as I passed the Statue of Liberty on a ferry, I could not help wondering how long it will be before I actually steam down that same river, headed for Ecuador. It gives me a shudder whenever I see those big ships now— and it is nearly every day that I see them.

But even as they thought to the future, they couldn't help reflecting on the past.

Your reminiscences awakened memories which I have not thought of for some time. The Lagoon—oh, the scenes and emotions which come—the heavy mist that night when the watchman surprised us! That was the first time you ever put your head in my lap. We sat quiet, and watched a piece of moon rise from the dim lake. You took my wrist in your hand, and slid your hand up my sleeve to the elbow—another of those "first times.". . .

And, oh, I can remember the anguish of walking back to the dorm. The prospect of never seeing you again. The fears that I was not pleasing God even then by allowing myself the bliss of being with you for the few days that remained.

One night—it must have been the following September when I was on my way to Prairie—we stood on the steps of the house where Van was living. You were a few steps below me, your foot up on a step, your elbows resting on your knee, your head down. You said nothing for a while. Then, "Betty, to marry you would be an admission to myself that Christ is not sufficient." And then, in such a wistful tone, ". . . but I always thought He was." I don't know what I said. I only know that I crept softly up the dark stairway to Van's room. I got undressed without waking her. Then I lay there and sobbed.

At the end of this particular letter, with its long recollection of memories, she curtly said, *"I must stop."* Having taught me from a young age to keep boys at arm's length, as her own mother had taught *her*, she knew when enough was enough. Whenever she allowed herself to daydream about my dad during this time, she did it determined not to accept the luxury for too long, or else she'd descend into self-pity. And this, she would not allow. It was time to set this down and look only ahead. God had clearly confirmed the direction He'd given for Ecuador. He'd done it time and again during her months of learning Spanish, of living in a missions context, and of growing ever closer to His heart through hardship. Now was not a time for looking back. She'd be home in a few days, *"having bid our Brooklyn apartment adieu without tears. I have a booking on the Santa Isabel for April 11 from New York. Doesn't seem possible."*

She wrote to him again in early March:

March 7

Well, as you know by now, plans are already made, and I'm afraid I didn't consult you very carefully. Tidmarsh had written D. back in December, *urging* her to come as soon as possible.

"D." was Dorothy Jones, a young woman my father knew from among his assembly connections, who had come to New York earlier in the year with similar ministry aspirations as my mother. Dorothy and my mother even shared the apartment—a great blessing during this season of loneliness.

Then he [Tidmarsh] wrote both of us in January, earnestly asking that we not delay. As the steps of a good man are ordered of the Lord, He has once more ordered them, and I feel almost as though I had *no part whatever* in the present prospects. But I am thankful, and want to follow when He leads, as well as where.

You ask how I feel about our being within close range—as to whether it would "bother" me, and how I thought it would affect you. Well, if I had my choice, I would have remained in the States until you were in the jungle, simply as a matter of expediency. As to how it will affect you—I've no idea. You say you'll be "wild to see me." Can you, then, "serve without distraction"?

These are rhetorical questions—I have asked God to do all that is in His heart. He will lead us right. If He wants us to see one another again before we go into the jungles, it is not for us to set up barriers.

(Do you realize it will have been six months since we said goodbye? Hard to believe.)

March 9

I know I just wrote to you a couple of days ago, but I just feel like talking with you this afternoon, Jim. You said in a recent letter that you'd like to have forty-five minutes with me—now when, pray tell, have we ever been able to spend that little time together? Remember the night we got home from Franconia? We were going right to bed—and it was two hours before we even looked at the clock! But I'd give anything for even five minutes with you just now. But then—every meeting involves a parting. And I don't know how many more of those I can take. . . .

Had lunch last week in Kearney with an Irishman and his wife. My—he refreshed my spirit! Talked incessantly from the moment he got in the house until we left for the women's meeting, but often spoke of the Lord.

Asked me if I knew the young men who were going to Ecuador. Asked which one was "the one with the big shoulders." I finally decided he must mean Jim Elliot, and his face lit up. "My, that young man has a smile like the light of heaven on his face! There was no question about *his* call!" was his comment.

I smiled and nodded assent. I can always say I was at Wheaton at the same time as you and the Cathers. Then folks are satisfied. Sometimes I wish I could tell them more. But what? Oh—the Lord knows. He knows it all. But often I feel, "How long can I give silence—my whole life long?"

The Lord has dealt with us in mercy and judgment. I do not question His dealings. I praise—oh, I *praise* Him, with you, for the memory of *completely* happy hours with you. It never fails to bring pleasure when I recall the many good times spent together. "Who could ask for anything more?"

My dad's next letter (March 11) was chock-full of action points and equipment lists for her to consider bringing. How exciting it must have been to him to anticipate her soon arrival and feel protective of her as he provided counsel from his firsthand knowledge of the situation on the ground. He was not only protective but was quite thoughtful and gracious. He even asked if she'd be interested in letting him help her get an organ. She answered:

> How I would love to have one! As I've often thought, I could get along without almost anything in the world except a piano or organ—something to play on! . . . But I had really put it out of my mind for the field, knowing that I could get along without it, and regarding it as a needless expense. But I have now written to Mr. Anderson (a friend in the Evangelical Foreign Missions Assoc. Purchasing Dept. who has already helped me a lot) to ask him about organs. He gets 60% off on some musical instruments, though I don't know about organs. I will let you know if they are reasonably priced.

He soon sent a check which he hoped would be enough to pay for it. *"I fear that if I wait to get the exact cost, you may not have time to purchase. If there should be any balance, use it as you feel best. If it is not enough—bill me later. But on all counts—get one!"*

The amount was exactly enough, she wrote to report.

March 26

> Jim, how can I thank you enough for the check for $100? It was an excellent guess, as it cost $95, plus a nominal service fee from EFMA. . . . Ordinarily they run around $185, so you see he got a good discount. I am praying that it will get to the boat on time.
>
> As you may know, my sailing date has been pushed up to April 4, so things are pressing heavily now. Had a complete physical this morning, and was found to be outrageously devoid of disorder of any kind.
>
> Went to New York on Monday to get my yellow fever shot, and dropped in to see about the wood stove I mentioned—only to find they are not making them anymore! The days are filled with "trivial care, burdens too small for other hearts to share," but in so many ways I find that *God* shares them, and has helped me wonderfully. I am asking particularly that *nothing* may be forgotten which should be attended to. What a multiplicity of things are involved in getting out of this country—to say naught of getting into another.

For instance, *"I just heard the other day that it is not at all expedient for one to wear red in Ecuador. Is this true? If so, it's tragic for me! Half my clothes are red! Why don't people tell me these things?"* But red clothes or not, *"Is it possible that in eighteen days I shall be in Ecuador?"*

The boat pulled out on April 5.

Souvenir Passenger List

S. S. SANTA MARGARITA

VOYAGE # 93

NEW YORK TO WEST COAST OF SOUTH AMERICA

Sailing April 5, 1952

. . for . .

Cristobal, Buenaventura, Puna (Guayaquil),
Salaverry, Callao, Arica, Antofagasta,
Chanaral, Valparaiso

⚓

OFFICERS

Howard Ford	Commander
E. Calabrese, U.S.N.R.	Chief Officer
Frank Kadow	Chief Engineer
Joseph Gray	Purser
Logan Evans, M.D.	Surgeon
Domingo Salmeron	Chief Steward

LIST OF PASSENGERS

Alvarado, Mr. Oscar R.	Lima, Peru
Barsby, Mr. Henry	Nottingham, England
Blackall, Mr. Robert M.	Northampton, Mass.
Blackall, Mrs. Robert M.	Northampton, Mass.
Driver, Mr. Thomas T.	Maywood, N. J.
Driver, Mrs. Thomas T.	Maywood, N. J.
Driver, Mstr. Bruce W.	Maywood, N. J.
Harshman, Mrs. Dixie Fay	Philadelphia, Pa.
Hellman, Mrs. Olga	Eureka, Calif.
Hellman, Miss Margaret	Eureka, Calif.
Hellman, Mstr. Charles F.	Eureka, Calif.
Hockman, Mr. L. H.	Buckley, Wash.
Hockman, Mrs. L. H.	Buckley, Wash.
Howard, Miss Elizabeth	Moorestown, N. J.
Koziak, Mr. Edward A.	Stamford, Conn.
Koziak, Mrs. Edward A.	Stamford, Conn.
Koziak, Miss Kathleen	Stamford, Conn.
Koziak, Miss Regina	Stamford, Conn.
Koziak, Mstr. Douglas	Stamford, Conn.
Koziak, Mstr. Edward F.	Stamford, Conn.
Lovell, Miss Hildreth M.	Chicago, Ill.

Last goodbye picture taken on the deck of the *Santa Margarita*.
My mother is at right, along with Aunt Ginny and the captain.

APRIL 5: Exactly two hours ago we streamed slowly out of the dock in New York harbor. Is it actually I who sets out on this mission? "I, the Lord, have called them . . ." And so I go.

It means leaving all that is dear to me—except Jim, and he is dearest—behind. But God is with me—He has wonderfully sustained. I ask above all that He may lift up dear Mother, and comfort her loving, grieving heart as only He who is the God of all comfort can do. She was so brave—only a few tears, and visibly noble efforts when the hawsers were thrown off. . . .

How I miss them all now. They sang "He Hideth My Soul" as the gangplanks were lifted, and stood waving until the last great door was lowered to block them from view. Only then did I give way to tears, but the Lord stood with me and strengthened me.

I realize for them it is so much harder than for me—I have Jim to look forward to, though just now that is not much comfort, somehow. He seems so remote from all this. Home has always meant more to me than I ever expressed to any-one, and I know it will be harder than ever to think of it with equanimity when the newness of this experience has left me.

Oh my—to put down what I feel just now would be impossible. I love them all so much—each one so dear. . . . One day we shall know one another's hearts, I believe, and then there will be no need for words.

One of the only times Betty Howard was photographed in shorts.

A prayer of Amy Carmichael, she thought, said it best. *"'For my beloved (plural!) I will not fear—love knows to do for him, for her, as hitherto. Whom my heart cherishes are dear to Thy heart too.' Oh, I know it is true, Lord—I will trust Thee for them."*

Still thinking of God first, still thinking of others second, still thinking of herself last, even as she sailed off alone toward the utterly unknown.

SPRING AND SUMMER

APRIL 15: "Behold, I am with thee in all places whithersoever thou goest." This verse came to me with my first consciousness this morning, as I woke here in a somewhat shabby, very humid hotel in Guayaquil. The noises of the street and square below woke me, and I tried to realize that I am in Ecuador, the place of God's choosing for my life, I believe.

This was the same Ecuadorian port city (pronounced GWY-a-KEEL) where my father had docked, not quite two months earlier. He wished he could have been there to greet her. But the undeclared nature of their relationship called for not overdoing his level of interest in a certain young missionary arriving from America.

There was talk of it, *"on the quiet, of course,"* he said in his letter of April 9.

But you will know soon enough that nothing is kept that way here. Ruth (Stam) Jordan said something up at the station a couple of days ago that indicated someone has already got the word around. I find Pete most understanding in the whole matter. In the long run, you and I will simply have to develop a smiling patience. You must have done so already.

Oh, yes. If he only knew.

But just because she'd made it to Guayaquil didn't mean there was any rush to greet her. It would be a while yet—as it had been for him—before all her belongings were unloaded and cleared customs. In the ten days she waited for the final leg of her trip to commence, she got her first taste of South America *("I could scarcely believe that I was seeing the real thing, such as I'd often seen in pictures")* along with an onrush of encroaching fear.

APRIL 15: This morning I feel that nameless depression which comes to me when alone and in new circumstances. I wonder if I shall ever learn Spanish (I know, of course, that I will, God helping me), how long I shall have to stay in Guayaquil, whether I shall have to stay in Quito any length of time, when I shall be able to see Jim, etc. . . .

APRIL 18: Had I known that I would still be in Guayaquil today, I should have been hopelessly discouraged! But each day brings hope that my gear will come through and I will be able to fly to Quito. God has been so good in providing for me to stay with friends from PBI, new GMU missionaries. . . . It is a miserable house, but quite ritzy for Guayaquil in general. All the houses here have extremely high ceilings and are built in a narrow, rectangular shape.

They house dozens of children, as well as roaches, scorpions, rats, lizards, mice, etc. There is a dank, damp-plaster smell, and outside there is always the stench of "something burning.". . .

The contrasts are most notable. Indescribable filth and squalor, nestled right up against beautiful, shiny American cars, a few very fine homes, and modern public buildings. The average streets are unpaved (85% of them), with goats, children, skinny dogs, donkeys, mules, vultures, and rats all thrown into the melee. . . . Oh the filth! And many of the children wear no clothing at all. The men use the lampposts and fireplugs as do the dogs, unconcerned by spectators. Women sit on doorsteps nursing their babies. Surely this is no place for a single woman. Men here do not know the meaning of the "cold shoulder," and ogle and whoop at me. It makes me long to get away to the jungle, where at least it is not so filthy and populated. I used to have the idea that missionaries who lived in cities had it easy—now I am very thankful God has called me to the forest work. I don't think I could stand this very long.

APRIL 21: And still I wait! The Lord is testing the effectiveness of lessons hitherto laid before me. Just the delay, when time seems to be lost, would be difficult, but the prospect of seeing Jim in Quito makes it doubly hard. To think that every day here means one less day with him—O Lord, *Thou knowest.* . . .

Yesterday afternoon we went for a walk along the waterfront. How it saddens me just to see the common sights. Literally almost every person one sees is pathetic. Such misery written on faces, I've never seen before. Such rags of clothing, such utter lack of industry or desire for improvement. The street by the river is by far the most popular thoroughfare, yet by the shore were some nude men, bathing and washing clothes. My whole being recoils at such sights—not that I am shocked, in the sense of "surprised" or horrified, but it is a shock to my nature. I cannot express just how it affects me. . . . I kept thinking, as I walked along the shore, of A.C.'s poem which ends, "When shall the goddess flee away, and India (Ecuador) walk her shore with Thee?" How true it is that here (as in any mission field outside of the States or Europe) one is faced with life in its primal state, life stripped of all tinsel and show—bare, ruthless reality—a vale of tears in very truth. It makes one long for the coming of the King, "more than they that watch for the morning."

But at least *one* element that had kept this "vale of tears" impression so prevalent in her 1952 thinking was finally drawing to a merciful end.

She came today;
Stepped off an airplane
And watched her feet walk down the steps;
Looked up at friends
And frowned a little.
The sun was brighter than the plane,
That made her frown;
That, and the not seeing me
Among the friends.

She hesitated
Wondering which side the fence
To walk up toward the building
Where I was waiting,
Watching her. And then
She saw me;
Came straight on,
Stepped up and stood
Before me, wondering
What I would do.
I took her hand, smiled
And said,
"Sure good to see you."
So it was, and so it is
Now that she has come.

Hard to say it any more dramatically, I think, than how my father's poem captured their reunion. My mother, in *her* journal, said it this way:

APRIL 28: I arrived here on April 24, having flown from Guayaquil in 1 hr. 20 min. (450 miles) via Pan-American. I am at present living with a cultured Ecuadorian family, Arias by name. They are very kind and helpful. Speaking Spanish constantly, of course. Yesterday I spent most of the day at HCJB [the mission's radio station]. It is a remarkable place, and God has honored it abundantly.

And what can I say of Jim? He is here, of course, living with Tidmarshes on the other side of town. The last three days have been maddening—not a moment alone with him.

But this morning after our class in homeopathy with Dr. T., we went for a little walk down into a eucalyptus grove . . .

JE: Having prayed last week that the Lord would arrange a time for us to be alone together, this seemed ideal, and I took the great privilege to embrace.

EH: He took me in his arms, and he told me once more that he loved me—for being willing to wait God's time for us.

JE: I could not find another woman like her who would wait without commitment indefinitely.

EH: With his arm close around me, he asked if I was happy.

JE: "Are you happy?"

EH: Oh, what to say? Even at such a moment of bliss, there is the stabbing pain and dread of being separated from him even for a moment. I feel sometimes that I can bear no more.

JE: "Is there anything I can do to make you sure?" "I don't know". . .

EH: God knows (and only God—not I) what I can bear, and He will lead us aright.

JE: ". . . it's just that it gets worse all the time."

EH: We talked of marriage—Jim says it will of necessity be years before we can think of it. He believes he must give the prime of his life to the work, which means living in Shandia (T.'s jungle station) for at least two years before doing itinerant and pioneer work, pressing on to other tribes. I have asked God to give me the same steadfast assurance and peace that Jim has in this regard. I had felt it could not be more than two years hence before we could marry.

JE: Tears, quiet sobbing.

EH: Lord, do Thou fulfill this Thy word unto Thy suffering servant—preserve me from evil, sustain my trust in Thee, and lift up my soul that I may praise Thee for these my sore testings, for I do love Thee, and long to fulfill Thy will.

Surely just being there was part of God's will. And because He had led her there so clearly, she knew His protection and care would stay with her and keep her. Whatever the difficulties and the hazardous possibilities, whatever the outcome of her and my father's relationship, God would help her (and him) be the missionary He wanted.

Now just to be clear—Quito was the site of their in-country training and orientation. While there, they would be taking classes, obtaining skills, practicing the language, and becoming acclimated to the culture. In time, they would narrow their focus onto the specific openings for ministry that were then available in the area, as well as those that were continuing to develop. Both my mother and dad were affiliated there with the same missionary organization, under its general umbrella. But exactly what form their individual assignments would take was constantly in flux. The nature of "pioneer work" is that you don't know. The bridges and paths, though somewhat explored, are still largely untested. Primarily then, this season of theirs in Quito was one of working and waiting.

Nice, though, that they could finally do most of their working and waiting in the same location.

My father in Quito. I believe my mother took this picture.

Yet because of this, they naturally had no need for writing letters to one another during this time. So we lean on their journals now in following them through a compelling spring and summer that once seemed so unlikely, even a year ago.

I'll mostly stay out of the way and let their writing do its own describing, connecting the two whenever their separate journals recall the same event.

EH (APRIL 30): The Lord has answered prayer and given me peace once more about Jim. He allowed us a wonderful morning yesterday—we sat on a sunny slope of a beautiful valley, where we could see for miles across great fields to rugged peaks.

JE: Overlooking the Valle de Guápulo. She seemed small before me, almost frail. "Are you comfortable?" "Yes, and happy." Broad daylight!

EH: Then we walked down into Guápulo, a village in the valley, late in the afternoon. It was misty and lovely.

JE: Spoke of engagement. She thinks I'm inconsistent, Lord, seeming to be self-contradictory so often in speaking plainly of marriage and then seeming to be so unsure about it all. I guess You understand, Lord. So long as I can do a work in reaching a primitive people *better* as a single man, I will stay single.

"And that brings me to the other thing we've been digging around," he added in his journal of April 30, pondering where he felt the Lord might be sending him after this training phase was completed. *"The Aucas. I see no reason now to stay single if I'm only sent to the Yumbos—Tidmarsh didn't, Cathers hasn't. But Aucas! My God, who is sufficient for them?"* Indeed, they would prove another class of savage entirely.

JE (MAY 4): Dorothy Jones arrived Friday, and it looks like my "larks" of last week are over. *[She and my mother lived together.]* D.J. and Betty came over for breaking of bread *[Sunday Communion]*—refreshing, and I trust pleasing to God. Worship is excellent exercise for the soul. Makes a man big inside, makes him feel like he has found what he was built for, though he is conscious that he is inept.

"Inept." I realize, in his saying this, he was referring more broadly to the shared nature of our human depravity, our brokenness as fallen people. But as the spring and summer wore on, an emergent sense of inferiority, especially in comparison to my mother, became a real issue for him, quite maddening in its intensity. This entry of May 4 is his first real disclosure of it—of "it," you'll see him say—meaning he must have been grappling with "it" for some time.

JE: Couldn't keep my eyes off Betty. She is attractive in so many ways. I had to catch myself from breaking into a laugh of joy as we all were at Frank Cook's for supper. She knows *so well* how to handle herself in public—artistic in conversation, a ready and refined laugh, and always a soft look for me. Sang with HCJB chorus over the air again, and she has a beautiful voice, too. Well, do I thank God for her; she is on all counts unusual!

She brought me three letters from Thomas *[her younger brother]* to read. There is something strong between them, something so like about them that they are closer than any other members of the family. They exchange Latin phrases, or hymn quotes, or tidbits from some author I've never read. Felt a strange envy creep over me as I realized what a place he has in her.

I had to face *it* again—I can never be all she ought to have in a husband. Too dull witted, too slow a reader, too poor a memory. Her ability to hold tiny details in mind over years (she told me what coat I wore at Saint Michael's cemetery in '48 just yesterday!). Lord, let me make up to her in other ways what I lack in supplying that sort of thing for her. I just wasn't raised a scholiast. She will ultimately have to be satisfied with my body in exchange for what I lack in mind, and I, with her mind in exchange for what used to appear to me a lack in her body. Strange how I am quite satisfied with it now, and having such boyish fears.

He'd come a long way from making comments on her "angular figure" or criticizing the acerbic impression given off by her posture and demeanor. (My mother never forgot him saying, "You've got the brains, and I've got the body!") But apparently it was mostly bluff, a masking of hidden insecurity. Here, though, seeing her at a much more mature twenty-five—spiritually, relationally, yes, physically—he was surprisingly taken aback. God was bringing them together, and purging old attitudes, in ever new ways.

JE (MAY 8): I can't get her to believe that I am really satisfied with her body. She still has me holding my first impressions stated in our former days together: "banana nose . . . sandpaper . . . skinny." I don't know how to explain or clarify the change in this which has come since I really knew that I loved her last September 20. All I know is that it doesn't matter if her breasts are small, or her shoulders are slight, or her nose not finely shaped, or her front teeth set apart. I wouldn't like her any more if they were "ideal"—partly, I think, because she would not be what she is psychologically if she were anything but what she is physically.

Conscious of these things, she has become realistic in her outlook on life generally, and has developed a humility through them she might not have, had she been built otherwise.

This much I know: we were made for each other—if I for "comfort," then she for "speed"—though I have not found her *incómodo [uncomfortable]* in the least! My arms are for her "homing," a place to rest. Shelter, shield, and strength. What having her there means to me cannot be said. God has brought her there and prepared her before He brought her. I am *wholly* satisfied with His doing.

And yet the uncertainty about their future continued to cloud things. Marriage, they knew, would definitely need to wait. Though saddened, they were in full agreement that my dad couldn't afford the distraction of setting up house as he was being inserted into the jungle. But what about engagement? Why couldn't he go ahead and declare his intentions now? What would that cost him? How would it undermine or negate these reasonable convictions of his?

In reading Scripture one day, he believed he'd found the biblical parallel that supported his view for staying uncompromisingly single. Uriah the Hittite, removed from battle by King David after the incident with Bathsheba, refused the king's appeal that he go spend time with his wife. "The ark, and Israel, and Judah abide in tents; and my lord Joab, and the servants of my lord, are encamped in the open fields; shall I then go into mine house, to eat and to drink, and to lie with my wife? as thou livest, and as thy soul livest, I will not do this thing" (2 Sam. 11:11).

> **JE:** It was not *time* to return to his house, though he had the right to do so and the encouragement. It was the *time* for battle, and Uriah was a warrior; there could be no mixing of home goodness and the business of his life.
>
> So it came to me. Marriage is not for me now; it simply is not the *time*. (I do not say, and never did say, "It is not the *thing* for me.") With tribes unreached which I now believe reachable only by unattached men, "I will not do this thing."

There. That sounded strong. Biblical. Unassailable.

> **EH (MAY 9):** Today we walked in the streets of Quito. Jim spoke to me of his having asked God again for reasons for not being engaged. He answered him with the story of Uriah's refusal to lie with his wife and enjoy his home when there was a battle on.
>
> **JE:** I don't know why, but it seemed unreasonable to her, and she laughed at me.
>
> **EH:** Jim said, "Do you realize what it may cost?" (speaking of the possibility of his going into work among the Aucas). Yes, I realize what it may cost—death. And it is not as though I have not considered this possibility before.
>
> **JE:** Flaring back at first, I soon lapsed into silence, and by the time we reached her bus stop downtown, I was seeing only sidewalk and biting my lip.
>
> **EH:** As Jim tried to explain his feelings, he broke down.
>
> **JE:** . . . and then I cried, and we walked. I couldn't understand why I was unable to explain sensibly just *why* it was not time for engagement.
>
> **EH:** He feels that if he were to become engaged, he could not take the risks he may be called upon to take. For me, this is a purely technical difference, for I don't believe it could cost any more if we were engaged than in our present status, for I love him with such utter completeness and abandon, and feel myself so one with him even now, that the prospect of his being killed is unthinkable! I could not love him more at present, though I believe God can increase our capacity for loving.
>
> **JE:** My reasons didn't hold up today, not even to me, and I am now aware that my reasons for not getting engaged are hidden in the counsels of God's Spirit, the same as my reasons for loving her. . . . It may be that there are no reasons to be given. She says it is enough to know that I know, that I don't have to summon reasons (thanks, Lord, for a girl who not only will *wait* here, but be *happy* to wait here).

EH: I need know no reasons for our present state—I only need know that we are doing the will of God, who will never fail us nor forsake us. O the comfort of His words, the peace that keeps our hearts and minds through Christ Jesus! And may the grace that is all-sufficient make of me a true child of the Father, loving, trusting, praising, and resting in His acceptable will.

Apparently, despite their lack of total consensus, they'd left the matter in God's hands, contented in His will and gracious toward one another. But the more my dad thought back on this day's conversation, the more troubled he became (again) by that now familiar "it."

JE: I learned something about Betty today. She makes me feel "on the defensive" in arguments (in the kindest sense of the word). She often sees clearer than I, and faster, to the end of things, and moves ruthlessly and rapidly to state what she sees.

From her point of view, we ought to be engaged—though she is not trying to force me to it. . . . When I couldn't explain well why we shouldn't be, and I choked up, she immediately changed her attitude and went on the defensive herself, saying she understood, that she was sorry she had to say anything, that she hoped I didn't think I would have to produce "reasons" for staying apart.

I was sorry I couldn't control myself, because I fear to make her less expressive than she is in these matters. I *want* her answers, suggestions, outlook—no honest man could fear them—and today I may have been too sensitive to them, so that she thinks it hurts me to hear her "debate." But I swear it was not against her that I cried, rather against myself, that I could not say what I know, or even against the Lord, that He had left me verbally defenseless.

Most surely it was not against her. I kept saying to myself of her, "You're right; you're so damned right—but there is nothing for it, nothing to say, nothing to admit. I agree with you, but somehow I can't ever make you see what I know."

I've thought of how my including the curse word from this last paragraph might refresh some who are burdened with trying to be perfect, though it might shock some who would never use such a word. Either way, I hope you see his genuine humanness and his natural, fleshly writing, so that if you've idolized my dad, you will instead give thanks and bear with his faults, as we must do for example when reading the lives of many characters from the Bible.

In larger terms, I simply view this whole event as tension between the flesh and the spirit. He and my mother wanted desperately to do God's will. To my dad, this meant being able to sense God's showing him exactly when he was supposed to engage her. He felt strongly that even though God would ultimately bring them together in marriage, it had to be after a length of time spent in the jungle. But to my mother, it meant an agony of waiting, trusting, trying to be quiet and content. *"Oh, it is agony—to act unconcerned and distant when I am all but overwhelmed with tenderness toward him. When shall I be free to tell him???"*

But thanks to their sincere, devoted hearts, God kept their days afloat with blessed and divine distractions from their inner turmoil.

EH (MAY 15): Yesterday was one of the outstanding days of my life. At 2:30 a.m. Bill Cathers, Rob Gill, Abdón (an Ecuadorian), Pete, and Jim came for me, and we started up Pichincha [*a 15,000-foot volcano*]. It had been very rainy and doubtful, but as we began to climb, the moon shone out brilliantly.

JE: Nearly wept with the beauty of it . . . wonderful with Betts.

EH: At about 11 a.m. we reached the pinnacle—a steep, jagged rock formation quite strikingly resembling the Matterhorn. It took some pretty rugged rock climbing—at least, I thought it was something, though for Jim and Pete, who have climbed in the Northwest, it must have been tame.

We came partway down the mountain together, and then Jim and I took a different route. We spent some time just resting in the warm, soft grass on the slope of the valley. Jim went to sleep . . .

JE: . . . feigned sleep in her arms . . .

EH: . . . and I drank in the incredible beauty of the vast vistas before me.

JE: And unless I am mistaken, she pressed a kiss on my cheek as I lay there, desperately trying to keep my breathing slow! At least she went through all the motions.

EH: Oh, it is good to be with one who also loves God's handiwork.

JE: "I'm glad you're the kind of man that likes this sort of stuff"—mountain climbing, that is.

EH: It was so much fun, pointing out to one another all the loveliness about—from tiny, exquisite flowers to the brutal grandeur of the peaks and cliffs about us.

JE: The tranquility of being with her is indescribable, and I find it has a mellowing effect on me, makes me easier in social converse. Also, I find it "sensitizes" me, makes me more alert to *feel* situations. Praying that God will make me wise enough to treat her right, love her well, and control our playing. And He deigns to do so, insofar as I can now measure it. The joy of just loving, giving and taking, waiting and holding, is at peak now.

True, as she notes constantly, there is a pain in it, being unable to consummate now as we are, but then there is no real love without suffering of some sort. I pity her as I see she worries over the future—loving and losing. God, let me be faithful to her. And let me live to love if it please.

EH: The Lord has given me some happy times with Jim since I last wrote—two afternoons up at the bodega, and one evening coming home from "the station" (HCJB). He got a bit piqued at my attitude about something he said. Every so often, when I want with all my heart to take his arm or tell him that I love him, I say something sarcastic or cutting or very offhand, in order to restrain myself. This is what happened Thursday night. He reproved me for my attitude (it was only an *apparent* attitude, for such thing *never* represses my feelings toward him), and finally in some measure I brought myself to explain the reasons. He seemed to understand in part, and almost melted me with his gentleness.

JE: Her restraint from speaking of her love—to me or to anyone—is a hard thing for her, and I must learn to be satisfied with answer responses for now. She cannot be aggressive until engagement, she feels, and I am glad there is that restraint, for I feel none.

How I thank God for her! I find He is answering my prayers for wisdom to treat her properly—not through my understanding of how far to go or just how to love her—but through her attitudes, restraints, and liberties. She is a marvel for having the right "feeling" for things. And after I try to figure out her feelings, I find that they are often the best *reasons* for doing or refraining from any given thing.

I'm so glad to hear my father say that. I don't think he'd have been one bit surprised to know she maintained this same "right feeling for things" her whole life long. I was a living witness to it in our home. And while I know his impulses urged him to want more from her physically than she was willing to give, I treasure both of them equally for their inner commitment to purity.

I can say, without any risk of overstating, much of my own decision to stay pure until marriage came from my mother's joy in telling me about *their* marriage, and about her and my father's determination to keep their promises to God during this time in their lives. They each ached for the other, as all lovers do. But as the woman, she understood well that she, even more than my dad, was the one in greater control over how much leeway they allowed themselves in touch and enticement. There's much wisdom on display here, amid much tension. Be inspired by it. This is an actual demonstration of God wanting His children's best and of His children believing—despite their passion, despite their feelings—that nothing, *nothing*, offers any substitute. Times may be different today, but this truth is not. And never will be.

So with the arrival of summer came an awareness that the call of the jungle was drawing nearer for my father. Up until now, he'd felt *"liberty to allow myself luxuries in getting acquainted with the country,"* wanting to both learn and love everything about this place where God had called him. Intent on fulfilling his missionary calling, he knew the time was approaching when he must *"necessarily curtail"* some of these adventures.

Sure, there was value in every new experience. *"Learning a language means meeting people in all their circumstances and trips. As long as you are with nationals, it will always contribute to the end."* But he couldn't afford for his Spanish to be merely passable, not if he hoped to accomplish what he'd set out to do there.

JUNE 8: Giver of the gift of tongues! Let me speak to them as they ought to be spoken to, so they do not have to hide their real reaction with polite praise. Glad to be in a national home—at least to hear it spoken as a living-thought medium—not merely as English translation.

It meant, of course, striking a balance between work and love.

The discipline of distance has passed into the discipline of proximity for me these days. Living right across the street, eating a meal a day together, on the bus, walking—it puts me on an entirely different basis than I have ever known with her before. . . .

So far the Lord has given a good balance, it seems to me. I don't feel like I've really abandoned my Spanish for her or any of the other big purposes of being in Quito. I've had to keep myself from staying out too late and from going out too often. And love never gets "full" to the point of satiation, although at times I have the sense of having had "just enough for now.". . .

JUNE 15: Still, we haven't kissed. I can't believe it sometimes, but it's so. Who ever heard of people in love, like we are in love, sporting as fondly as we do and as often, who have never met at the lips? Can it really be there will be *more* thrill than now?

Yes, but *"life cannot be all love,"* as my mother said. And events were coming together on the ground that directly influenced their subsequent missions tasks, as my father recorded in this journal entry.

JUNE 23: Wycliffe Bible translators made public the news of their recently signed contract with the government to enter tribes in Ecuador and reduce their language to writing. This will bring changes in our plans for the Oriente *[eastern region of the country]*. Especially does it seem to affect Betty. Where will You send her now, Lord?

Meanwhile, he was venturing out on some reconnaissance excursions.

JULY 2: Buzzed Shell's deserted field at Ayuy *[Shell Mera, headquarters of Mission Aviation Fellowship]*. Made inquiries about Quichua population in the Canelos region. Estimates uncertain. Would guess one thousand to fifteen hundred. Saw the necessity for our being single to reach these people—too scattered to reach with the mission-station method.

Through experiences like these, he was learning to experience God in new, unexpected, invigorating ways.

JULY 11: I wonder sometimes if it is right to be so happy. Day follows day in an easy succession of wonders and joys—simple, good things like food well prepared, or play with the children, or conversation with Pete, or supply of money for rent and board within hours of its time to be paid. Grace upon grace in the outside sphere of living.

But, simply because I am not really studying the English Bible, fresh truth for inner soul refreshment is rare. . . . I was reading my diary notes [of 1949] and noting the contrasting soul soreness of those days with the freedom and joy of these. Those were certainly more productive from a point of view of getting things from the Word; these are more casual and less fruitful, but for reasons. Spanish must be gotten. I want badly for God to speak as He did then, but I want Him to begin speaking in Spanish, and I am not yet used to that—perhaps not ready for it. . . .

How well I see now that He is wanting to do something in me! So many missionaries, intent on doing something, forget that His main work is making something of *them*, not just doing a work by their stiff and misunderstanding fingers. Teach me, Lord Jesus, to live simply and love purely, like a child, and to know that You are unchanged in Your attitudes and actions toward me. Give me not to be hungering for the "strange, rare, and peculiar" when the common, ordinary, and regular, rightly taken, will suffice to feed and satisfy the soul. Bring the struggle when I need it; take away the ease at Your pleasure.

And my mother, though journaling only seldom throughout the summer, found both her love for the field and her love for my father growing steadily.

JULY 20: For some reason, I've not felt like writing in my journal. But there is so much I could have said. It has been a month in which God has helped me wonderfully with the study of Spanish, and also one in which I've grown to love Jim more than ever before.

We have many perfect times together, in the fields, through the eucalyptus groves, and on Quito's lovely hillsides. One day we set out at 3:00 a.m. and climbed Pichincha [a second time]. Jim had been sick at his stomach just a few hours before we left, so he was very weak, and we could not go far without resting. It was very cold—frost coated the grass in solid white, and the moon shone full over the lighted snowcaps to the north, east, and south. It was enchanting. At dawn the sunrise was appallingly lovely, with the fading moonlight on the other side of the valley. We were exhausted, and Jim looked so pale it almost scared me. I took turns carrying the heavy pack every hour or so.

Near noon we found ourselves skirting (and half scaling) a great rock wall at the head of a ravine. This really scared me, and Jim was a bit dizzy. If he had lost his balance for a second, there would have been no recovery. Then after the strain of this piece of the journey, we had to cross a great field of volcanic ash and sand. When we finally reached the valley by which we were going home, we found it a quagmire of mineral springs, into which we sank over our shoe tops!

Discovering at last a patch of dry grass, we flopped down and fell immediately asleep for an hour. Then we followed a long, long trail which dropped very gradually, and at 7:30 arrived in Quito.

Other pleasant times have included reading poetry together, exploring sections of the city and surrounding country with which we were not familiar, and just short walks, to be together.

In love, in Quito.

But time for such enjoyments was drawing short. The prospect of parting within a few weeks, not knowing when (or if) they'd ever be this close again, began to wear on both of them.

JE: Sense great moving of heart wanting to be fair to her, wanting to marry her, wanting, wanting. But now I feel no guiding from God, not even for engagement. The "years" weigh on me often, awake and going off to sleep, thinking of the length of a year, worrying over the real view I should take of engagement, feeling my previous arguments fall, one by one. . . . We talk of it freely together, she and I, and my reasoning must be making it worse, but I know—reason or not—now is not the time. . . .

The acceptance of that as the will of the Father is no gladdening thing—not that my wants (for her, for the work of God, perhaps among Aucas) conflict. They are not contradictory, but they do not seem to mesh. They have come at the same time, so that instead of fitting into one another, as cogs would, they grind against one another, sometimes with awful concentration. . . .

It is too soon for me, not having seen the Oriente, to believe that God may not want me there entirely unattached. . . . But all the while, I'm mad for her, wanting to be with her night and day, the haunting hunger of body, the loneliness of mind making book study a farce at times and making life itself seem useless without her.

EH: This morning I feel overwhelmed once again with the thought of Jim's going. This time next week he will have left, if things go as planned. Time is slipping away, and we have no time to be together.

Saturday and Sunday he was sick, and we could not go out. Monday we went to Alangasí, and hence were with the others nearly all the time. Tuesday I had hoped to be with him in the afternoon, but instead he went home after lunch and studied. At four o'clock, when I thought surely we would go for the mail together, he came over and said that he and Pete were going down to the Tidmarshes. So I hoped for the evening—he had not come to call for his mail when I went in to supper; good—he would have to come in the evening, and then perhaps he'd stay on a little while. No—in the middle of supper he appeared to get his mail. So the evening was spent alone. . . .

Oh, sometimes I feel that I simply cannot stand it any longer—this present set-up of love and intimacy, about thinking with one mind, and yet the great chasm of not being engaged. The strain, when I long in utter anguish to tell him how I love him, and cannot.

JE: She noticed today, as she did not on the twenty-fifth, the spirit of heaviness that comes over me. I told her that I felt weepy, sighful, and that I couldn't tell her why now, but that I would later, when she could do something about it. Also, that it concerned things about her that I didn't want changed; and that I would get over it. Not very clear. It isn't to me either.

I don't understand what there is about loving her that makes me such a damned woman. I can hardly begin to describe it; I only know that I feel it strong and that I can't talk of it without twists coming to my mouth. Lips get dry and tears seem to brim at my eyes, and there is a crushing sense in my chest. At the bottom of it is a tremendous weight of sheer unworthiness. I don't feel fit to be in her company; I can't think of things to say if she doesn't readily come back in conversation. . . .

I know it would help to talk to her, but can't bear to think of speaking of this thing in daylight when she could see me cry. She wouldn't believe me, anyhow. I don't give the impression of feeling underdog, and I don't usually display any humility that would suggest I felt myself the lesser.

EH: This separation now, for example, when I am here in my room sobbing because I cannot keep from it, sobbing for love of him, and praying only, "Thy will be done"—while he is laughing and cracking jokes with Sanchez and Pete. Oh, if he knew—but he cannot know, and I cannot tell him. There is *no one* to talk to. O Lord—forgive me, give me grace, patience, unselfishness.

JE: Oh, if only she felt that she could tell me she loved me and why, perhaps that would bolster me somehow. . . . If only she could come to *me* instead of my having always to go to her, letting her control, having to follow so many times when I feel that I should be leading. But what is to be done? She *can't*, simply *can't* do otherwise until engagement—says it just has to be that way now. My God, what a vise I'm in.

And just as the pressure was feeling its most acute, news arrived that— while good—required a stiff upper lip of surrender.

JE: She had word the sixth that Ginny was engaged to Bud DeVries on Sunday.

EH: I am stunned—but, oh, *so* happy for her—my "little" sister, seven years my junior.

JE: Crying when I came over to ask her for a walk in the evening. . . . "Is Ginny engaged?" "Yes—and two letters from Dave about his new baby." (Long pauses.) "It's just that I can't see why they should have it so, and we have it this way.". . .

Thursday was not much better for her. But we went downtown together, took a taxi up the Panecillo *[a prominent hill in Quito]* and walked down. She was much freer to chat—her very touch filling me with tenderness. We played in the grass down below the house, and she taught me to "two step" in the street afterward—after midnight!

But in the dark of the next Friday morning, he was gone.

August 17

I walked over to your wall and stalked the length of it while Pete checked the room for the last time. Almost called your name to your dark windows, thinking you might be awake. . . . Then I dropped into silence, knowing I was leaving you and ending the happiest weeks of my life, sorrowing a little in the silence.

This was the first of many letters that would begin sailing again between them. But only to his journal did he commit the thoughts that had run through his mind as he lay in bed the night before, his final time of being just across the street from her in Quito.

Slept restlessly, with recurrences of last night as she knelt over me in the field. I told her that I had gotten liberty to hope for engagement in less than a year. She said, "That's good to know." Feel more and more that my reasons against engagement do not carry the weight of those in favor of it.

It will mean years of "promised" life, likely, and that involves some problems, but they do not compare with what I am assigning Betty to, in this uncommitted period, with her great reserves and pressures. For us both, I believe engagement would be a release for easier thinking, both present and for the future.

Thinking now of asking Ed to bring a ring.

AUTUMN

Shell Mera was to be only a brief stay for my father. After two weeks there, helping lead a Bible camp for boys, he would be on to Shandia, the Tidmarsh's station among the Quichuas. But despite his many responsibilities, despite all the adjustments to a new location, and despite the prying eyes of nosy young students wondering if he was writing again to *"a certain señorita whose picture they found under the lid of my suitcase,"* he managed to compose a number of letters to her, even during this tight time frame. He closed the first one with an appeal to *"write, darling,"* along with a charming P.S. comment that read, *"Sanchez just dropped by and sends 'casual greeting.' Mine is not so."*

"Sanchez just dropped by and sends 'casual greeting.' Mine is not so."

My mother's response was equally quick.

August 19

What a surprise it was for me when I went out to the tea at the Station to find a letter from you this afternoon. It was so good to hear, Jim, and I want you to know I appreciate your thoughtfulness in sending one up so soon. . . .

Oh, my, I hardly knew what to think when you told of coming over to our wall on Friday morning looking for me. It's just a good thing I wasn't out there in pajamas, but if I'd had any idea you'd do that, I would have been up and dressed to see you. It's not that it didn't enter my head to get up, but I thought it would be another case of standing there alone, aching for you to come, yet knowing that you were not aware I was there, as I've done several nights when I wanted to see you.

That night when I was alone in the house, longing to see you, I stood outside by the front wall for nearly an hour—seeing you rise from the dining room, saunter into the *sala*, play with the kids a while, light the light in your room (was hoping you'd gone for your coat!) and then (my heart sank again) I saw the desk light go on. After you started typing, I walked up the street till I could see just the edge of your face through a crack in the curtains. Well—I thought it would be easier to let our goodnight at the gate on Thursday be the last. But, oh, I'm sorry, Jim—you know I would have come!

The Lord has been so good. I can't describe the peace He's given since you've gone. I have no tears to tell you about, except just a few (and not really bitter, desolate ones). The feeling that predominates is one of deepest thanksgiving—first of all, for the blessing of your love, and then for all the time God gave us together. It is, to me, literally, "peace that passeth understanding.". . .

It seems strange to be seated by my window now, writing to you instead of expecting to see you at the gate at any moment. As I go upstairs at night, I don't see Pete swinging his arms in the living room, or you hoisting one of the kids up in the air. But somehow it seems just as normal this way, and I find that I can be perfectly content even though I'm not looking forward to seeing you at noon! The only explanation I find for it is a miracle of God. He is abundantly able.

This peace from the fading summer of 1952 is reminiscent of what she'd written in her journal the previous Thanksgiving: "*I believe that perhaps the most effective 'balance wheel' in a believer's life is just this. In each event of life, we are to give thanks.*" And that's exactly what she was doing here—giving thanks for what God had given them, rather than bemoaning what they'd lost.

My father's next letter from Shell struck the same thankful, peaceful, contented tone:

August 21

This will have to be a short one, Betts. It is after 6:00 a.m. and I have just come over to one of the sheds facing the airstrip to get away from the wake-up skirmishes of the bunkhouse. Tidmarsh arrived yesterday afternoon and said he would drop by on his way out this morning, and I thought it would be a good opportunity to drop you a note. I suppose you will be like I was yesterday, expecting against reason that word would be in the packet of mail. Knowing how sharp is even the smallest disappointment, and wanting to spare you as many as possible, I will try to get this away. . . .

Thoughts of our Quito days are refreshing and restful. I find my mind always turning to you when I am ready for sleep. You and my relation to you are one of the surest "relaxers" I can bring to mind—the one subject over which I have prayed and thought and studied sufficiently to be completely at ease about.

Back and forth they wrote, nearly every day now.

August 23

Tidmarsh came up yesterday a.m. with your letter. It was a second surprise. But so good to hear, Jim, so very good. . . . Sitting in Tidmarsh's living room the night they went to Shell Mera, I remembered those mornings of April and May, when I waited for you to come in for a minute or so before class. There has been marked development in my feeling since then.

August 25

Thanks so much, Betty, for your letters and the enclosures. I need yours as badly as you need mine. And now somehow they make you seem so much closer than our other correspondences, not merely because you are nearer but because I can read more of *you* into your letters, knowing you so much better than I ever have before. And feeling too, as I do now, hardly without knowing how it happened, that I can share all with you—your family letters and affairs that I felt quiet about before, like meaningless happenings in my own life and family. Quito was a get-acquainted period, and we needed it more than we know. . . .

You won't know how glad I was to hear of the hardly-believed-for peace you describe. May the Spirit who gave maintain. More than once the feeling of being cruel has come, accusing me for leaving you without engagement or more promise, making me wonder at the ways of God, a wonder that shaded into resentment. And it is easier to know that He who led gave grace.

He knows better than you, Bett, why, and how intensely and how long I have desired you, and the struggle it has been to commit you to Him alone to comfort when I wanted devilishly hard to have you committed—insofar as engagement would make it possible to me. But now I know that His loving kindness, forever better than life, is better too than further human loving; for I doubt if even engagement could have wrought the impossible peace you speak of. Praise, then, praise for Peace.

A few days later—Thursday, August 28—he sat down to write one final letter from semi-civilization, hoping to *"get some fresh word through"* before moving on to Shandia, delivered by those who were returning to Quito with the boys the next day.

> You will know whether Tidmarsh preceded us in. If he arrives this afternoon, he will likely go to Pano the first time the weather breaks and get the house swept out for our arrival. The only thing we have to wait on is the arrival of the school-teacher. He is due Saturday afternoon, and if things go as scheduled, we will be going in then on Monday, the weather being the only foreseeable variable factor in the plan to date. I personally hope we will get in for the weekend, as we sense we are a burden to the missionary folk here.
>
> Our first move will be to get settled comfortably, trekking with Indians with all our stuff the 4–5 hours to Shandia from Pano, and getting housekeeping established next week. Then we settle down to language again and cleaning and building.

Even as he hurriedly, prayerfully tried to finish off this letter, writing of how *"I hope for you and the McCullys"* to come join him someday, Dr. Tidmarsh arrived—but not alone. The gear he'd needed to bring down had been too much to fit inside a single vehicle, so his wife, Gwen, had accompanied him in another car. With one extra passenger.

> **EH:** Jim, it was so good to see you. Just to walk with you for that brief half-hour while you shared your mother's letter with me was good. And the next morning . . .
>
> **JE:** Woke at 3:30 a.m., unable to sleep knowing that she is here. Up at 4:30 with the boys. Packed, breakfasted, and said good-bye to them all. . . . But she was here, and we talked odd bits—about the greetings Monday night, about the unfinished letter I gave her because her coming caught me in the middle of it. Then, as we stood, stalling at the kitchen door with the others outside . . .
>
> **EH:** . . . I'm still trying to figure out just how we came close that minute.
>
> **JE:** Suddenly we leaned toward each other and pressed hard, face to face, only for an instant.
>
> **EH:** I don't remember you pulling me, nor do I recall coming to you. I just know that your face was against mine suddenly, warmly, briefly.
>
> **JE:** That's all—but, oh, it was a full instant, full of telling things. She came toward me without being pulled, full of quick passion. Then we went out to the car together.

EH: Jim, I know that His mercies are new every morning—but *that* mercy, *that* morning—I think it was an especially great one.

Another goodbye, but a dear one.

Returning to Quito, she read the half-written letter that her visit had blissfully interrupted, the letter he'd been able to place directly into her hand. In it, he picked up on a line she'd recently written, where she noted "marked development" in her feelings for him. Those words had intrigued him enough to ask:

> Next time you write me, would you mind enlarging on a theme embodied in this lone sentence in your last: "There has been marked development in my feeling since then"? It refers to the days when you used to sit in the living room at T's waiting for me before class. For me, there has been change in nothing but intensity, from the day we held hands coming in from the airport. Not that that is a small thing, but I am tantalized to know your attitudes then and now.

He longed to hear her saying more, saying *anything* about her love for him, realizing (of course) she might not choose to go into it any more deeply, demurring with *"one of those wonderful, 'Jim, I can'ts.'"*

No, she was glad this time to oblige.

September 1

> Regarding your question of the statement I made about my feelings having shown development—I, too, of course have felt an intensifying since April 25. But in Saturday's letter you say that you feel now that you can share everything with me. That's what I mean.
>
> I find in this an analogy to our relationships with God. The man who doesn't know Him intimately brings to Him only the great needs, the "significant" things. The man who dwells in His presence knows, as did Jeremiah, that "I know the thoughts that come into your mind, every one of them"—but he knows also that, apart from His omniscience, God also has an intimate and loving interest in the "small" things.
>
> > There is no great with Thee,
> > There is no small—
> > For Thou art all, and fillest
> > All in all
>
> Perfect love casteth out fear. It is this simplicity that constitutes in a great measure, I believe, God's profundity. And so with us, Jim. I find happiness in sharing with you not only the many things we have in common—the things which drew us together initially—but now also the little things we don't have in common: my family, your family; my daily happenings, yours; the things that make us individuals; the things that are involved in your being a man and my being a woman. I think you will understand what I mean.

Yes, he understood. He just hoped she understood *"how intensely and how long I have desired you, and the struggle it has been to commit you to Him alone to comfort, when I wanted devilishly to have you committed to me—insofar as engagement would make it possible."* His experiences of the coming months in Shandia would confirm to his heart that he'd been right all along in not needing to be married yet. The conditions were too primitive; the demands, too all-encompassing. *Engagement,* however, was something he was bending on. And in thinking of it—in thinking of her—he missed her all the more.

September 2

Woke wanting you, squirming in bed at the remembrance of the sudden and short but somehow full embrace here at the door of the kitchen. I can hardly remember how it happened, but I think I felt you coming toward me with hardly a suggestion from my outreached hand, and I remember to this moment the hard pushing of your face against my neck. *Thanks, darling.* It seemed very fitting for that moment, fitting to the place and the brief occasion of your visit. The next one can hardly be fuller—but I hope it can be longer.

He went on to write of pulling flower samples up by the roots to take with him into the jungle: *"shoe orchids, white with brown-spotted centers, growing on a fallen tree over the creek. They are now in a small packsack—the one we took up Rucu together—with other orchid roots, roses, naranjilla, a coffee root hibiscus, geranium starts, and a poinsettia shoot. I hope things grow like folks say they do—I've got the flower craze worse than I get it some springs in the yard at Portland."* My mother loved this, she said:

That is one of the things that pleases me so about you, Jim—your love of the lovely things of life. Not just the grand and the wild and the majestic—things which, knowing your apparent personality, I would expect you to like—but also the small, the exquisite, the aesthetic, things which indicate another side of you, not so apparent at first acquaintance. It has been one of the happy discoveries in the past year, along with your devastating tenderness and thoughtfulness. No longer do you seem "crude" to me, but rather I recognize a certain polish—not the artificial, surface polish of convention, never—but, shall I say, intrinsic. And I appreciate it.

He wrote also of a man being brought to their location *"who, in a drunken scrap Saturday night, had been cut across the back of the neck, from ear to ear, with a pocketknife."* Many of his later letters from Shandia would be dotted with heartbreaking accounts of local people they tried to assist with medicine and basic health care.

And your letter—I almost laughed out loud in reading your remarks about "The Embrace," after writing almost the identical this morning. The sweet smell of Tweed is a tender comfort, Betty—do keep them scented. . . .

Now I will close. The afternoon has cleared, so that the big pillars of cloud, rising in a haze over the jungle (I am writing in the kitchen and can see the Oriente through the door), stand pure white against a blue sky. Silhouettes of distant birds are sharp against them, going east.

And tomorrow, happily, and in the will of God, I will follow only too well, I know, against the inner weakness to return, to go back to you. But I feel that I have set my hand—and to look back now would be dishonor. He knows the inner part—and He knows how much of me I really leave with you. And He knows why I leave, and for how long.

Lovingly, Jim

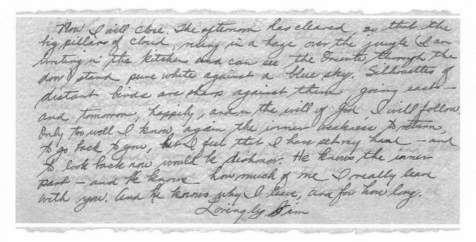

"Now I will close . . . and tomorrow, happily, and in the will of God, I will follow."

Despite the pangs of heartsickness he was feeling, this pioneering adventure is what my father had always prayed for, hoped for, and seen himself doing. It's why he came to Ecuador. It's why he'd trained and worked and traveled and sacrificed.

And with similar anticipation, and similar longings, my mother also began feeling waves of excitement, seeing that all her devotion and linguistic study was ready to be put into use for mission work. She wrote:

September 4

The days are amazingly full for me. I don't know just what I manage to do to keep so busy, except that I've been studying so consistently that I find it hard to do anything else. The mornings that used to lag so, when I was waiting for you to come to dinner, seem to fly by, and likewise the afternoons. I've hardly finished dinner before it's 5:00 and time to go down for the mail.

Again, it is of the Lord's mercy. I never thought it could be this way! And already five months (yesterday) have passed since I left home. And if the time is flying for me, I'm sure it must be even more so for you, with so much to get done. I am so anxious to hear about everything. . . .

I want to know all about what you're doing, what you eat, what it's like there, so that I can picture you, Jim. That little taste of Shell Mera sure gave me *ganas* [desire] to get into the jungle. May God speed the day.

As always, Betty

But days never really "speed" when you're missing someone as dearly as these two were now missing each other. The ministry tasks before them were often challenging, sometimes in the extreme, especially in my father's case. Yet rarely did a day pass when they weren't sitting down at some point to add another page or more to a letter already in progress. This season of their lives was by far their most prolific season of correspondence, even though the mail delivery coming in and out of their various locations was subject to unpredictability and delay.

Much of the content of their letters involved details of jungle life and missions work, as well as the lively stream of updates on news, family, and personal matters you'd expect from two people eager to share and hungry for information. I wish I could include it all. Any reader would find their exchange of experiences fascinating. They were discovering that even the "small details" held great interest. But rather than going into the triviality of those exchanges, I will let the profundity and poignancy of their letters speak for themselves with only an occasional comment.

Here's my father, recalling the trek into Shandia:

September 7

We made the three-hour walk in two-and-a-half, sloshing through streams, sliding over roots, greasy with mud. It's not a hard walk, but one can hardly enjoy the forest for having to watch each step so closely. The forest here is not unlike the west—only, of course, much bigger and much emptier, but for that, much more interesting.

You came to mind in one spot on a sharp ridge where the trees slid away on both sides into a deep green which seemed bottomless—those queer trees, not with round trunks but with concave surfaces between the roots that ribbon out in all directions. You came to mind because I could look up and see the notched horizon of hills that hid you up there in Quito. And I wondered what you were doing, and of course, why you weren't there to share it with me

Even more forcible thoughts of you flooded back as we burst, a little surprised, into the clearing of the play field. Right ahead and to the left, a huge, full moon was balanced between the forest and a straight cloud, and in sixty steps the river below caught up with the reflection. . . . I had a few moments alone to think of the past four moons *[May, June, July, August]*, and how we warmed each other watching them. Oh, Betty . . .

Oh, how I want to share, share, share hourly, momently, the wonders of this forest with you, Bett, and I am not resigned in the least to the poor compromise of letter writing. There are times, for sheer bulk of the things to be shared, when I just have to say, "We'll talk of this later." Sorry, but I'm afraid even words in conversation won't do—you'll just have to come and visit! . . .

This morning I was reading Psalm 13 in the Spanish Moderna *[Spanish translation of the Bible]*, and felt as though it spoke for me in verse 2: "How long will I join counsels in my soul, bringing longing in my heart every day?" Whenever I take time to think about us, "counseling" with myself, it brings longing to me, Bett—man's wanting for woman, and more keenly, my own personal reasons for wanting you. I can't help "counseling," and it brings you automatically before me. I don't always follow it to the end that David did, but usually I can "sing to the Lord" (v. 6). I hope it is the same for you. But there remains the problem, "HASTA CUANDO?" *["Even when?"]* There is still no fulfillment in sight for us, as I see the work ahead here. It is, like it or not, still to be "a long, hard wait.". . .

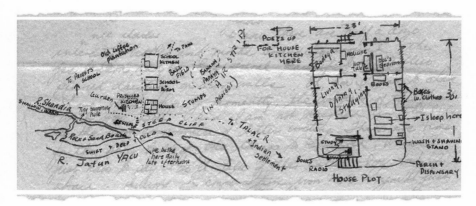

She had asked for details about Shandia, and he sent them.

Now, Betts, dearest, I think eleven pages will suffice! I hope it is not scattered, as to give the impression of being impersonal—an accusation you've made of my letters before. There is lots of detail yet to be filled in, but I want to finish the page telling you how thankful I am to God for you, for our history together, and for the present rest we have in loving as we are apart. And then, too, I believe Him for a happy future for us—so much that I often feel myself thrill—just imagining doing some little social act with you. I don't know why, but I went to sleep last night thinking how nice it would be to have you at my elbow while I drove the car—like coming home from the Pacific that night, and like times *en route* in New England.

Goodnight, Betty

Her answer, when his letter finally came . . .

September 20

It was two weeks ago that you began your 11-page letter, but only two hours ago that I read it. Oh, thank you, Jim, for such a long one, and for telling me the things I want to know. Now I feel that I can picture you at least a little bit, whereas up until now I've been at a complete loss. I wake in the morning and try to imagine how it is with you, what your room is like, what the day holds for you. . . .

It is really too late for me to begin comments on your letter or relating Quito things, but I just wanted to talk to you for a few minutes. As always, it is difficult, when I have to restrain the pen from writing things that come to mind. But I will let you know this—when I came home (a dark, rainy, very cold evening) and read your letter over for the second time, tears came. I'm not sure why, besides the fact that I missed you tremendously—unless it was the sentence about "no prospect for fulfillment—a long, hard wait."

Jim, it is not that this is *news* to me, or that I am not at least as aware as you are of the price we are asked to pay—it is just that I don't want you to say it. It brings it home with brute force, making me face it again, when I have been living only one day at a time, in peace. If the inklings I have now prove to be the will of God, it promises to be longer than we know.

These "inklings" included a long talk the day before with Doreen Clifford, the missionary she'd met the past January in New York, who had returned to Ecuador as well. *"She is beginning lessons in the Colorado language,"* my mother wrote in her journal, speaking of a work taking place to the *west* of Quito, whereas my father's work was off to the east. It would put them on opposite sides of the Andes Mountains—requiring longer plane trips, and longer bus trips, with many stops and often breakdowns in between. Yet *"when I came home,"* she said in a September 19 journal posting, *"I began to wonder if God would have me to go down there and help her with the classifying and organizing of material, since of course it is an aboriginal language and no one has as yet done any formal work on it. In a way, I do not want to go down there. I cannot help but feel that Jim and I will become engaged sometime within the coming year. And it will be hard to settle in one place and then pull up stakes and perhaps go to the Oriente. But God knows that I want to do only His will, and all of it, without thoughts or consideration of my own feelings."*

Oh, Jim—how I need the grace of obedience—of obedience with cheerfulness, without shadow of hesitation, without any "But Lord—it's been so long already!"

I want to be one of those who "follow the Lamb whithersoever He goeth." He cannot be unmindful of us. He will make up to us all that we feel is lost—all the "years that the locust has eaten."

I often think—perhaps I should say, of late it has come to me—of the analogy of you, in my relation to you, and heaven, in relation to us as Christians. Both to me are synonymous with *rest*. We think of the "bosom of the Father," of that eternal rest that remaineth for the people of God—of the joy of adoration, a complete service in itself—of the many references to the "rest" which is heaven. And here upon earth, as I have told you, I have found in you *rest*. To bring it down to very mundane things, I've not been sleeping well lately, and often long to be in your arms, as you have let me do so often, and just rest.

Jim, I just can't get out of my mind the way you said, "Were you asleep, darling?" I don't know how many times, in the strangest places, that has come to me. But now I must go to bed, the next best substitute for rest, I suppose.

She continued writing him every few days.

September 24

A year exactly since I felt God was pointing the way to Ecuador—never shall I forget that day, alone in my room, struggling to discern between my own feeling and the Shepherd's voice, until He kindly showed me that there was no discrepancy between the two. And about this time in the morning, peace came, and I began looking forward to seeing you Friday night at Tidmarsh's farewell meeting in Plainfield. That was the night of our first embrace, that Friday. "O God of stars and flowers, forgive our blindness—no dream of night had dared what Thou hast wrought."

Last night I went over to T's and the doctor showed his pictures of Shandia for Bill and Irene and me. It was so good to see the place where you are—I could see your window in one picture. It looks lovely there. Of course Dr. T. related numerous incidents in his inimitable way. I nearly died when, after Gwen had spouted off about the terrors of the crossing every adjective she could scare up, Dr. T. said, "Yes, it's a veddy (sic) trying experience." I am sure the word "trying" could never be called an exaggeration.

He gave me the bird you sent up—it's beautiful, isn't it? I don't quite know whether to thank you for it or what. The doctor simply said you wanted it kept up here in Quito, so had asked him to give it to me. However, I appreciate that, anyway, and for the present it is hanging in my room.

Now as for your letter—a wonderful one—You say the forest there is "bigger" than in the west. I wonder if you mean in area, or if the trees are bigger. I must confess I was a bit disappointed when I saw the western forests, as it just seemed to be bush, without many really big trees—none, it seemed, with thick trunks. The birds and flora must be beautiful, and those rivers, judging by T's pictures, looked quite different from what I would have expected. I am glad you don't have your nose in a vocabulary book all day—you have more than a one-track mind. It must be a lot of fun to see what you can make out of nothing, so to speak. I'm just dying to try it myself. I was sorry to hear that you're using a plastic tablecloth, but sorrier still to hear of the meager fare you put on it—rice, plátano, yucca. I do hope you'll be able to add some variety later.

List of things my father needed in Shandia. Thankfully he drew pictures of certain items she might not immediately recognize.

Now as for the stuff from the bodega: you asked for a yellow card with a set of steel drills. The only yellow card in the barrel had hacksaw blades. I couldn't find a leatherette case with steel punches either, but I found a leatherette case with what look to me like steel drills, so I'm sending that down. I took everything out of the barrel looking for the punches, but couldn't find them—so sorry. It surely is a good thing you drew pictures—I'd never have identified some of the items. (Incidentally, your list says that the punches should be in the blue barrel, so since I couldn't find them there, I didn't go through every other piece.) The 3 x 5 papers I'm having made—there was no such thing in Quito. Hope they're ready Saturday, as they promised. Pilar escorted me up to get the honey—good stuff, and cheap, so we bought some, too, for the Arias.

Your notes about the onomatopoeia of the language were tantalizing—how I'd love to get my talons into something like that! God knows my heart—I believe He is going to lead that way sometime (to language work, I mean).

Doreen has been up since Tuesday a week ago, and has spent two nights with me and is coming back tonight. We've had some wonderful talks together.

I feel a unity with her that I've not felt with anyone since Bunny. We talked till 2 a.m. both times, and then I've been with her several afternoons.

September 28

As you will have discovered, I'm sending quite a few letters for you to read, along with mail for Eladio and Pete which I picked up. . . .

I was so glad to hear from Van. I'd written her when I was in Guayaquil. Funny that she speaks of our being in Peru—she had the address on the envelope correct. Her letter is an honest one—in contrast, I fear, to many of the "missionary reports" Dr. Nida used to speak of. Oh, Jim, yesterday I just beseeched God for truth in the inward parts. . . . It has been shattering to realize the things that have gone on in the name of Jesus Christ. People always said that a great many disillusionments were in store for us when we reached the field. Dr. Harris impressed this on me. But I shall never forget the conviction with which Mrs. Harris quoted, "When thou passest through the waters, I will be with thee . . ." I have been praying lately on the ground that the psalmist used—in English often, "for Thy name's sake"—in Spanish (and I think I like it better), "por amor de tu nombre." It is a sure ground. God must preserve His own glory, but there are times when we must leave it entirely up to Him, when it looks to us, as Service puts it, that His glory has been "dragged in the mire." I read through A.C.'s *God's Missionary* again last week. "Crooked patterns"—may God have mercy upon us, that the only pattern shown may be that "of the light of the knowledge of the glory of God, in the face of Jesus Christ." For the kingdom of God is not in word, but in power. It is no game we find ourselves in. It is the war of the ages, and we wrestle against principalities and powers. And without purity in us, there is no power. The hymn "O Make Me Pure" has been running in my mind.

It has come to me that part of God's reason for taking us (you and I) through suffering is for the answer to this prayer. When I think "Why should I have to go this way?" I realize that there may very well be special testings ahead for which I could not be prepared in any other way. Had a letter from a close friend of mine who is now entering her first year of med school, and has just become engaged to a man who is going to Indonesia as soon as possible. She has five years of med school ahead of her before she can think of going to the field. She says, "It will be a hard road, Bets, and not the one we would choose to travel, but we rejoice to think that the Lord has called us to go the hard way." She knows nothing about you, but it was encouraging to have one more evidence that we are not the only ones! (Sometimes I feel as though we are.) What Van says about the lonely way for those who choose Christ cannot be denied. I realize (if not fully yet, to some extent) that loneliness would not end if we were to be married—partings would only be that much more poignant. And if now, when we are one only in mind and in spirit, I feel torn when you go, what would it be if we were "one flesh"?

Tidmarsh tells me that Ed and Marilou expect to be here before Christmas. That's wonderful. And of course I cannot separate the idea from what you said about coming out to meet them. I wonder if we shall be able to see each other. Oh, Jim—here I am anticipating it already! The Sra. Navarrete says their apartment should be finished in November, and she'd love to have Ed and Marilou there. Says she could help Marilou with shopping and such that would be difficult at first. I think it would be an ideal set-up. Bill and Irene are looking for some sort of apartment that they could use for bodega and for living quarters while in Quito. I do wish we could find such a place for all of us. Incidentally, I have my suspicions that Irene is pregnant—but I didn't ask. Neither she nor Bill look too well, though the baby is fat and healthy. . . .

I guess I had better let this suffice. If I leave now, I may get to T's before the rain. You should have seen the hail we've had—one day a whole shoulder of Pichincha was completely white, just like snow, and it didn't melt for almost twenty-four hours! Thank you again, so very much, Jim, for your eleven pages. I really appreciate it, knowing how much there is to do.

Following these three of my mother's, here are the next three letters my dad wrote.

September 27

Pete and I should be doing something besides writing letters this afternoon, as there are plenty of things which the doctor left on the list to be done in his absence which we haven't completed yet. But we were waylaid between 2:00 and 3:00 by a siesta and haven't recovered yet. It's hot, humid, and threatening rain, not at all conducive to walking back to the school and cutting down bench and table legs for the smaller boys—our scheduled project for this afternoon. Besides, since it was too hot to sleep during siesta, and all I could think about was you, and since I want to have something ready to go early Monday morning, I really should be writing you. . . .

No one, not even Pete, really knows how close we have been and, resultantly, are. I have not made secrets with you to broadcast them but to keep them for my lonely thoughts, looking out at the stars from my bed, or smiling at the dawn, or watching cloud forms come to pieces in the blue afternoon heavens—like today. I was reliving that afternoon in the little straw hut while it rained just now. *Were those two really us?* And the day I found you running down the road, hoping to beat us to the bodega, and ripe with tears. *Was it really broad, sunny daylight?*

Yes, yes, I shout back at myself, and what *was* may well be again. I wonder if I could stroke your cheek tenderly now, with broken nails, calluses, and a dozen blisters all in different stages of development, a dark, hammer-smashed thumb, and singed hair all up my hand and wrist from working with gasoline stoves and rubbish fires? I know it would not feel the same, but I would sure like to try.

October 1

It is such a pleasure to write you now, Betty. I'm beginning to feel what you said several times—that you often had to resist writing, almost as a temptation. So I find it these days, composing ideas at odd moments that I should write down but feel that I *must* not, that it would be something akin to extravagance to write to you every time I wanted to. So I desist, to study, to repair an Indian's gun, to go out and see how the men are working and maybe lay a hand to it with them. And now, when I am seated to write, I always wish I had set down the rush of ideas as they came. Those seem better, somehow fresher.

And, if writing is pleasure, how shall I describe receiving? Especially now that you seem so much freer to express yourself. . . .

But why must I always make you cry? I'm sorry I stated what we both know, Bett, but it doesn't help me any to say "I'm sorry." It is a serious *molestia* to me *[an annoyance]* occasionally to think how far I can really be from your feelings, and completely failing to understand how things react in you. . . . I really feel sorry at such times, for I sense that it is a basic distinction of nature between us, that I can write or say a thing without a thought, and find it wounds or troubles you. I wonder at myself, because it is not hard afterward—hearing you explain *why* you are troubled—to understand clearly. But why, now that I know you so well, should I still have to blunder out such things and be told afterward? I don't know, Betts, dear, but I wish I could be more sensible to you. I suppose it will take living together to adjust such things, and I hope I am not too hard on you in the meantime.

October 8

This time a year ago, I was sitting a little self-consciously and quite sunburned in the Howard's home in Moorestown. All day today my last birthday has come back in daydreams, and I have lived a hundred little things we did together in making it "the happiest birthday ever."

And now, with rain and thunder bringing on bedtime, come back those hours lolling on the shore at Great Bay Harbor, and the remembrance of how thick that quilted jacket was to feel you through—and walking to the beaver dam, thinking how hard it was to really be comfortable walking with my arm around you on that sandy, rutted road—and how you pushed me off in the moonlight by the Keswick lake and went and stood away from the bench—and how you slept in my arms at Birdsong.

It makes me downright happy, Betty, just to remember it, and so thankful that God led us that way then, when you and love itself were so new and fresh to me that I didn't know quite what to make of it all. My diary notes are scanty, but sufficient to reveal the bewildering joy that overtook me last fall.

I shall never forget going into Dave's room one of those nights, and standing for a moment—more than a moment perhaps, almost a full minute—realizing that *this* was it, and telling myself, "Elliot, you are in love with this woman." It had never touched me so keenly before, never really shook me with a thrill until then. And the suddenness of it (my naiveté and absolute lack of direction or plan in coming to Moorestown amaze me now!), with the realization coming simultaneously that I not only could love as a man ought (I had doubted that seriously since Wilma), but that I actually did so love, made the sheets coldly memorable that night. And a phrase came back from some snatch I wrote years ago as I tried to sleep, something about curling inside myself and "glowing in amber gladness over you . . ."

Well, it remains the happiest birthday of all for me, and marks the beginning of the happiest year of my life so far. I never knew, no, not in dreams, the joy of really loving, this giving of oneself, not to be made happy, but to make another so, and finding in it what happiness is. Oh, thank you, Betty, for the bringing of love to me—by just being what you are, and by sharing what you are with me.

"Elliot, you are in love with this woman."

Perhaps this is why, lost in such beautiful musing, the news of my mother's decision to go west with Doreen struck him with such force. She had written in her journal, "I lean strongly toward going down to San Miguel to help Doreen get a start on the Colorado language. She hasn't had linguistics, and since I have, it seems almost incumbent that I should go." Her only real reluctance (other than the obvious) was whether she should commit to a place like "tiny San Miguel, where most of the residents are Christians—and vast reaches of the northern Oriente without one witness! O Lord—direct!"

By mid-October, though, she'd made up her mind. "The Lord has given peace about my going down to San Miguel." This news, along with other standard relays of communication, had been reported by shortwave radio to the others, including the men down in Shandia, during one of their scheduled

linkups. He told her of his reaction to it, in the remainder of his October 8
letter:

> I don't know why the sudden word over the radio this morning about your going
> to San Miguel should have affected me as it did. Formerly, I had even hoped you
> would do just that, but now that it actually comes to seeing you leave Quito—
> well, it made me quietly pensive all day. It was something like saying "goodbye"
> all over again—it puts you so much farther away, and I know that if I ever should
> make a sudden trip out to Quito now, you wouldn't be there. There is, of course,
> no prospect of any such thing, but the idea haunts me. It has been a help to know
> your surroundings and something of your schedule there, to be able to think of
> you different times during the day, and picture you. . . .
>
> But remember, it will mean your letters will have to be full and frequent, for
> my sake, even if they do pile up in Quito. I'm glad you have decided to go—glad
> when I'm in my right mind, and grateful for guidance for you now. But I'm not
> always in my right mind.
>
> Oh, I don't know how to tell you, Betty, or even if I should, but our months
> in Quito put me on an entirely different emotional level toward you than I was
> on before. Does it sound wrong to say that where you have been given rest since
> parting, I have had only uprisings of stronger want than ever? Where you have
> had peace, I find myself at perfect war.
>
> Continually I am experiencing things now that I heard you describe of your
> pre-Quito problems, and of which I knew little then, but which I feel fully now. I
> mentioned last letter the strong urge to write, write, write, and the something that
> makes one restrain. I could add the crazy wish of wanting years to pass suddenly,
> the old rebellion of "why should it have to be so with me?" The needing of a place
> to rest. Could it be that we are crossing the same river, but far enough apart to be
> at different depths, wisely kept so that we would not sink together? I seem to feel
> it all much more keenly out here. There comes a sighing even as I write.

On a recent Wednesday, in fact, *"in the cool of the day,"* this sighing had
turned into a little *"chat with the Lord"* out on the airstrip.

> Decided finally what I have been thinking for months. Engagement is the best
> thing for Betts, for me, for the work. Wrote Ed to buy a ring for me and bring it.
> I am withdrawing all my feelings about long engagements and getting ready for
> one. When? When God brings Ed.

And whenever God brought Ed, my dad's plan (as he wrote cryptically to
my mother) was to be the one who went to meet him in Quito. And wouldn't
that be a good time for her to come back for a visit as well? *"So let's plan in
the Will to meet in Quito after Ed arrives—Christmas, or June! Not a very
definite date, but I hope we can keep it."*
There might be a little surprise waiting for her.

"Christmas, or June!" He hoped they could meet in Quito then, once he was able to find an engagement ring to give to her.

———

Funny, she almost found it out by complete accident, when the surprise ended up literally in her lap one day at the mission office. If she hadn't been such an honorable woman, with such a sensitive conscience . . . let's just say I'm not so sure I would have had as noble a response as she did to the dilemma in which she found herself.

> **OCTOBER 15:** Yesterday I faced one of the greatest temptations I've ever had. I found that Jim had written a letter to Ed McCully, and put "please forward" on the envelope. Knowing his correct address, I thought I would just transfer it to another envelope with the right address. In doing so, I allowed myself to unfold it, and found that there was a page which began, "Dear Buddy—this is a private letter . . ." My eyes caught the words "Betty." And "engaged." I immediately slapped it into the envelope and sealed it.
>
> But my heart asks, was he confiding to Ed the things he can never tell me—telling him, for example, what has made him hesitate to become engaged, what barriers exist in his mind, what doubts he may have of his love? Or was he, perhaps, telling him that he has been thinking of engagement? God knows. I must be honorable with Jim, above all others.

Secrets really stayed SECRET with my godly mother! And even as curious as she must have been to see what was inside (can you even imagine?), she knew she couldn't read it. *No!*—it was private. And she didn't want to hurt my father or breach his trust, even in this wholly innocent way. What an upright and wonderful trait of hers. I admire it so much, just as I do her commitment to follow God's will without reservation . . .

October 17

> Gwen tells me you seemed a little taken aback when she told of my going to San Miguel. I guess it's not to be wondered at. I would have told you in my last letter had I been absolutely certain, but it was still in the question stage.

You may remember our talk the day before you left—we were by the piano. I told you that although it seemed very simple to you, for my part I was not at all sure of going to the Oriente, and felt no special urge to learn Quichua.

You know that for six years I have been sure of God's call to linguistic work—and I felt it was to be pioneer. This is my opportunity, and I am as clear about it as I was about my call to Ecuador. The way God led me was unmistakable, as I had practically put all thought of San Miguel out of my mind, for various quite logical reasons. But the Lord leads us by paths we know not, and I am grateful for knowledge of the next step. What it may mean to you and me personally, I cannot consider now. I know that you will understand and agree that neither of us owes anything to anyone but obedience to God.

I had one of the happiest dreams I've ever had of you, the other morning. I had waked early but went back to sleep, only to wake an hour or so later with the most delicious, relaxed, peaceful sense of having been with you. The details were all erased with the coming of consciousness, but, oh, it was wonderful to wake and know that you love me, which, I believe, is not only a dream. . . .

Thank you, Jim, for your kindness in apologizing for "making" me cry. I felt no need of apology of any sort, but your tenderness is always a wonder to me. Just your phrase "living together" did something to me. The thought had somehow never come to me in just those words, and your saying them left me shaken. The joy of such an idea is unimaginable at this stage.

A phrase from a song I love came to me . . .

> I bring a prayer that God will bless and keep you
> Through every moment with its joy or tears;
> I pray His arms may tenderly enfold you,
> To guard you . . .

Sometime perhaps I can write the whole thing. But I do pray, and trust that He will be your Rock and Deliverer from every peril of the Enemy and the forests.

As ever, Betty

When she wrote again, it was nearing the time of her leaving, and the tears were flowing again.

October 25

Jim, I hardly know how to write to you tonight, but I cannot help writing. I have been crying, and I fear I will not be very coherent. Why am I crying? I suppose it is a number of things, none of which ought to bring tears. But you say that even as *you* write, you "sigh." I wish that's all it were with me.

Oh, Jim, there are days when I am *sure* I can't stand it any longer—the uncertainty, the constant restraint, the "rising doubt, the rebel sigh." Your letter intensified this feeling, knowing you are at last experiencing something of the same. On top of all this, I spent all of yesterday and half of today in the bodega [*sort of a storage shed*]. I can't tell you what it does to me to go through your things, and even to go through mine. I see your handwriting, your clothes, some things familiar. In the unfamiliar, I see you buying them, packing them, using them there in Shandia when I send them down. I am glad to do this for you, Jim, getting stuff out, I mean. And it is in no way any "trouble" to me. It is only the association that makes it hard.

As I went through my stuff, in packing for San Miguel, I opened my barrel for the first time, and floods of memory came back over each thing. The barrel was packed by Dad, Mother, Jim, and a couple of professional packers. There was little Jim's prized, shiny jack-knife that he wanted me to have. In the list of equipment contained in the barrel was the handwriting of all three, Dad's with Scripture verses related to many of the items. Homesickness came over me, and I wanted to go to Moorestown, not to San Miguel. If it were not that I know God has called me, I would never in the world go down there. There are reasons for dreading it, and there are moments, verily, when I do. . . .

It is not with a light heart that I leave Quito. I have been happy here, God knows, and feel that I'd like to build three tabernacles. The thought of being that many more days away from you, as far as mail goes, is not easy. If I write more fully and frequently, as you have asked me to do, will you too? What happens to all those theories that were expounded last fall, in connection with Vine's exhortation on missionaries getting heavily involved in correspondence? We cannot blithely ignore things that were serious issues with you a year ago, Jim, unless God definitely leads on, farther, or in another direction.

I pray for you, for strong preservation from the Enemy of souls, for facility in Quichua, for clear guidance and direction, and that He will "grant to His servant strength, and bless with peace." You are in my heart, and I miss you.

Betty

October 27

Oh, Bett, how I thank you for pushing through all that stuff again. I know it was a "flunky" assignment, and no job for you, but it saved us days here, and will make any further getting things from the bodega a real chore, not having anyone to do it.

And now, I suppose you are in bed, readying for a long day tomorrow. The room is bare and cleaned to a pin, I know. And I know something else—that I would give nearly anything to walk in without knocking and slip quietly into an embrace.

It is 9:30. Your last night in Quito for a while, and your going leaves our meeting as uncertain as mine did a year ago when (in that blessed green suit and red leather bag) we pressed cheeks in public at the station, and I was on *my* way west. This I know too—that if next year is as full of sweet surprises and things to be wondered at, as has been this last one (and I have no reason now to expect anything less; the situations are analogous in their impossibilities), it will be but stronger evidence of the good hand of God upon and over us, keeping His promise and confirming all we have hoped in Him.

Is it not, for all its sting, a wonderful way to live, Betty? To dream and want and pray, almost savagely, then to commit and wait and see Him quietly pile all dreams aside and replace them with what we could not dream—the *realized* Will?

With this indomitable charge in hand, my mother took off by banana truck to Santo Domingo, where she stayed with the Cathers for a night, before leaving next morning on horseback for San Miguel. *"Here I am tonight, sitting by a gasoline lantern in a bamboo and thatch house, having just come from a good prayer meeting of the believers here. It is my hope,"* she continued journaling, *"that God will give the key to the Colorado language. On Monday, Doreen and I hope to begin our work together."*

My father, meanwhile, along with Pete Fleming, kept up the hard work of building out their little school, station, and clinic, even as they continued drilling on their language studies, in prayerful hope that Shandia would be their launching point to other tribes in the rain forest.

Sadly, though, it wouldn't be launching him to Quito by Christmas, as he'd at first alluded. My mother was disappointed but understood.

November 23

When I'd read of the impossibility of your coming out for Christmas, I went out in the kitchen and cried. . . . I have been counting the weeks. This morning I thought, "Surely a month from today—together!" I have been planning how perhaps you could come down and meet me on the trail between San Miguel and Santo Domingo. We would go together to Quito, have Christmas together. God knows the disappointment. . . .

If I had not perfect confidence that He is ordering all things after the counsel of His own Will, I should implore you to come to Quito, no matter what it involves. But Jim—do not think of any of what I have written as reproach. You know well how sure I am of God's hand in all His dealings with us, and I ask only, whether they be of joy or pain, that through them *we shall be brought to Him*. I have no doubt that we are to see one another again sometime—but, it's just that I wanted so much that it be *Christmas*.

Why do I write all this to you? As I have said, not because I hold you in any way responsible. It is simply that it's what I am thinking. Perhaps it is what you feel too. And I want to share. I don't like to hear of your tearing up pages you've written to me. No matter what you've said, it is something *thought*—and lost (to me, at any rate). For this reason I write in my journal many of the things that I cannot write to you now—that nothing be lost, if perchance the day may come when *all* can be given.

Your letters were new strength to me (and, oh, you do not know how I need it). Even the details, the lovely descriptions (and the sad ones), the account of your little parrot, the plane accident, the happy fellowship with Bill—it helps me, Jim.

Oh, there are times, of course, when I laugh at myself, and think life is wonderful and complete, engrossed in my Colorado work. I enjoy tearing around in jeans on horseback, walking with one of the girls in the jungle—with that, "Reuben, Reuben, I've been thinking . . ." attitude. Tomorrow Barbara and I are going on a fishing trip with a group of Colorados. We will be gone three or four days. I love that sort of thing. I also love the linguistic work. But always, and underneath, I try to imagine you there, working alongside, coming "home" to the house, riding the trails with me, struggling over some phoneme or allomorph. And such a thought is always better than *this,* no matter how much fun I may be having.

I really can't imagine how this letter would sound if I were to read it over a week from now. I'd probably tear it up. But I won't have a chance. I shall leave it here for Bill to take when he comes in on Tuesday for his Bible class. . . . I was going to sign it "As always"—but it seems a little different now.

Betty

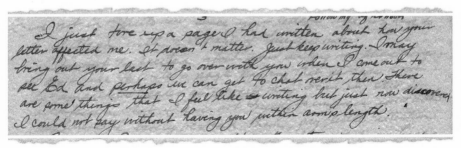

"I just tore up a page I had written." My dad's longing for her.

December 5

The doctor came in this morning, and after the frenzy of getting supplies stacked away, I had a chance to get at my mail about midday. Usually I save yours and the family's until last . . . but I couldn't today—just tore yours both open and read them slowly, eating every phrase like a morsel. It had been too long, Bett, too long since receiving your last, and I don't think it's good for me to wait too long. Not for you. That's why I'm writing tonight. . . . It can only be a note, as I have nothing especially to recount, and little time to recount it, but I want you to know, though I seldom put it on paper (because I think it looks strange here), that I love you. . . .

You make me sorrier than ever that we cannot be together for Christmas. I had gotten over the disappointment, from sheer weariness of it, and your first page brought it all back. For you see, I *chose* not to come out at Christmas. T. gave us several opportunities to state our preference about the thing, but it would have meant leaving Pete alone here, for Gwen is insistent that the doctor be in Quito then, and I think it is only right that it should be so. Do I then care more for Pete and feel sorrier for him alone here than for you there? Not exactly. But how can I say it? I feel like I really need not, knowing you and trusting your love to interpret the thing in my favor. There will be no way to make it up to you now—I only hope I can come out in January.

But even *January* might be wishful thinking.

The doctor, apparently forgetting all that I told him of my hopes for going up to Quito when Ed gets settled there, casually remarked today that he didn't know if he would come in January or not. So please, Betty, don't be saying to yourself anymore, "a month from today, surely we'll be together." I will come when I can with a clear conscience before God, and I will let you know of our plans if it is humanly possible.

I write this, not in rebuke, darling, but that you may not have to go into the darkness of the kitchen again to cry. If you like, I will come and meet you on the trail to San Miguel. I promise to make the next time we are together conform as closely to your preferences as is possible.

Wonder when that "next time" might be? My father tried to guess.

December 6

There is a very good possibility that I will not get another letter to you before Christmas and your birthday. That means this should contain all I want to give you for those events, but it cannot possibly. . . . I know you are not silly in expecting impossibilities from me out here, and I am grateful you are that sort—I know certain other women are not. So I will hold my surprises until we can be together again in Quito—asking only that you be patient with me, as plane travel is very uncertain, and that you make some attempt to be on hand up there after the first of the year, if you can get some gauge of my date of leaving. I will try my best to keep you informed by a letter, but if you should be unable to get any clue—stick it out and I'll go down to Miguel and see you. . . .

I strongly sense the rightness of God's leading you and me as He has, Bett. I could not be doing now what I am doing and needing to do (such things as letting the Indians invade my bedroom anytime we're here) if I were a family man. As it is, I feel we are making contacts and friends on such a level as is most advantageous for the future of our work here, playing and sharing with the Indiana in a way I could not have time for if I were married. It is temporary. I, like you, don't feel that a plastic tablecloth is for life, but in our present circumstances, there is nothing else for it, and we gain by having a table the Indians can touch with muddy hands. . . .

Reading in Psalm 119 the other day, I was struck with the verse you wrote in my gift copy of *Toward Jerusalem,* or rather referred to. "Thy statutes have been my song in the house of my pilgrimage." This is what all houses are, and I feel it keenly about this one. There is a poetic sense in which it may refer to the body, as you seemed to suggest, but I am thinking now of life, and particularly my present experience of it, as a pilgrimage. And the goal of it, I see not only as heaven, but as a certain culmination with you which will sort of be an end to a great deal of wandering I've been doing since 1949—Oklahoma, Milwaukee, Huntington, Chester, Portland, the East, and now here. Or, at least, so I am led to hope. . . .

Sometimes—this month especially with its rush of pressures—I have felt lost without you, Bett, felt like the world was going by in a whirl of wonder, and I was dazedly letting it go by, my body participating but somehow standing apart, looking for something that didn't show in all the wonder—and aware that that something was *you.*

It all goes over my head, it seems, and I go through the motions of keeping in the tide, but if anyone was watching closely, they would know—by the quiet sigh in a rowdy game of volleyball, by the faraway glance up the river and over the treetops, from mid-current to the clouds way off to the west . . . they would know I was not really all there where I seemed to be. . . .

Your picture, the framed one you gave me for Christmas, has been a great help somehow. It depicts you as I like to think of you . . . the dozens of times it has surprised me by looking up sideways from a suitcase. It makes it seem like it has been forever with us, through everything, the way it is now, and seems to say, "Take it easy, Jim, we are not through the story yet, and you have no basis for believing it will turn out to be a tragedy."

Still I do, Bett, I do fear sometimes, like a worrying mother, that something would happen to you and I should lose you. And then what would I do? Where would I be when I wasn't where I seemed to be? Which way would my imagination go when I went to sleep?

Funny, but I never think of *my* having the accident and your losing *me* . . .

His final letter of the year sparkled with a bit more joy and—what shall we call it—boyish jitters? *"You will know that Ed is to arrive this weekend, and it is maddening to think that I'll have to wait weeks to see him,"* thanks to the now familiar delays of passing through customs. Even so, *"it brings our being together again within sight, of course, and I have been losing some sleep over it."*

December 16

I think sometimes that it will be impossible to meet and speak casually with you, saying, "Hello, Betty," in the presence of other people, feeling sure that my voice will crack or I'll do something that will embarrass us both. But I suppose it will be like always—the greeting, the not-too-long glance into your eyes, the handshake and the small talk about things that really don't matter. Well, if the Lord preserves me in my right mind until then, I shall be grateful, for quite frankly, I have never been this way before.

And nothing, he knew, was going to be the same about this visit.

Does Dorothy's case of jaundice, along with several others who have visited HCJB folks, to say nothing of themselves, give you any qualms about a ten-day or two-week visit there? I don't care how thin and healthy you are, I won't hear of risking jaundice just because it might not look right for you and me to be quartered at T's. Betty, I beg of you, this once, not to let what people think influence your decision about us being together. I want to be as near you for as long as I possibly can, this one time. . . .

Oh, may it be as you said, Betty!—that "we shall be brought to Him," brought to Him in a new nearness and with a new weight of joy, for having denied, by the grace He supplies, for His sake, this special sort of want. "There is no man that hath forsaken—*for My sake*—but who *shall receive!*". . .

You may think my suggested stay at T's is a little strange. It may be. What we may discover is that there won't be room for us both with Emma there—although

I don't know why, unless the room I used to have is really packed with stuff. We'll see, but please don't disregard the suggestion. I want to see all I can of you.

So with this tingle of excitement in the air, my mother made her final journal posts of 1952, trusting she would *"see Jim in a few weeks. He plans to come out on Dr. Tidmarsh's next flight in. It worries me somehow, but yesterday I read, 'Jehovah guardara tu salida tu entrada.'"* ["The Lord shall preserve thy going out and thy coming in."] *So I will trust His promise."*

DECEMBER 28: As Jim said in his last letter, he wonders if he can possibly meet me casually in the presence of others—"hello, Betty," handshake, etc. I sometimes feel that I shall not be able to restrain myself from rushing to him. For him, however, this seems to be the first time he has felt thus. For me, it is the sixth (I mean, the sixth meeting after long separation). . . . At times the thought comes to me that it can't be again that we should see one another, that surely something will happen to one of us. "But the Lord is kind—be not blind, be not blind." And His is the Will that willeth only good. "We rest on Thee, our Shield and our Defender."

What is this Lord Jesus
That Thou shouldst make an end
Of all that I possess and give
Thyself to me?
So that there is nothing now to
    call my own save Thee
Thyself alone my treasure
Taking all, Thou givest full measure
Of Thyself
With all things else eternal.
Things unlike the mouldy pilf
    by earth possessed.
And in God's garments
    dressed am I
With Thee an heir to riches in the
    spheres divine.
Strange I say
    that suffering loss
I have so gained everything
In getting me a Friend
Who bore a cross.

JIM ELLIOT

I cannot give myself to thee
For I am not my own.
Christ claims this life—His sacrifice
Made me bone of His bone.

Upon thy life, beloved, too
Our Lord has set His sign.
Will, purpose, and command are His—
Obedience, yours and mine.

He is the object of our love,
And He is love's great force.
"We love because He first loved us."
Love finds no other Source.

If, in mysterious design,
He sets our paths apart,
Can we not gladly take the road
Planned by a Father-heart?

But that these lives should be as one
Is His alone to give.
To separate or to unite,
Divine prerogative.

ELISABETH HOWARD

QUITO ★ 1953 ★ ECUADOR

LOVE TRANSCENDING

"I am almost beside myself with longing for Jim," she said in early January, writing in her journal in San Miguel. *"The suspense is harder than ordinary waiting. Everything depends on when Dr. T goes back to Shandia."* And, as she went on to say, *"That could be any day, or it may be weeks away."* My father was equally on pins and needles—not only from the waiting, but also from not knowing how to get timely, reliable word to her of any updates on his schedule.

January 6

Bett, it will be impossible for me to advise you of the date of my coming out. Seems strange that this is the only time so far that the doc has not seemed anxious to get in here and leave us without any stated reason for not coming.

Well, I suppose we will have to wait, but I don't have the same spirit of hope that possessed me when I last wrote. It may be a month now, as he tells us he has hardly begun on the purchasing for this trip in, and he brought in such small quantities last time that nearly every item in the store has to be replaced. I'm not sore at the doc for this, but a little surprised at myself for having set so much stock in the hope that I might get out this weekend. I do hope you get these two notes together so that you don't make plans to go up to Quito and have to cancel them. Forgive me, Bett, for being so extravagant in my hopes.

As to how I will finally get word to you about coming out, I have no idea. I don't know what you want me to do, but it may be best to wait in San Miguel until I can get word to you from Quito. But if you want to wait it out in Quito—well, that will bring us together maybe a day or so earlier. If there was just some sure way of contacting you down there . . .

Eladio *[the schoolteacher]* is here and the walls are on the clinic and I didn't get any language study in and hope deferred makes the heart sick and I'm missing you terribly and I love you with all my heart.

The madness was causing him to write long, lovesick, run-on sentences. After all these years of waiting, now even a *day* seemed to him an eternity.

Daily there is word from T that he has begun to purchase supplies and will be down shortly. Ed came to the radio yesterday morning and told us he might not come in for two weeks yet. I hear Gwen is sick and that he is busy painting.

If he has any idea what young love is, and that we intend to be in Quito together, he is being cruel. All I can say is that he has little memory or little foresight! Every day ends the same—with a wondering, Betty, and a wonder charged with wanting to be with you and hoping it can be a good length of time.

But almost as hard to take is the absence of your letters. Today makes the ink on your last letter seven weeks old—it made the last mail seem very empty not to hear even a word from you. . . .

Several folk here come down from Quito, so we could have mail every ten days. As it is, we get it about twice a month. I suppose it's the same with you, but I do miss word from you.

"Even Pete is getting letters from Olive posted December 19, and your last date is the second," he moaned. *"Can San Miguel be farther than Seattle?"*

My mother said she was "beside herself" too. But hear her classic, spiritual thinking, as written in the following journal entry, nearly a month past the Christmas reunion she'd hoped to enjoy.

JANUARY 21: I want to enter into full sonship with the Father. The present test is one of God's means for effecting this. He is dealing with me as with a son. Let me not respond as a child, kicking and screaming and pouting. Rather, with a mature acceptance of His dealings, let me understand and adore. Then only will the chastening contribute to my spirit's development.

How many of us can honestly say, "Let me not respond as a child," when our whole being wants to kick and scream and wail? How willing are we to accept God's plans maturely when all human reason and affection shouts to "do something about it!" She chose to accept the Lord's timing, His way in this whole drama. And how glad I am that she loved to write, so that her honest journal can be published now. I know she taught these principles from the platform, but it's good to see in her own hand what I saw her practice in real life.

My father, of course, expressed a similar trust and faith. And I'm glad he wrote of it too!

JANUARY 18: Maybe the Lord is having me wait for a full moon to be in Quito— that would be the twenty-ninth. I wonder if that is His design. . . . But it has already happened inside me. I have given myself over to the love of her, and there is no desire, purpose, or sense in any thought of withdrawal. It only lacks her word, and I could not believe that will not be given, with such square-shouldered confidence as I believe I have gotten from God. There is the "It is finished!" tone in my spirit; morally, I am already engaged. There is, or can be, no other woman now for my children and my wife, and there is a quiet, glad knowledge in writing it. I have sought slowly the will of God, and the slowness has brought strength into the conviction of it, and joy in the realization of it.

Soon, he could almost taste his long-awaited prize.

JANUARY 26: Yesterday afternoon Ed came to the radio and told us that the doctor would likely be down on Thursday. If Ed comes with him, we will probably go out to Quito a week from today together. It is barely possible that I may be engaged in ten days.

Oh, that it were certain, that I held her already after she said yes or whatever she will say. This waiting has built up pressure and released it so many times that I feel it has changed me somehow. I sense an aging and a waning—not of desire but of spirit—as though strength were washed out of me from so many nights standing alone on the cliff and watching so much water pass. It is the oldness of hope deferred, the borderland of hopelessness.

A week seems unbearably long this rainy morning; intolerably slow the river runs, though it is in the rush of flood. Pass, water; get on down to the sea. Wash away the Was, the Is, bring down What Is to Be. I'll need special tolerance of things these days, kind Lord, a steeled patience—with rain and poor radio communications and trying schoolboys. Help me this week, and do let it be the last of waiting.

Mercifully, it was.
And here's the account of it, in my mother's words.

On January 31, Jim and I became engaged. I am overwhelmed with the wonder of it all. I arrived in Quito Saturday afternoon, Jim having arrived on the previous day. We had supper together, and, beside the fireplace in "Maranatha House," he asked me.

J: "Do you want to marry me?"
E: . . . (my answer) . . .

(My dad's journal says her answer was, *"I have no reason to hesitate."*)

J: "I love you and I want to marry you. God has given me peace." And, after quietness, and—our *first* kiss—he put a ring on my finger.

"O, God of stars and flowers . . ."

The relief of being able to tell him my love, of feeling free for the first time, is simply unspeakable. I literally ache with love for him and long now for the day when he will be my husband. O, I want to be *possessed*. I desire him, and his desire is toward me—Oh, perfect love, all human thought transcending.

Picture taken the day after their engagement.
On the left, she's turning her hand to show the ring.

——

What joyful relief! Her waiting for his proposal, her prayers, and her natural longing for the man she loved—his waiting to know from God His timing for the engagement—it all culminated on this last day of January 1953. Their well-thought-out words, reticence, and steel will paid off on this joy-filled evening. Would they both have said it was worth the wait? I believe they did, and they were certain of God's timing and blessing for their union.

All of the unusual, brilliant, agonizing, trusting, hope-filled words in these journals and letters have made me wonder: Was my dad unwise to tell her of his love way back in June of 1948? He was quite sure then that God wanted him to be a single missionary, but of course didn't yet know God's plan. Was he too precipitous? How would I advise a young man who felt sure he had fallen in love?

I think I would say: Be very careful how much time you spend with her until you've met her dad and asked for his blessing on getting to know her in an intentional and serious way. And even if you're wildly in love with her, try to keep your mouth shut until you are absolutely sure that she is the one for you. The practice of saying "I love you" has become so commonplace and cheap that it has caused untold misery by dashing one's hopes and damaging one's heart if there is no determination to marry as a result. Men are to seek God before seeking a wife. Women are to place all their hope in God to bring the right man into their lives, should that be His will for them. This is how God protects and provides. It reminds me of a T-shirt that one of my sons used to wear: "Seeking Him to find her."

I believe my mother and dad would second that opinion.

The waiting is why they could experience love now afresh.

Not much was normal about the next two weeks. Their journals briefly itemized the doings, including every dinner and outing, sometimes even down to the selections on the menu. Among the more interesting events, right off the bat, which my mother summarized in a single journal entry from later in the month:

> **FEB. 1**—Church, breaking of bread, HCJB in the evening. The whole choir burst into "I Love You Truly" as we entered the studio!
>
> **FEB. 2**—Greetings broadcast when we announced our engagement to whoever was listening.
>
> **FEB. 8**—Jim preached in church, I sang, dinner at Gwen's . . .

Probably the most insightful encounter happened on February 10, as described in my father's journal several days later:

> **FEBRUARY 14:** The other night, Tuesday, I believe, we had a lunch together at the bodega and afterward a long discussion about limits to engagement relations— everything from touching her breasts to intercourse.

Earlier the past summer, he had argued in his own mind with 1 Corinthians 7:1—"It is good for a man not to touch a woman"—and concluded from the context that it was likely *"speaking of an unmarried man sharing another's wife,"* not an unmarried man who was planning to marry the woman. *"It does not apply to my play with Betty,"* he felt, which meant he could enjoy *"further liberty with her body"* without being guilty of fornication, once they were engaged.

But how sweetly he honored my mother's self-discipline and determination to set the lines of demarcation more strictly. This deliberateness in declaring boundaries gave them a depth of freedom that wantonness (which only *seems* like a freedom) would not.

> Oh, how glad I am she knows just how much of herself to give. . . . When I came home, so I spoke, "A garden shut up is my sister, my spouse; a spring shut up, a fountain sealed" (Song of Sol. 4:12). She is that until marriage, by her present attitudes.

But where this February 10 encounter had been notable for its delay of future unknowns, February 15 was notable for bringing unthinkable unknowns directly into their present.

> **EH:** Dr. Fuller informed me today of an active tubercular lesion in one lung. Jim was with me when he told me, and we faced it together when we got here to Gwen's.

JE: She held a brave face until we got home here; then, in telling Gwen, her voice broke. In the *sala* she cried bitterly, hard sobbing and much tears.

EH: I have never been so crushed by anything in my life. It may mean going back to the States, for three months of absolute rest in bed. How can I leave Jim? I cannot be a hindrance to him.

JE: She fears she can never marry me—says that I can't be nursing a consumptive all my life. Told me that I couldn't kiss her on the lips anymore, but she let me—in the hall just now—forgetting, I suppose, that there is a bacteria eating at her lungs.

EH: Jim and I had a letter from Dave and Gibby of congratulations on our engagement, which brought tears to both of us. Little do they know this latest dark cloud that comes on the horizon.

JE: As for me, things are unchanged. She is the same woman I loved last night before I knew the tubercles were formed in her chest. If I had any plans, they are not changed. I will marry her in God's time, and it will be the very best for us, if it means waiting years. God has not led us this far to frustrate us or turn us back, and He knows how to handle T.B. . . .

If she really has it, it may mean a trip to the States for three or four months, or it may mean a lifetime of being an invalid. I don't know what it means. Only I know that God is in the generation of the righteous and guides their steps aright. Beyond His counsel and will, there is no going. I am there now and want nothing more.

Either way, it surely put a damper on the rest of their time together. And back in Shandia, when he later learned that *"the 'tuberculosis' proved to be only a shadow, which disappeared in the third x-ray,"* he was none too happy—not about the false alarm, of course (praise God for that!), but about how it had needlessly interfered with their long-anticipated, once-in-a-lifetime visit. It was good news, even with the disappointment it had wrought. He would simply need to count his blessings another way.

February 23

I'm afraid I would not deal kindly with the gremlin who saw a black spot on your x-ray if I could get my hands on him tonight. When I think of the kisses his ignorance robbed from me the last three days in Quito, I could choke him outright. Oh, Betty, I knew it could not be all that you feared it would mean for us. And I think that for this—because I never fully realized, never really believed all that could be—that I didn't break down one of those three nights. And, oh, I thank God that it was not so.

He couldn't get those days back, and he couldn't have her by his side at the moment. But he did have something new to be thankful for: their engagement had brought to her letters *"a difference in tone and material"* that hadn't been present in any of her previous ones. Now, for the first time ever, he could read the words of love and affection he'd always wanted to hear.

> ## Engaged
>
> Mr. and Mrs. Philip E. Howard, Jr., of West Maple ave., announce the engagement of their daughter Elisabeth, to Mr. James Elliot, son of Mr. and Mrs. R. F. Elliot of Portland, Ore. Mr. Elliot and Miss Howard are both in Christian work in Ecuador. No date has been set for the wedding.

Will I ever be able to tell you, Betts, what it does to me to have you call me "darling"? And to know that we are wholly and for always committed to one another, given over to one another's power and pleasure, sold out of ourselves, each for the other's good? The absolute goodness and rightness of it is unspeakable.

How shall I say what I feel in gratitude to God for the rights and responsibilities of your love? And, what shall I say to you? I don't know. Only this, my darling Betts, that I am drawn to you with a fondness I can never exhibit, and held to you with a love that is at once all tenderness and all strength which my very body, at either peak of gentleness or power, does not suffice to declare.

I love you. Once that meant "I trust you," and "I appreciate and admire you." Now it means that I am somehow part of you, with you, and in you.

But his next paragraph is perhaps the most significant of all, and is such a needed observation in our day—worthy of all attention. How wise had been my mother's determination not to give too much of herself to him, both in commitment and physical touch, before she could be sure of his intention to marry and could say "yes." As a result, she had saved up her words of love for this important moment. *That's* why her words were coming out in such a rush now—like a dam breaking, its waters tumbling freely into the channel. *That's* why even her written words could communicate such tremendous blessing, could be such a gift to him, because she'd kept them to herself awaiting God's perfect timing.

And how touching of my father to recognize this, to apologize even, for not being able to give her the same distinctions of stored-up expressions that were giving him so much joy to read from her.

> You will not find in my writing now what I see you have saved for me in yours. Forgive me for an early eagerness. And if I seem in this as I did in my last, be kind and remember that I was not able, from lack of conviction, ability, or desire, to hold myself as closely as you were. There may not be in this the "burst" that a letter following engagement should contain, and I am sorry, in a way, knowing the keen pleasure there is in seeing things I have waited years to see in your hand. You should know by now that I really do not lack fervency.

Yes, his love was just as deep, even if already shown and spoken of. *"I need a wife,"* he wrote in his next letter—quite a contrast from the Jim Elliot who had once been so determined to go it alone. But not just a wife, he needed *her*.

March 8

> When lying on the cot at night with the quiet loneliness of the dark, or seeing a very poorly washed T-shirt, or looking at a picture of you, it comes to me anew that I was meant for something else besides myself and "the boys"—specifically that I was planned and made for you . . . and that life itself was meant for me to share with you in its very smallest part. I love you, darling Betts, and pray that God will soon clear the way for us to be together.

I once heard a Christian professor say that when he began looking for a young woman to marry at his Christian college, he could have married any one of them on campus, as long as she was a Christian. I was shocked and incredulous. "Do you mean," I asked, "you don't think God planned a specific partner for everyone?" With an air of kindly condescension he said, and I paraphrase, "No, I don't, because God could help any one of them be able to be compatible with me, and with His help we would be able to have a good marriage."

This went against all my teaching and upbringing. I'd been taught that God had a specific spouse for every one of His children who married. If someone's husband or wife dies, of course, He may have another that He brings into a person's life, as He did for my mother God gave her two husbands after my dad. Addison Leitch became my stepfather during my later teenage years. I called him Dad. He died of cancer four and a half years after their marriage. Lars Gren, my mother's third spouse, is still living.) My parents both held this belief about God's will for marriage, as attested by their own words, and I felt the same way when I fell in love and married my husband. He was the man God made for me, and I the woman for him. When God created Adam and Eve, did He not specifically plan them for each other? Would this not be the same for all history?

I'm sure that's what my father believed when he said he wanted *"to live with you all the hours of every day I live, to share what I am at close range, and just to rest in being loved by you."* He needed her, and she needed him. *"The work too needs you, dear, almost as much as I."*

Like, he said, when *"a favorite little Indian girl of mine came wailing out of the forest,"* saying that *"her father had been drinking and picking on her, and her stepmother began repeating stories about her that made her feel sick and outcast."* Apparently they'd been accusing her of coming to the school to have "relations" with the schoolteacher, and were also spreading other lies about the work of the missionaries there.

> Today when her father came, I chewed him out for saying such things, and he was sorry—he was drunk. He invited me to go "instruct" his wife (that's the word they use for "rebuke"), and all the Indians concerned insisted that I do so.
>
> Eladio and I and the father and the girl went to see the hard-hearted one— who promptly denied all, blaming the "lies" (as everybody says they are) on a sister-in-law now up-river. I never sweated through so much Quichua all at once in the six months I've been here! And now I must "instruct" the sister-in-law! . . . Seriously, I think a wife would solve many such difficulties.

The medical part of their ministry was difficult too. They'd once been giving vitamins and shots of medicine to a man who came in *"vomiting great mouthfuls of bright blood last Monday. . . . He was getting along fine until Friday about 3:45, when he vomited again and became exceedingly restless—dangerously so, for one so weak. He was gone by 4:30."*

The first man I ever watched die. And so it will come to me one day, I kept thinking. I wonder if that little phrase I used to use in preaching so much was something of a prophecy: "Are you willing to lie in some native hut to die of a disease American doctors never heard of?" I am still willing, Lord God. . . . But, oh, I want to live to teach Thy Word. Lord, let me live "until I have declared Thy works to this generation."

How helpful it would have been to come home to a wife, after such a mortal eye-opener.

And then there were the construction projects—*"building houses for other people"* when he wanted so badly to be building the first home where he and my mother would live.

March 11

I cannot see beyond concrete and nails and planks and aluminum now. I keep hoping some miracle will happen—something that will upset all our plans—even our hopes for the work here. Like a carpenter coming to do the building, and freeing me now to travel . . . anything that would get me doing something besides building houses for other people. (If you think *living* in other people's houses is distracting, try *building* one in my state of mind!) And yet I feel, Betts, that God has sent me here for it, that no one else can do it who is now on the field, and that God has put me here for it, personal likes and dislikes aside.

It's strange, but I both hope and dread some cataclysmic upset that will bring you and me together. I feel like it would have to be that now, with things so well formulated and going along so nicely.

Little did he know, God would do just that.

SPRING

"The Lord has met me in new ways in the past few days, Jim," my mother wrote from San Miguel sometime in this spring of '53, *"and I give Him praise."*

Oh, darling, there's so much I want to talk with you about. I do hope and pray that we can be together for the conference next month [a missions gathering in Quito]. I still don't know when it begins. You mention my suggestion about your coming over "just to see me." I realize your situation is different from mine. You cannot simply pack up and go off for a week just any old time. . . .

I find that I very soon get stale and fed-up with life here. Contrary to your life—too busy and too full—mine is slow and event-less often, and the days drag by. . . . I find that the fact that nothing actually presses me to activity, leads me to dawdle in quiet time, let my mind wander in prayer, and daydream when trying to study. Sometimes, I confess, after a long time on my knees and very little praying done (for the thousand trivialities that beckon my attention) I finally call it quits, saying to myself, "This isn't prayer. Might as well be up and doing something," even if it's only making a cake or sharpening a pencil. . . . I feel that I have lost much since college days.

Well, to be realistic, she wasn't actually doing "nothing." She was laboring to decode an alphabet from an unwritten, oral language, in hopes of opening new vistas of opportunity for the Colorado Indians, not the least of which was the opportunity for them to hear the gospel in words they could understand. Many of her letters to my dad that spring tell of *"stewing over these old glottal stops and h's,"* sorting out problems with *"nasalized vocoids"* and *"consonant clusters,"* or trying to differentiate between *"so many individual variations in pronunciation."* ("I'm having an awful time with T and D," is one of my favorite lines.) In every interaction with people from the tribe, she was carefully listening to each sound of their Tsahfiki language, then writing down copious notes of new data. *"There are some things I don't see how I can ever be sure about."*

No, doing linguistic research may not have been the same as cutting down lumber by hand in the forest and converting it into subflooring, as my dad was often doing. But it was important work just the same—cerebral, demanding. It was something she'd studied hard to prepare for, to do well.

What I love, though, in hearing both of my parents update each other on their daily activities—in letters that were now painfully slow in arriving, thanks among other things to a national gasoline shortage—is how frequently and vulnerably they sought the other's prayer in helping them stay on task and in the right spirit. I've pieced together the following excerpts from a number of their letters to one another throughout the spring.

> **EH:** I would be glad if you'd pray for me in this matter, Jim. The inability to concentrate, the lack of any real will or desire to get anything accomplished—it is not a light thing, and I feel convicted about it.

> **JE:** You asked what else to pray about. Do remember this week of meeting. Pete and I will be taking a meeting each, every day, and we are going to attempt it in Quichua.

> **EH:** Yesterday I was able to decide on four phonemes [*symbols which represent sounds*] for the Tsahfiki alphabet. I trust they are correct. . . . Jim, do pray that I may be given special wisdom in this. Barbara just *has* to have a workable alphabet. Pray that they'll be right.

> **JE:** And I hope you are praying right along for souls—genuine conversions to Christ among our schoolboys and many Indian friends. It has been more and more on my heart since coming back—the turning of these folks from darkness to

light. True, we do not have the language well, but they are understanding some-what, and I long to see their comprehension brought to convinced believing. God is able for this, and we are asking. . . . Do pray that we will have the power of God in our devotional talks this morning. . . . We have begun the house floor, but are still short of boards and men to cut and plane them. Pray definitely about this.

EH: Jim, my darling, I pour out my heart in thanksgiving to the Lord for you, every time I go to pray. . . . I pray daily that He will keep you from harm or sickness. . . . I would be glad if you'd pray, Jim, that I may be "girded up" in the "loins of my mind"—disciplined in study and prayer. It cannot be excused because I am get-ting old, or because the devil is tempting me more—the Lord has promised to "lead us in triumph."

JE: Pray that it will be so here, Betts, that God would take this work in hand and do it ON HIS OWN LINES. To see Christ honored and testified to publicly by one of these young Indian fellows we now know as friends would be something like seeing a miracle done before my very eyes, I believe. Indeed, it *would* be a miracle, but I have never seen it as clearly so before now. "Except the Lord . . . in vain . . ." God *must* do His work, or it will not be done, and we stand waiting for Him here.

EH: How I wish you were here to consult with me! But there are also other rea-sons I wish you were here. How I'd love to know once more the strength of your arms around me, and the wonderful sweetness of a kiss. . . . I think of you so much, and talk to the Lord constantly about you.

JE: Good-night, my brave lover, and may the God who loves you stronger than I stand guard over you. . . . Don't discourage your folks from praying for a wedding this summer—I wish I had the faith to pray similarly. All I can do is cry to the Lord for His time and tell Him what it's like having to wait. This summer! Bless them, and God honor their faith!

And yet he was praying with similar hope and faith, despite knowing *"they are asking for something that I am afraid would be quite upsetting to present conditions—not disagreeably so, but not without taking either Pete or I out of Shandia. There is still only one bedroom in Shandia, and not much prospect of another empty turning up."*

However . . .

March 17

The only thing I can think of is what I mentioned in my last—a change that would be so shocking and catastrophic that you and I could be free to marry soon. . . . And God knows how often and how confidently I have put the desire before Him, Betts dear, saying, "Lord, Thou knowest how I desire her and how long we can take this, and Thou knowest, too, our plans for Shandia. Oh, God, direct us!"

Even others were starting to wonder when he and my mother would be marrying.

> Wittig startled me when he was in with a load of cement and kerosene on Friday by pointing over to the concrete piers and saying, "Who knows, Brother Jim, that may be your house over there."
>
> But I don't know how the girl of my dreams would go for that. For all the talking we did in Quito, I never really did press you as to *your* expectations for us out here. I remember telling you that I didn't know what to expect for us, but all I can remember about what you wanted was a house "bien metida en la pelea" *[in the heart of the activity]* and talk about fireplaces and a blue-green bedroom. . . .
>
> I know, Betts, that you feel as I do—you'd be happy on a dirt floor if only we could be living together, but what do you really hope for as far as location and proximity to other missionaries and house type and so on? Or do you feel it dreaming too far ahead to think on just now?

He was right, she didn't harbor any real preferences about their housing arrangements. Who *could*, in a place such as this? But the previous winter, prior to their engagement, she had made mention in her journal (December 6) of feeling a bit taken for granted—not only about her desires for basic amenities in their future home, but even about the assumption that her calling and gifts made sense in Shandia at all.

> **EH:** He goes ahead building, actually thinking in his own mind that I shall some-day be in Shandia, but not so much as asking me how I feel about it or what sort of house I might like. I have no desire to go to Shandia, actually, and much less to live in a house planned and built by someone else. What is there for me to do in Shandia, anyway?
>
> But this morning the word of the Lord quieted anew. "I would seek unto God, and unto God (not 'unto Jim') would I commit my cause." "I will give them one heart and one way." "In the way of Thy judgments, O Lord, have we waited for Thee. The desire of our soul is to Thy name."
>
> There are times when I feel I should let go and "tell Jim off"—tell him how I feel about the way he is handling me. There are other times, when I think of his love for me, and my own unspeakable desire and love for him, that the former thoughts are overwhelmed and lost. It is God that maketh my way perfect. In Him do I trust, and I will not be afraid.

By spring, then, she was well past making demands, and only wanted to be with him. *("Oh, Jim, I just find myself living for the day when I leave here to go to the Oriente.")* She'd been wise, then, to hold her tongue in winter, to wait on God to quicken these kinds of thoughtful questions in my father's mind. Several times during this period, we hear him asking, *"How do you feel? Please tell me what you are expecting in a home out here,"* trying to figure out how he could paint bamboo walls blue-green.

Writing to her in April from Dos Rios, a nearby, more established missionary station, he said:

> I wish you could just see Shandia once so that you could think with me about such things, but I have no idea how it could be worked for you to visit. This Dos Rios house was built with machine tools and by real carpenters—and how I envy their doing it so well. We will never be able to produce such a place, and I wonder just how we, you and I, will ever fulfill dreams of blue-green bedrooms. Hand tools leave lumber so crudely finished and so poorly fit that painting to any degree of beauty is a practical impossibility. We may have to settle for bamboo, Betts, so be thinking how you want it!

By this time, though, he had already been expressing his *own* lack of any frivolous demands and expectations, as in this letter from March.

March 22

> You asked about a wedding dress and my preferences. Bless you, darling, but you're comical in your sincerity at times. Whatever difference would it make to me? . . . As far as I'm concerned, you didn't ever and won't ever need a color to flatter you. Generally I have preferred long dresses to short ones always, but that, too, is irrelevant now. You looked lovely, I thought, the night of Dave's wedding in a short, white suit. I may have a word to say about the length of your hair if you ask me, but beyond that, darling, it's your show. I am a most interested by-stander waiting to see what you'll do! . . .
>
> How shall I tell you, darling, after all I've carelessly said about your features, that now I think them all wonderfully framed and that I know when it comes time for me to see them, I will remark with Solomon, "Behold, thou art fair, my love.". . .
>
> And now, Betty, my promised and longed-for wife, good-night. May the Shield of our spirits hover over you tonight and give you rest in sleep, making you glad and effective in His service and preparing you for me as a fellow worker. It may not be very romantic, but I like to think of you that way—as one who can sensibly share the problems of this type of work and conscientiously partake in the solution. I doubt if my comrades have any such hopes in their wives. And for this, my dearest, I love you tonight—for that part of you that is so practical and wise and helpful.

It's humorous how my dad thought the other guys' love for their fiancé or wife was nothing compared to his for my mother. Perhaps every couple who are wildly in love think their romance is the perfect one, greater than anyone else's in the world. But when others would tell him of problems or difficulties in their relationships, he celebrated privately what he considered the superiority of my mother's character and their sure ability to navigate the waters of marriage.

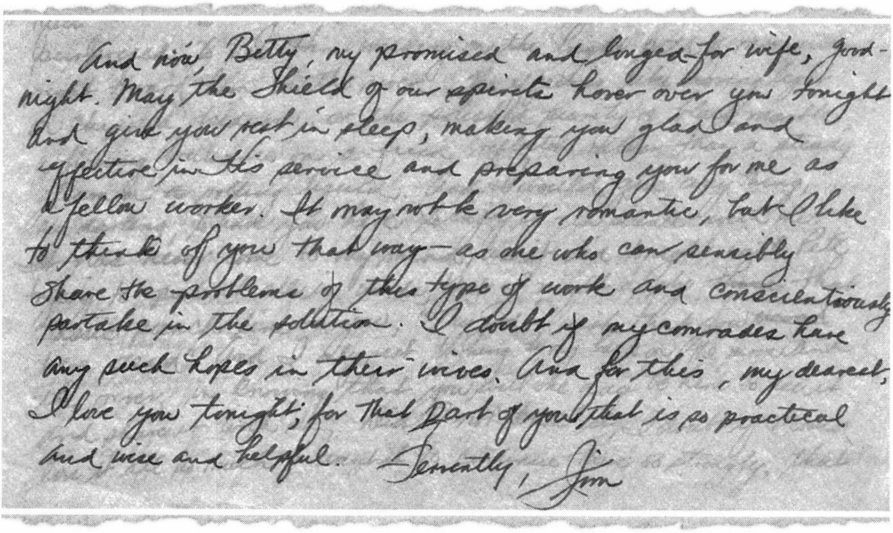

[handwritten letter reproduced in facsimile:]

And now, Betty, my promised and longed-for wife, good-night. May the Shield of our spirits hover over you tonight and give you rest in sleep, making you glad and effective in His service and preparing you for me as a fellow worker. It may not be very romantic, but I like to think of you that way—as one who can sensibly share the problems of this type of work and conscientiously partake in the solution. I doubt if my comrades have any such hopes in their wives. And for this, my dearest, I love you tonight; for that part of you that is so practical and wise and helpful. Sincerely, Jim

I have wondered if it were true what Ed said about there being times when real love, exhibited both in physical attentions and in a striving of words to understand, will not succeed in bringing you out of a "mood." Up until now they have, I think . . . because you were willing to tell me. It would disturb me, Betts, if we came to such an impasse and you refused to complain—just shut up and wouldn't be plied. So I think I'll ask you to put on paper a promise of some sort that when there is something—usually described as "oh, it's nothing"—that you will *tell me*. However small, I want to know what is troubling you, and I am a poor guesser when it comes to such.

This comment reflects a noticeable trend in their writing at this time, as they each tried imagining what life together as man and wife would be like. Again, these excerpts come from their various letters (and one journaling note) throughout the spring.

EH: You know, I was thinking today—although we must face long separations after marriage, you won't be going to an office every day of your life, eight or ten hours a day, having me at home. We shall be together *more* perhaps, in the long run, than the average couple in the States. I want to work with you, in the Lord's service, as much as I can, and I know that you will be far more of a father to our children than many would be in the States. I long for the day when we can share everything.

JE: There has been so much to make me think of a home and children this week *[in Dos Rios]* that I have gone to bed and awoken every morning with wonderings of what it will be like. I know it will be a delight with you, but just how it will be to really go at it—how we will teach our children the difference between Spanish and Quichua and English (a most interesting diversion in the home of three little ones)—how you will handle giggling kitchen help—and how we will be when company comes and the kids, sitting at a separate table, have a quarrel on.

EH: I think constantly these days of our first home together, a one or two-room shack, with cane and paja [straw]. But to be with you, Jim—what will it be?

JE: And to do it with you! Betty Howard, the Austere, the Thoughtful, the Woman with the Man's Mind (all that from Wheaton), and the Betty who doesn't like overhead lights, nor doubles [twin beds], nor men who spit—my Betty with the lovely legs and flat stomach and slender shoulders, and, oh, such soft cheeks. My darling, I love you, want you, need you, *crave* you now.

Anything could set them to thinking of the other.

EH, JOURNAL: A beautifully clouded moonlit night. Full moon, but only visible at intervals. I've been sitting down on the porch, watching the movement of the luminous clouds, asking God for just one uninterrupted, clear shining of the whole moon. Sort of a promise or omen. He gave it. Thought, too, of Jim's observation: "By George, that moon is round!" Wonder if he is able to see the moon tonight?

JE: You will see by the date that it is a night of full moon, and Pete and I have just come in from standing on the cliff, awed at the utter exquisiteness of this setting under a nearly clear sky and a brilliant moon. The river is wide here at the point of its big bend, and the path of the reflection of the moon strikingly broad. The solid black of the forest broken by the sheen of moonlit water and capped with the deep blue of evening sky is sufficient to silence one and set him thinking on the wonder of Creation and the power and beauty of our God. . . . The glinting water seems solid from its lack of any transparency in the black and silver, and one would not be surprised to see Him walking on the bright path of moon right toward us on the river. The effect is like moving light or chipped obsidian, rather than a steady gleam on rolling liquid.

And I would give anything, my darling, to have you here to enjoy it—in silence—with me. It has never come to mind as it did tonight. . . . I only rest turning my back on the moon and the river, in knowing, that you will one day be here to see it with me. Did I not know it, I doubt if I could love it all so much and want it to continue thus so strongly, that we might know it together. I cannot help pressing the query to the Father—"How many moons hence?"

Many of my father's thoughts of their life together included, naturally, its sexual, physical expressions.

JE: I went to sleep last night with one of those not-too-insignificant, but meaningful night-worries—an old one. I think I mentioned it in Quito—about whether or not you would *play* with me. Not only let me play with you, but be aggressive with your hands, toy with me when I'm sleepy, kiss me when I'm too tired to do anything but lie down, pull my ears and punch me in the stomach, do all those great and silly things that women should do when men want to love, but, for weakness or weariness (I get that, way down here) cannot be aggressive in it.

Will you ever come to me, on a bed and dozing, and cuddle up to me without my moving a finger to encourage you? You haven't done a number of these things yet, darling, and I'm just wondering when I'll experience them. I think of one time you came up behind me while I was typing at the doctor's and bent over and kissed me—oh, Betty darling, do you know what that long, audible sigh I just gave means?

JE: Oh, Betty, I love you. Do you know how? I love you *strongly* tonight, with a sense of power, a huge, surging hope inside me as to the fulfillment of our love. It is not the quiet longing that is usually on me, but the upflung fists and the shouting for possession, and both arms eager to crush you to me. It is the bursting heart and the wild eye of passion, the laugh that makes the stomach tighten.

You cannot possibly understand this, and I really don't ask you to—it is just one of the ways I love you, and it happens to seize me as I write. Love is not all a resting in me. It is a tenseness and a daring, a call to crush and conquer.

But my mother, too, ached to be held and loved by him, and to share every joy that God would one day give them to experience.

EH: Oh, I miss you just terribly, Jim. I hunger and thirst for you, with a vast aching feeling. Sleep is the only relief I know, and that has to begin and end with the realization that I am in bed alone. I love you. . . .

EH: Oh, Jim, my darling—I love you now as never before, in an intimacy never dreamed before, in a peace and confidence not experienced before. I love you as my own soul—as if you were my very soul. I feel that I belong utterly and absolutely to you, that I was made expressly for you, and that I shall never truly live until I live with you. How, oh, how shall I tell you my love? I have told you some of it. There will be a day when I can tell you far more. But never can it all be expressed, either by word or action.

Hearing her speak so ardently of her love does not surprise me at all. She was an honest, logical thinker, but also had the beauty of femininity. Unlike some of the stoic impressions of her, she was a very passionate, vulnerable, and even a hilariously funny woman.

But she was also highly cognizant, as a yet unmarried woman, to surrender all such desires to the loving command and will of the Father.

MARCH 20: Teach us, Lord, both Jim and me, to rest in quietness, knowing that Thy will cannot be improved upon. May the peace of our relationship to Thee, and the beauty of the love Thou hast given us, be unspoiled. Let no unholy impatience enter, I pray.

This combination of self-discipline with the fullness of her love gave evidence to her humanness, her realism, and I find joy in seeing it here. I rejoice seeing *both* my parents writing this way, fully in love with God, and fully in love with each other, and tremendously unashamed in each aspect—both the spiritual and the physical. They embraced the truth that "perfect love driveth out fear." They were right to want one another, just as they were right to wait until they could fulfill their desires under God's full blessing. God made men and women to be attracted to each other and to be obedient to His timing. This is how we become whole, free, utterly sanctified people.

Let's not then gasp to hear them speak of their full-bodied hunger for one another. Maybe each of us can learn from their determination to bring all things, even this irrepressible and often unruly thing, under the total authority of our Head.

> **MARCH 25:** Oh, how I long for her—all of her, her help and counsel and just her presence here, but most of all this morning, for her body. . . . I don't know how long I can take this. It leaves me useless to study or pray or read or work. Every little thing seems to irritate me, and there is nothing that would satisfy me this morning but Betty herself—all of her. Lord God, how long?
>
> Little did I know for what I dealt in those days I said I was willing to live for celibacy—nothing did I know about the power of love for a woman, I believe. *So help me, God, I did not know!* Had I been aware of what I should feel this morning as the rain falls heavily out of a low sky, I doubt if I would have made any sort of vow of willingness to stay single. Lord, can it be that this must go on for hundreds more rainy mornings and hundreds more fitful nights? How shall I bear it apart from some inwrought miracle of grace?
>
> Father, if it is possible that the work here in the Oriente not suffer, and that Your design for the Kingdom plan in the jungle be in no way thwarted or slowed, O merciful God, give me permission to marry her—soon!

Back in San Miguel, my mother understood, too, that their waiting would continue unabated for now.

March 28

> I've just been making an inventory list of substantive-like sequences in Tsahfiki, but I'm hungry for a little time with you, Jim. I miss you so much, and want to sit down with you and just be together. But that is not possible, so I must try to be satisfied with this.
>
> Barbara has just come home from town and informs me that Bill and Irene, who left here last Monday, are still in Santo Domingo, there being no gasoline to get the camioneta [van] to Quito. Reason: wash-out on the railroad between Quito and the coast. You've probably heard about it. So we are really stuck in here. Dorothy got out just in the nick of time. I wonder if it affects the plane at

Shell Mera? Prices have gone up here terrifically, and there is no rice, salt, sugar, etc.

I hear they have to build a bridge for the railroad, which will take three to four weeks. I only hope they finish it by May, so the trucks will be running from here again! If not, I'll just start walking around the first of May . . .

. . . because she was hoping the two of them could at least meet for a visit at that missions conference in Quito. To be clear, though—seeing each other as an engaged couple meant something different to them than it would, not only to the majority of people today, but even to those in the culture and time where they were currently living. My mother wrote in the same March 28 letter:

Last night I had quite a chat with Edelina, our girl. She is engaged, and is much interested to hear about our customs of engagement and marriage. She's never heard of a wedding (except the civil formalities, of course) and asks me about them. But last night we discussed fornication (she'd always wondered what the word meant) and purity of body, etc. She had not known that extra-marital intercourse was sin, and simply couldn't believe me when I told her that I have two aunts nearing fifty who are virgins!

She thought that you and I regarded ourselves as married (with all its implications) before God, even before the ceremony. The whole discussion was a revelation to her, as she herself was born out of marriage, and she says she doesn't know any señoritas who have no children. And—remember—her family are evangelicals, her stepfather one of the leading brethren, and her mother in fellowship. No doubt everyone here thinks we really must have ourselves a time when we go up to Quito.

No, it wasn't like *that*. But she could hardly wait for it.

April 5

It has been entirely too long, Jim dear, since I sat down to tell you how much I love you. I didn't realize it had been such a time till I looked at the date on #9, which is still sitting here, waiting for some way to be mailed. There is still no gas in town, and Bill and Irene had to give up and go to Quito by truck yesterday, leaving the camioneta in S.D., so we hear. Dorothy and Doreen have not been heard from— in fact, nary a word from the outside world has reached us for two weeks. I am to be quite honest, lonely, darling, and feel that I need you more than ever. At least I need word from you, or even *of* you, to know that you are well. Yesterday was three weeks since I had a letter from you, and it was written a month ago!

And do you know what else I miss? Music! Doreen took her organ with her to Quito, and I miss it dreadfully. Quite often I used to go downstairs in the twilight and play from memory or the Keswick hymnal. This is the first time in my life I've been entirely without music even to *hear,* and it's awful. How I wish I had the lovely organ you gave me—but Dr. T. said it was definitely leaking air, and was going to fix it for me. It wasn't fixed by the time I came down here. But I appreciate now as never before what a lovely thing it was for you to give me, Jim, and I thank you again from my heart.

And then the ring—! The thrill certainly hasn't worn off. I catch myself, sometimes in the presence of others, gazing at it, thinking of its loveliness in itself, and above all the wonderful significance of it. Will I ever actually grasp the fact that it is I who is engaged to Jim Elliot, the man of my very dreams? "What have I done to her?" you say. You have given me, in offering me what you are, the complete fulfillment of life, the balance, shall I say, that my personality lacked. You have called forth all the love of my heart, and it amounts to more than I thought I had saved up, these ten or twelve years since I've been capable of loving! You are everything to me, Jim, my darling, and I, too, want to live every hour of every day of my life with you. . . . Right now, for some reason, working on this Colorado business makes me feel so far from you, because you cannot in any way be a part of it, nor I a part of your work. It is a comfort, however, to know you've been here and are acquainted with the place and the Indians.

Yesterday was Sábado de Gloria, and you know what that means! Barbara says it was wilder this year. But what a sight! And I had no film in my camera! Dorothy was going to bring me some. She was to have been back on April 1. The Indians began coming around 10 a.m. and by noon the plaza was a mass of every color imaginable—red, of course, predominating. Abram, the chief, came and sat on my porch and talked with me and played his accordion for me. He is quite an intelligent fellow, and seemed to be running a little "Mr. Anthony" clinic all day, giving advice to various Colorados. Samuel, the one I've told you about, is his brother, and apparently next in line to be chief. He proudly brought his wife and two children to the house to meet me and stayed overnight downstairs. Manuel, son of Soledad, was as drunk as a sailor, and came panting into Doreen's house where I was, hollering for protection saying they were going to fight with him: "Soy chiquito! No puedo pelear! Soy muy chiquito—muy díbil. Después de 3 años seré grande para pelear." [I'm little! I can't fight! I'm very weak! After three years I'll be big enough to fight!"] If you know Manuel, he is one of the biggest, strongest brutes of the tribe! He was swinging his gun around in a most promiscuous manner, so I finally managed to usher him gently outside again. Another Indian proposed to me three or four times, but I convinced him I was too *gigante* for him. He claimed he was nine years old—he was at least twenty! The drinking and bulla [ruckus] went on all night. They gradually drifted (or stumbled, or were dragged) home just before Sunday School this morning. . . .

Barbara and I went to Patilé's on Monday, and found ourselves in the midst of the denouement of Saturday's feast! Dozens of drunken Indians lay around on benches and the ground. . . . I got another proposal, this time quite insistent, from a fellow who said he was tired of his woman and thought it time for a change! So, actually the trip was en balde *[for naught]* except for seven words I managed to elicit from Radolfo on the way.

Still no word of or from the outside. Don Miguel is going up to Quito tomorrow, so he'll take this for me. I can't imagine what's become of Doreen and Dorothy.

"And then the ring—! The thrill certainly hasn't worn off."

Of course, being in Ecuador in the 1950s, and being missionaries in such obscure places, nothing was definite anyway, including the prospects of my dad and her making connections in Quito—of *any* sort. According to him:

April 10

I can give no definite word about just when I'll be out. Pete came back from Quito with word that he has a great deal of dental work to have done. I am trying to persuade him to go out the week before conference so I can have leave to perhaps pay a visit to San Miguel with no time limits on the other end as there would be if I were to go out first. I still am dubious if we can persuade Eladio to stay more than a day or two alone. But Pete feels like he just got back from Quito and doesn't want to head out too soon.

No sooner than a day later, however, he wasn't feeling quite as accommodating.

April 11

These next two weeks will be long ones, I fear, as the rains have come and we must be inside most of the day. I cannot spend hour after hour studying phrases like Pete, and I get wild as a stalled stallion waiting in the radio room, studying the forest across the river and facing the gray empty sky. I will come out regardless of what Pete does or whether Eladio likes being left alone—I need you, darling, and need you soon!

By the end of April, barring an ever-possible weather delay, he was putting his plans in writing.

April 29

Please be patient if I'm not in Quito by Tuesday night, May 12. I finally had to tell Pete that I was going out then, (Monday, the 11th) if weather permitted, no matter what he decided to do. . . . So he is to go out Friday now, with dental appointments all next week and running over into the following week, with some idea of coming in Saturday (the 14th), so that one of us will be here for both Lord's Days. I doubt, frankly, if he will make it back. . . . But that's his business—I'm staying my Sunday.

Weather is very unpredictable now, Betts dear, and I have done everything possible to arrange to get out Monday morning and be in Quito by Tuesday, but we must wait the hand of God over any plan now. We had a siege of rain that lasted 36 hours *constantly* last week, and it was impossible to fly in the Oriente the whole week. So take courage, darling, I'm coming.

That week will be one of those unhappy ones for us—committee meeting mad. Rosales will have us up to our ears in appointments. . . . I suppose we will just be seeing each other. But, Lord willing, week number two will not be so. I am leaving it open. We will plan it together, and you will have the final say on what goes—and I have liberty for anything short of marriage! I have thought of a visit to Miguel together, if you would find that pleasure—you will know our restrictions there better than I. Or there is Quito, and with Bill and Irene gone—the bodega. So I must get me ready—a haircut and a face stiffened to shaving perhaps twice a day.

The day finally came.

MAY 11: Flew out of Shandia at about 10:30 a.m. with Luis Andi. Picked up Gerry Conn in Tena and flew to Shell Mera. Waited for a bus until about 2:00 p.m. and had difficulty getting out of Baños. Made Ambato about 8:00 p.m. and Quito after midnight. She had waited up for me at Tidmarsh's until very late, but had gone to bed thinking I stayed in Ambato. Pete let me in, and Doc got up to welcome me. When things were quiet again, I tried to waken her by rattling at the door, leaving the bath water running as a decoy. After some trying, I went in and woke her with a kiss. She rose into my arms in one of the warmest embraces I can remember, and it was the beginning of two most intense weeks of embracing.

MAY 15: Late evenings alone with her by the fireplace were the best. If there was before anything tentative in our loving, it is since then destroyed. Our love is now and always and only the true love I can know, and if I should lose her, there could be nothing again in life like this.

MAY 19: Happy days, like none before I've known.

My mother didn't take time to recount this delightful May visit in her
journal, but in its afterglow, she thought back to a May several years ago.

May 28

When I think, Jim dearest, of the lovingkindness of the Lord in just simply giving
us to one another, when we had each just come to the place of true surrender in
the matter—five years ago on Sunday—May 31. By "giving," I mean just bringing
us together, or "revealing" us to one another in love, for of course we were not
really *given* until January 31, 1953. But we had not *sought* one another. We were
not out to get a mate. What might I have gotten had I sought? Surely not *you*.
And I am, oh, so grateful and glad, dear, that you are what you are, and that your
love is so full and pure. May God make me the woman you need and desire, and
prepare me for you.

Sunday—our "fifth anniversary!" (Now you'll say I'm sickly sentimental!) When
I think of that day—of the leap my heart gave when you came to me so casually after
the FMF breakfast, and said you'd like to talk to me sometime! Then as we sat at
the Lagoon, after you had confessed your love for me, I remember your touching
me slightly with your shoulder, and I thought you shamefully bold! (I still do, darling—and, oh, how I love you for it!) Oh, the Lord has been wonderfully gracious in
preserving that love, through all our times of doubting, coldness, and separation,
and bringing it to such fullness now. I feel that I have done nothing, *could* have done
nothing, to "keep" you. God has kept you, and will continue to. . . .

Oh, darling—as I compare you with others—indeed, with all others that I
know—I can only exclaim that thou art chiefest among ten thousand. Thou art
my beloved, and I am *thine*.

In loneliness, your very own

Bett

And so they were parted. Again.
That the work may continue.

June 2

Have had some interesting chats with Pete. He wants Olive to take Wycliffe after
Biola, and hopes that she will be here in eighteen months. He wants her to learn
Spanish on her own, but not Quichua. And he is glad he is not in a frenzy over
her like I am over you, because he thinks it would be rough having that drag on
for years. But he is certain that the "madness" will be on him again when she gets
within range, and thinks it's a good thing that I feel the way I do. He also told me
quite bluntly that he in no way stood in the way of our marriage, and I made it
plain I felt the same way.

That leaves me the only wall in the way, and I get to thinking that is the crazi-
est thing I ever did—to stand in my own way of marrying you, when I want it so
badly. And believe me, darling, were it not that I am firmly persuaded of the will

of God in this untried, unheard-of "itinerant evangelism," we would be married, quite unceremoniously, like you promised we could be if I did it suddenly, tomorrow. I want so badly to be with you now—day and night, like it was last month, by fireplaces and in the warm tropic nights, across the table and in my arms, with your voice coming through the doors as I lie in bed.

June 10

I miss you these days, my darling, waking in the morning always with the desire for you strong, and often beginning the day with what few bars I know of "When the dawn flames in the sky, I love you." It does, and I do. . . . And my prayers are full of you. . . .

Last weekend we took the school to Pano for a paseo *[a walk]*. Lost every game of soccer we played, but it was a good experience for the boys, just the *seeing* of an orderly directed school and something of discipline. Ours is quite hopeless, but schoolteachers are not easily found.

Lord's Day morning (Pete came back to Shandia on the flip of a coin Saturday), I dedicated Miller's new son, Carl, in Quichua, and preached on Luke 16 in the morning service. The Lord gave me unusual liberty, and coming home on the trail, two girls who live halfway between Pano and Shandia, and who had come to Pano for the meeting, accompanied me, and asked for baptism! They had come often to Shandia on previous Sundays and shown live interest in the Word, as it seemed to us. But if they are serious, and they *seem* dead serious, they are our firstfruits here. . . .

One of them (Carmela) was here today, and I spent an hour with her and her little sister, explaining to them memory verses in Quichua. She seemed very alert, and prayed more diligently than I have ever heard *any* Indian pray when we had finished. Pray for her.

But oh, Bett, how I wish I could give her to *you* to train and teach. It must be a woman who does it, and I covet these as *your* heritage in Christ. But it is now you are needed, not a year hence—right now, to take up the work and share with me in it all!

God grant that it may be soon.

Fondly, your Jim

SUMMER AND . . .

As eager as my father had become to marry—"*Love for her inside me says wait for nothing*"—he'd actually placed one condition on my mother before he'd agree to a wedding. She must first learn Quichua.

That's why, near the end of June, she wrapped up her linguistic work among the Colorado tribe and moved west to Dos Rios, roughly a six-hour walk from my dad in Shandia. As always, the trip itself was an adventure.

June 27

Now about my trip from San Miguel to Dos Rios—(I shall probably have to quit in the middle; lights out at 9:00 here!)—I left there on June 18, having more or less completed the alphabet on the 16th. The trip to Quito was not unusual, with only two delays of an hour each. Nothing stolen, thank the Lord. . . .

(My father's bag had been stolen on his own recent trip from San Miguel, costing him not only clothes and equipment but also a box of irreplaceable color slides.)

I spent Monday and Tuesday unpacking and repacking in the bodega (and missing you just awfully) and got a bus out of Quito to Ambato on Wednesday afternoon, as they told me there would be a plane leaving Ambato at 5:00. I got to Ambato at 4:30, and raced madly to the airport, only to wait till 5:30 when the plane got back from Shell too late to make another flight!

So there I was, stuck out at the airport, having to wait till next day for a plane. I was sitting there in my cotton dress (having thought I'd get straight into Shell that night) freezing to death, when the wife of the commander at the airport came up and invited me in to her home to spend the night. They are lovely Christian folks, and gave me dinner and a nice bed. It was surely one of the Lord's provisions.

The plane didn't take off again till noon, so I was thinking all morning that every hour there meant one less with you! I'd hoped for something like you had suggested—flying in to Shandia in the morning and spending all day there!—

The letter breaks off here, saying (as predicted) she feared the lights being turned off mid-sentence. *"Goodnight, my darling. The moon is there tonight, but clouds hide it. Oh, to be so near to you! It's so much better this way. It's the first time, you know, that we've been separated by a short distance! I love you ever so much, Jim."*

She picked up the narrative again next morning. *"Well,"*. . .

When we got in to Shell, after a wonderful trip, with all the big Nevados [snow-covered mountains] gleaming in the sunshine, Bob met me at the plane and discovered it was going right back that afternoon. This meant that he had to rush right in and get those women from Pano and bring them out. I had just time to swallow a bit of lunch before we took off.

My hopes were already shattered of spending any time with you, but it never occurred to me that we wouldn't land at all. As we were nearing Shandia, Bob suddenly handed the earphones to me and said, "Do you want to hear a handsome voice?" You were just calling Shell Mera. What a thrill to hear you speak just as Shandia hove into view.

Then, after circling near you the first time, when Bob hollered at you out the window, he said to me, "Well, we might as well go in and see them." Another leap of anticipation! But as he circled around, he said, no, he didn't think he could make it. I was just about wild, seeing you there so plainly, and knowing full well you'd be waiting for us to come down.

As you vanished from sight, I couldn't keep back the tears. (Don't worry—Bob didn't notice. He kept up his usual line.) I still haven't seen Shandia—I was looking for you, and then *at* you, the whole time, darling.

Close, yet so far. But maybe soon . . .

You said in your letter you'd be glad to come in here "when I get settled." I was settled an hour after I got here and, oh, so ready to see you! I am going to gradually lose my mind if you don't come soon and tell me about everything. I think the house sounds fine—anything, darling, absolutely anything, so long as we're together. . . .

The Bowles say they won't be here next Sunday, so I wonder if you would feel you could come then. Just whenever you think is right, and I know Carol will be glad to have you anytime. Jerry was just saying, "Oh, there's always room someplace." You know I'll be eagerly awaiting you. . . .

And if you surprise me when I've just washed my hair (or even when I'm in the river washing it) or when I've just come in soaked from a canoe trip, like Friday afternoon, I will be just as glad to see you. *Come . . .*

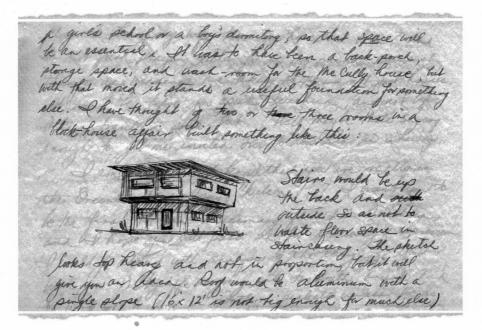

My father's ideas on their first house in Shandia,
though he ended up building it in Puyupungu.

Their bamboo house in Puyupungu, after five months in a leaky tent.

My father's next letter (June 29) was basically a primer in Quichua, including charts and guides that went back to his days at Wycliffe, as well as field analysis they'd gathered since being on the ground. He wanted her to learn the language as quickly and completely as possible, even though he admitted he was still grappling with much of it himself. *("Please don't judge me too harshly on this stuff.")* Apparently he was still in need of the work too.

June 29

The thing I am sorriest about is that we are not doing it together, this language analysis. I have dreamed of sitting down with you and going over things that I do not understand. Pete is so "know-all" on many points (he *does* know, usually) . . . but I know you and I would not bicker over some of the points that are bantered about here.

It's true, they weren't in close enough proximity to go over to each other's houses for an evening study session. But the shortened distance at least allowed their mail to become a little more reliable, shuttled by courier from station to station. *("I am looking out for every Pano face that pops out of the forest,"* my dad said.) But a time or two throughout this summer, when the need for supplies allowed him to justify a days' hike through the forest or a few hours' ride by canoe, they were able to be together—to talk housing plans, to talk wedding plans, to whisper the sweet truths they each loved saying and hearing. In his journal of July 5, after returning from his first trip to see her in Dos Rios, my father wrote:

> **JULY 5:** They were our three most intimate days ever. House planning and Quichua study—with those silly, spasmodic embraces interspersed and making it all so worthwhile and fun. The evening was spent on the clinic porch. Forget not in age what tenderness you knew there, my soul.

As far as the current status of their housing plans, he'd written her a few details on June 29:

> I hope the 12' x 16' two-story affair appeals to you. I have spoken to Pete of it, and he approves. I've built and lived in the thing in my mind night after night since the idea came to me. But if you want to be away from the others very strongly, I will get to thinking of something else. Because more than anything else I know, Betts dearest, what I want to do is make you happy.

And as far as wedding plans, he'd written and sent this note on July 4:

> What would you think of having a civil wedding, go on our honeymoon, and return for a reception evening in Quito? The uncertainty of dates makes me wonder this.

But a looming pattern was emerging that threatened to put housing and wedding plans and even plans for the entire mission station in jeopardy.

July 5

> The river is at one of those awesome stages where another day's rain will bring it to dangerous proportions—and it is still raining. . . . I thought I would get a note back to you with the Dos Rios boys who are not going back until the weather lets up. They got stuck in the dark about twenty minutes' walk away last night, so had to bring in the aluminum from where they left it on the trail in the rain early this morning.

Yet even as he kept a wary eye on the skies and the river, my father was learning new lessons in love. As seen from his writings of earlier years, he could be quick and occasionally insensitive with his judgments and advice. The same bold, aggressive temperament that served him well as a daring disciple of Christ could sometimes come across as harsh and abrupt, even meddling, especially in dealing with a woman. And here we see it again—the fix-it mentality that surfaced in conversation.

July 7

I have been wondering how you could best make use of your time in Dos Rios, and it came to me yesterday that you should help Carol plenty. I don't want anyone saying, "Oh, yes, she learned Quichua, but she didn't do anything else."

That Indian baby came to mind. Why don't you offer to assume full responsibility for him—clothing, bathing, and feeding? I want everybody to know all that you can do, Bett, and realizing the reticence that is in you, I would press you into it, could I do so. I know you will help in the school, but don't wait to be asked, will you? I want that you should show yourself fruitful in every good work, and I believe there is plenty to do.

My mother's response, in a letter from three days later, was gracious, with only a hint of defensiveness.

July 10

I appreciate your advice on how to spend my time. It is hard to know just how to help Carol. She never gives me anything to do; I just have to try to figure out what I can do, and with three Indians apparently doing everything obvious in the way of housework, I'm not always sure how to help. But I shall try. As you know, I have chapel twice a week, Sunday school this Sunday, recreation twice a week, and Bible class. Also play the organ for various meetings.

But his July 7 letter hadn't stopped there. He also said:

Frankly, I was not satisfied with your attitude toward [Pete] in the few remarks you made in Dos Rios. It is not sufficient to say that "there is something about him that just *gets* you." All the more reason why you should make an effort toward true compatibility and understanding. I threaten to make it hard for you, if you are going to be continually criticizing him—regardless of how he "gets" you. And I'm afraid I'll be adamant on that point, darling, as I regard it a development of Christian grace in you, and will be happy with nothing less than a spirit of sweet reasonableness in such matters when you are my wife.

Until he'd begun pointing such things out to her, during my mother's senior year at college, I don't think she realized how blunt or cutting her words could be. There are people who would never say anything to hurt someone else's feelings—even in honesty, even in love—and then there are those, like my mother, who call a spade a spade. But over time, she'd grown to recognize her need for being careful with this rather pointed tendency, not letting it become a weapon. And while pride can enter into any heart whenever exhortation or rebuke is given, I believe her response to his challenge shows real growth and humility at this time in her life.

I must say I was rather stunned at the way you put your rebuke to me about my criticism of Pete. It is the first time you have mentioned it, and I felt that I'd really been "chewed out," as Ed would say. I'm truly sorry, for I do not dislike Pete, but what I said was "just between us two," and I did not mean it to be "continual criticism."

But immediately I realized that I must begin now to be subject to you, Jim, and take your correction with a true womanly spirit. It is a role I must learn, for my first impulse was to argue. I would beg you, though, to give me some warning first, and then if I do not obey, say you "will threaten to make it hard for me." It almost made me feel like bawling, that idea.

But I ask your forgiveness for criticizing the one whom God has sent you to work with, for I know he has many fine qualities. I fear that the spirit of discernment is not in me.

Here I must recognize similar growth in my father's humility as well. He received her response as a welcome light shed upon his own weakness.

July 12

I'm really sorry, Bett, that I cannot seem to temper things I feel strongly about with some modifying or softening strain. I didn't really want to make it sound so stern as I see you have taken it, and it doesn't seem to me to be a point where I must be obeyed over your own will. It's simply an attitude that I have felt lurking and finally saw rising in our last visit, and wrote about as a thing I do not want to see grow.

I suppose I am more critical of [Pete] than you are, and should be "threatening" myself. Your attitude on receiving my letter was enough to humble me greatly on the subject, so that I don't feel like writing of it now. We can't talk it over now anyhow, so let's save it until we are together again.

This was good. They were learning each other, valuing each other, growing more and more appreciative of what the other was bringing to their lives. My mother had said it this way in a recent letter:

July 7

Your letter written Sunday and received yesterday morning left me weak. The depth and completeness of your understanding of my love, your perception and perfect appreciation, are things utterly beyond the scope of my dreams. I could not ever have imagined those qualities in any man, darling, and you have opened doors for me that I did not know existed. You seem to take nothing for granted. You ignore nothing. You regard nothing casually. You read me, Jim, as though I were made just for you to read!

Even his muscular frame seemed to be made for her, meeting a need in her heart, answering one of her self-conscious insecurities.

You are the first man who ever made me feel small. When I was with George, I was always more conscious of my height, for some reason; thinking, I suppose, that people would remark on how tall we both were. But when I am in your arms, I feel very small and helpless! When looking at your back in the mirror, when you have me in your arms, you seem just tremendously powerful. For all this, I am glad, and know that the Lord in very truth made us for one another.

She loved simply hearing him talk, too. One of the everyday sounds in her new location was the intermittent chatter on an open line of radio contact with nearby mission stations. The reception could be spotty at times, not always clearly distinguishable. But her ears perked up each time she heard the radio crackle with activity, thinking it might be the voice of my father, checking in from Shandia.

I've just been straining my ears for forty minutes trying to hear your voice, as you haven't come through once now since a week ago. Just at 2:00, I heard you and Henry talking and saying you guessed you were the only ones on the network. I felt like busting in and saying I was there, as always, for I do listen to the whole thing, hoping I'll hear you. But I could not hear well. I heard Henry say Jerry was over there and had brought you no mail. I feel just terrible. Why didn't I do what impulse told me yesterday, and answer your letter just the minute I finished reading it? . . .

One thing about the radio contact is that when I hear your voice, even though I cannot read you, I know just exactly where you are and what you are doing. It is one time when I do not have to speculate, as I do a hundred times a day.

It was maddening this afternoon. I heard you well each time you said, "Are you reading us now?" and then when you went ahead, I lost you. I never did hear the end or hear you say, "Over." But I know you are alive and well, which is something.

What an unexpected joy and blessing this was, getting to hear his voice so often. She'd written to tell him of it, how the radio helped keep her informed about him, how her heart raced when hearing him.

July 9

I've just heard you on the contact, and since I don't know yet if Bob is stopping in at Shandia this afternoon, I better have this ready just in case. I sent a letter this afternoon with some Pano men, but why shouldn't I send off two letters a day to you, darling? I love you more than any number of letters could demonstrate.

It is so good to hear your voice, faint as it is. . . . I'd just like to shout it sometime, right over the contact, and shock everyone in Ecuador (and probably Peru)—"I *love* you, darling! I love you!" Because it's true. I do. More than you can possibly know.

Their July letters really do read more like a conversation, now that the lag time in their mail traffic had been shortened to days, rather than weeks (and months). Here's a little collage of them, from various dates:

EH: I love you just madly, and think there just isn't anyone else to compare. Are you sure you're not perfect? I think you must be mistaken, because I just love everything about you.

JE: I didn't know I would get this way, Betty, but I am lost, utterly lost without you. I love you, my darling, and sometimes just have to stop where I am and heave a sigh.

EH: Every time I look toward the hills near Shandia, I involuntarily breathe out the word "darling"—and wonder just what you are doing.

JE: That long, low hill which I pointed out to you, and the knoll at the north end of it is a perfect sighting of Shandia. We lie directly in the gap between the two, if it helps you any to think of me "right out there."

EH: Jerry and Edna have just left for Pano, and I am kicking myself because there was nothing ready to send to you, dear. I am determined it shall not happen again, even though I did not know they would be going, so I am writing this right now.

JE: The closer we get, the more advantage I see in having you near. Thanks so much for your letters—they all arrived with Ablando yesterday.

EH (JULY 10): The letter describing Ginny's wedding made me want you all the more, Jim. How in the world do people live through such sublime events as a wedding? I don't know how I shall, once a date is actually set. When you spoke of the possibility of being married here, and having a reception in Quito, where did you think of having the civil ceremony? In Quito, with a reception following? . . . I still don't know what would be best. I cannot help thinking of the disappointment to our folks, Dave and Gibby, possibly Bert and Colleen. . . . What responsibility we have to the others, I'm not sure. I know the Lord will show us, and make us both happy whatever we do.

JE (JULY 12): The lush descriptions of the wedding didn't do for me what they did for you. For me, darling, "heavy ivory satin". . . "fitted bodice with designed off-shoulder effect". . . "embroidered iridescent sequins". . . "tiara of rhinestones". . . do not amount to what you describe as a "sublime event." Sorry, but as I say—to me, it is no more than an expensive tedium with little more than remembrance value, and although I shall do with all my heart whatever you desire in a wedding—whatever you want to remember—I must tell you that I dread the prospect of such a schedule, whatever the retrospect may be. I cannot tell you why, because I do not know, but there is something in me that resists the showy part of weddings with a passion I have against few other things in life.

EH: I wonder how the house is going. We've had some bad weather since you went back, which no doubt has slowed you considerably.

JE: We have been slowed considerably by the rains. All the post holes were full of water, and working the posts into line is almost impossible in such mud. . . . And to think we have to start a teacher's house before we can go to work on ours!

EH: Jerry told me today that once you put aluminum on a house, you cannot use it over again on another house. It's too thin, and it tears. The holes left by the nails, too, are unmendable. So maybe we should have thatch on our first house, huh? It would be a shame to waste hundreds of dollars on aluminum for a temporary house. Especially if it goes over the cliff! I saw several books advertised in *Popular Science* on how to build with cement blocks. Each was a dollar. Those magazines always strike me as being rather gauche. Would you be interested, or would it be better to wait and see if *Better Homes and Gardens* could give us the info?

JE: I agree about the *Popular Mechanics* mags generally and think *Better Homes and Gardens* more reliable. I'm still going to let you be the secretary on the cement house project. Hadn't thought of reusing the aluminum we put on the first little house, but of turning it into a girls' school or something when we moved out. But I think we will conserve the aluminum for a good house and use heavy tar paper instead—like on the Dos Rios store building. Find out if water caught from that roof would be suitable for drinking. Thatch-caught water is not good, they tell me.

EH (JULY 13): Have you been having cold weather there lately? Ever since I've been here, I've worn a sweater nearly half the time. Carol says it's "most unusual," but that's the way it always is when you go to a new place: "The weather was never like this." I'm wishing I'd brought some warmer clothes from Quito. And they say Shandia, being nearer the mountains, is colder still. So far we've not had one hot day. The afternoon you and I spent at the beach was the warmest. I'm more convinced than ever of the need for a fireplace.

JE (JULY 17): I am sorry you feel the cold so much! I have a standard remedy for that, and it is not a fireplace.

EH: Did you see the sky last night? "O Beauty, are you not enough? / Why am I crying after love?" But I am, dearest. I am crying after love, night after night, and day after day. How long, how long, how long? I long to wake with you in the morning, to dress with you, to cook breakfast for you (and it won't be banana soup), to sit across from you at *our* table, with our cloth and dishes and silver. To see you working outside, and to know you are mine. To sit and study, knowing that it is not beyond the realm of possibility that you should suddenly appear from behind and kiss me. To prepare lunch for you, and know you'll be in to eat it. To lie with you at siesta time, and to swim with you in the Talac—in the sunshine—and then to dress and eat supper together. And—oh, thought beyond words—to go to bed with you at night. To lie down together with no clocks or clothes or creaking stairways to worry about! Jim, I shall be your wife, but *you* shall be my *life*. (I wrote the enclosed while at Arias's, but had no thought of ever showing it to you until (if) we were married. But there are no barriers now. I am yours, and the thought, though far from poetry, is intensified now. So I let you read it.)

JE: Last night I was dreaming (awake) about our first overnight mountain climb together, and wondering how it would be to have someone really free to cuddle with for warmth. I have spent some cold nights in sleeping bags—do you have one, or will we fit into mine? I still am not through with Pichincha, and hope that next time we do it, it will be as old married folks doing something only silly unmarried folks would attempt. Oh, I love to be with you, Bett, wherever. And I want it to be everywhere—canoe trips and mountain climbs. That trip to Galápagos is for you and me, not me and Pete.

EH: In yesterday's *Daily Light* portion, I came across some interesting verses. *[Daily Light is a classic, yearlong book of collected Scriptures for morning and evening.]* I had been sitting here at my desk, trying desperately to concentrate, but overcome with longing for you, and with the ever-increasing hunger to be married. Involuntarily the cry goes up, "O Lord, how long? Speed the day!" I reached for my *Daily Light* and read, "If two of you shall agree on earth as touching anything that they shall ask, it shall be done for them of my Father which is in heaven.". . . "The Lord God said, It is not good that the man should be alone.". . . "Two are better than one." The verses were in just that order, and it startled me. Across the page, in the morning portion, I had marked "PJE, 1948," but the verses were of a very different theme. The Lord has led us by a way that we knew not, but by a wonderful way, for each phase of which I am thankful.

Such memories caused her to think back again on their circuitous paths.

EH: I've been thinking of those days when you were just "Dave's buddy," that "Elliot guy—you ought to get to know him—you two'd make a good pair." The days when you were just a wrestler out there on the mat, fun to watch, and of some slight interest because Dave was so interested in you. The days when you were the fellow who sat across the aisle in Ancient History with a high instep crossed over your left knee, and an interesting profile—a fellow in sharp contrast to that Oliver Somebody who sat in the next row in front of you, wore rubber overshoes, carried a briefcase, and always listened raptly to the lecture. How can that Jim Elliot be the same one who loves me now, and demonstrates it in the ways you do? The development of our relationship is one of the mysteries of life, and a most intriguing one. Oh, Jim, I am grateful for the way you have led me into love—gently, skillfully, and inexorably, with the most delicate touch, in a sense, and yet with the strongest compulsion! It is a great wonder to me, dear, and I am rather breathless in the contemplation of it.

As was he. In fact, by mid-July, he was making plans to return to Dos Rios for a visit, *"but the doubts pile up as my expectancy heightens."*

JE: News came yesterday with Bob that Marilou has jaundice or malaria, and that we will probably not be down this month, as he is chief tender in the affair. And then Pete got sick yesterday, one of those attacks (fever, chills, and weakness) that could develop into anything. So, my longed-for darling, we are cast upon the mercy of the Lord again for being together next weekend. Wish I could make it definite, but cannot do so now.

Not until later in the month was he able to get there to see her, spending an entire weekend *"speaking mostly of when we should be married: September, November, January, or March."*

A few days after his return to Shandia, after processing the things they'd discussed about marriage, and after talking through the ramifications with Pete, he felt good about where he'd landed. And as the now-frequent rain poured down on the rooftop, roiling the already surging waters of the Napo, preventing him from doing any outside work for the day, he sat down to write a summary of his conclusions to my mother.

July 30

As I see the wedding, it involves three issues: (1) your really getting Quichua, (2) my traveling at least a little as a single man, (3) the matter of housing. My feeling this morning after prayer, and chatting with Pete, is that we would do well to postpone the hoped-for November wedding two months until January. That will give you more time to clinch the language. (Where you will live seems to me a useless issue. God will declare that plainly, if we are discovering the Will.) It will also give a couple of months for traveling, and give us time to collect boards for building, a thing we need even for Ed's house. That is my suggestion—a January wedding—you pick the date.

Little did he know, however, the "catastrophic" thing he'd almost wished for in April as a way of speeding their wedding was currently cascading right at him, right at that moment, as the rains turned into torrents. And all my mother could do, hearing word of this flood, was write to him and pray he had survived it.

Letter from my mother, praying and waiting for news from him.

────

July 31

"Many waters cannot quench love, neither can the floods drown it." So I write you this morning, darling, loving you as never before, and not knowing in what circumstances you find yourself.

Ed McCully came out to the radio at 2:30 yesterday afternoon, and stood anxiously by until 3:00, but none of us heard from you. Marge and I stood by every hour on the hour until 6:00, hoping you might get your radio set up again. But if it was anything like it was here, I'm wondering if there is a building left in which to put your radio, let alone *yourselves*.

The crest was not reached until around 5:00 yesterday. Oh, darling—if only I could help. I've been standing by at the radio this morning, as Ed and Dr. T. said they'd be doing, but read no one, not even Shell. I'm going to ask Nate to fly in to Shandia as soon as he possibly can if I can reach Shell at 1:30 this afternoon.

I'm sending this letter with an Indian, also a little food, in case you've lost everything, including means to cook. I'm going to tell him if by any chance he should meet one of your Indians coming this way (I'm hoping you'll send word *soon*), he can send him back with this letter, and return here with any message your Indian may have.

I did not sleep well at all last night, wondering if you even had a roof over your heads. Wondering how much, if anything, you'd managed to save—even wondering about the possibility of your going over the cliff with the house! Oh, darling, I love you with all of my soul, and cannot imagine what life would be without you.

I wondered, too, at God's purpose in this. Will all your work be undone? I trust Him for it, Jim, after a fashion. (I had to add that, in honesty.) I really do believe He has a purpose which will "ripen fast," but I cannot help wondering and speculating. That's what I mean by "after a fashion."

I prayed this morning that you would be stablished, strengthened, and settled, after all these testings. That God will, in very truth, let you learn obedience by the things you have suffered. I long to be with you in this, and to share in whatever comes to you. Know that I am praying for you, as I'm sure they are in Quito and Shell Mera, too. I shall be eagerly waiting some word from you—if not before tomorrow, then with the return of the Indian. Let me know if there's anything we can do.

There really wasn't.

He wrote the next day, addressing it from what he called, simply, *"an Indian home."*

August 1

Shandia is no more. This is being written beside a fire outside with a dozen Indians looking on and telling me what to write. The first house went about 3:30 p.m. on Thursday, and we have spent the rest of the time moving our stuff away from the river—except for last night, when we slept the whole night with about thirty Indians in one house.

Most of the stuff is here now under temporary shelter, though the heavier items, barrels, motor, refrigerator, etc. are at various points in the forest—we hope out of reach of the flood. Most of our stuff was saved, thanks to the invaluable help of all the Indians, though we have lost a little through thievery, and the boards we tore from the houses, through simply being too weary to pack them away from the river. School went about midnight, and school kitchen in early hours yesterday morning. Clinics and our Indian kitchen went late in the afternoon. . . .

We will try to get our tent up today and get housekeeping underway again soon. It was so thoughtful of you to send bread. We found some butter and honey and had chicken soup for supper—the first good meal in thirty-six hours last night. Sorry I could not inform you sooner, but we were busy carrying stuff the very moment your carrier arrived, and I had no idea where pen and paper were until last night.

The new house is near the brink, and we lost about one-eighth of the air-strip. I don't know if they will dare land or not. If they do, we need aerial wire for the radio. Both our pens are out of ink, so will continue this in haste.

The flood.

And as he did, though the situation could hardly be any more dire, he immediately began drawing upon that well of faith he'd allowed the Lord to build in him his whole life long. In the days that followed, my dad's invincible spirit would show him to be the Jim Elliot who's still held in such high esteem today, a man who could stare death and destruction in the face and never flinch, knowing his God would never fail.

"Breakfast is on the fire," he wrote, *"and a beautiful dawn is breaking through the forest. We are both well and happy, waiting on God to show us His will for this station."*

And the same God, he knew, would also show him His will for marriage.

No, my darling, the waters have not quenched love. I do not know what this will mean for us—do not have even a hint as to how it will affect wedding plans. I wrote, but did not send (will send when I find it) a letter telling of Pete's reaction to a wedding, and suggesting that we plan for January, but I have no idea now what to do.

He just knew God would make a way. And my mother knew something else: she was going down to Shandia—to see it, and to see him, for herself. She wrote to him, after having just been there.

August 7

Darling, I doubt if I can express just what my visit to Shandia did for me. I want to thank you, at least. It was, in very truth, a benediction! I would like to apologize all over for my many tears, but you will not want that. (I see I was not the only one affected by the sight—Ed couldn't keep himself when he first got out of the plane.)

But, oh, Jim—if I've ever felt unworthy of you, it has been since that visit. Instead of my being a true "helpmeet" to you, and standing by at such a time as that, it was you who were a tower of strength. It makes me wonder if I can ever be to you what a man's wife should be. And it makes me know, more surely than ever, that you will be all I could ever have asked for.

It was such a joy to see you at work, cheerful and trusting, laughing with the Indians, exhorting them, binding up their sores, directing the workmen, doing your own share—in short, I was impressed with the fact that you seemed my ideal man and missionary. Not the "typical missionary," I saw *my* ideal. . . .

For all these things, for what I am discovering you are, I love you, Jim, with all my capacity to love. Knowing you only gives me more reasons to love you.

I try to imagine all the times my father had dreamed of being on mission, deep in the jungle, unattached to any woman in marriage, hazarding all things to carry the gospel to people who'd never heard the name of Jesus. Now he was actually looking forward to having a wife—having my mother. God had given Him *more* than he'd imagined.

I try to imagine all the times my mother saw herself doing pioneer work, putting the gospel in understandable language for a primitive people, but not in Shandia, which didn't really hold much interest for her. Now she was actually looking forward to being there, she said, with my father. God had given her more than she'd imagined too.

Don't think of my parents as perfect. They're weren't. Don't think of their relationship as perfect. It wasn't. See them as two people—a man and a woman—who willingly invited God to direct their lives His own way. God is the One doing things perfectly here in their story, even amid disaster, even after many years of testing and waiting, of separation and struggle.

Their struggles were far from over, of course. We know that. But for now—finally—He had brought them together in this place, for this season.

They were home.

I'm looking forward to being in Shandia, but, oh, darling, how I hope it will be the last place either of us has to live "in someone else's house." I am so tired of knocking around, living on other people's stuff. It's not the knocking around so much that gets me—I don't expect we'll ever really *settle* anyplace—but I do want to be independent of others' goods and services. And I want to make some sort of home for you, Jim.

For the short run, she would stay in temporary quarters in Shandia while my dad and his missionary partners scouted the uncharted areas of the Oriente, seeking to make connections wherever God led them, seeking their next doors of opportunity. He apologized that she would be *"dependent again on others' goods and services"* while he was out on the trail, but . . .

Next time I build, I feel sure it will be for and with you. And who knows when that will be? You know what I hope? I hope it will be before we have a chance to plan a wedding.

"Yes," she answered him from Dos Rios, before coming down to Shandia, *"I hope we won't have time to plan a wedding, too,"* that it would simply need to happen too soon for much planning.

Not November. Not January. Not March.

Mr. and Mrs. Philip E. Howard, Jr.

announce the marriage

of their daughter

Elisabeth

to

Mr. Philip James Elliot

Thursday, October eighth

Nineteen hundred and fifty-three

in Quito, Ecuador

They chose my father's birthday.

October 7: Quito

"They shall not be ashamed that wait for Thee."
"There hath not failed one good thing . . ."
". . . to give you an expected end."

Tomorrow, Jim and I are to be married. Praise, praise to Thee, my Lord and my God! Thy leadings have been wonderful these five and a half years. Thou hast shown the way, always lovingly, always surely, and hast kept us for one another.

From days of studying Thucydides together, through the time of renunciation and silence ("How can I give silence, my whole life long?"), the correspondence and despondence of PBI days, the days of Mt. Hood and Short Sand, the night of Dave's wedding, the uncertainty about the field, the night at the golf course in Moorestown and its subsequent heartache and healing, Shelton College, Franconia, and 3 West Maple . . .

Quito, Arias's home, the field above it, Pichincha, the bodega, separation to Oriente and Occidente, together again, January '53 engagement—T.B. scare, and Jim's unwavering trust in God and love for me, relief . . .

May, and Quito again, then San Miguel; Oriente in June, flood in July, Bobonaza trip in August, return in September, and a week of closeness in Shandia; this past week in Quito—and tomorrow . . .

O Lord—Thy lovingkindness is better than life.

My mother had dreamed of the traditional church wedding, wearing the white wedding dress, proceeding down the aisle with friends and family gathered. But in the end, the ease of simply going to the Quito courthouse won out, having a justice of the peace marry them.

Partly I think she made the decision because she saw the sense of my father's thinking. She knew he couldn't stand all the fuss and finery of church weddings. To him it smacked of the superficiality of all worldly attractions. He wanted their wedding kept as free of nonessentials and elaboration as possible. But probably their main desire for marrying at an earlier date was motivated by their almost five and a half years of waiting. They needed each other, more than they needed ceremony.

She wore a lovely sky blue suit that someone had made for her, adorned by a tasteful corsage. He wore the only dark suit he owned, a navy blue one. They invited Dr. and Mrs. Tidmarsh as witnesses, along with Ed and Marilou McCully. The affair was that small, that speedy, and that simple.

Wedding kiss.

———

Outside the courthouse. The boy with his pants down had
no idea of the solemn and joyous occasion.

———

October 21: San Jose, Costa Rica

We were married as planned, October 8, 9:30 a.m., and went afterwards to the Colon Hotel with Tidmarshes (our official witnesses at the ceremony) and McCullys. Had coffee and cakes, Dr. T. led in prayer, and then they took us to the airport.

Plane to Panama, where we went to El Panama, "Latin America's most luxurious hotel." Six days there, in pure luxury, then a flight here, where we surprised Dave and Phyllis almost to the point of collapse. We've been here nearly a week now. Lovely little city, lots of fun, good fellowship.

With eager, longing, and often breaking hearts, they'd anticipated this October 8 day, and the jubilation they felt afterward was a gift from God, the fruit of living for His glory and their realization of His perfect will. How could their honeymoon *not* be filled with happiness, thanksgiving, and absolute restfulness after all the waiting and praying and hungering that led up to it? For nearly three beautiful weeks, they were free from concern over the work in the field and able to celebrate what God had accomplished in them, what He'd given them. It was joy, joy, praise, and more joy!

Leaving for their honeymoon.

With Uncle Dave and Aunt Phyllis—joy-filled days spent in Costa Rica.

November 5, 1953: Shell Mera

Finished up a marvelous two-week honeymoon with three days more in El Panama. Flight to Quito on October 24, then ten days there, buying and packing for the Oriente. Today we flew down from Quito, but half of our stuff is in Ambato still. Lord, protect it from thievery and bring it down safely.

And now finally their life as married missionaries could begin, in keeping with the verse from Isaiah they'd chosen for their wedding day: "Lo, this is our God; we have waited for him." They had persevered in waiting on His timing, and the One who in His sovereignty plans our days and our years had brought them into this new phase ever confident in His ongoing calling.

Their story never stops capturing my heart. The Lord took my father's personality, so brash and bold—a young man who told his fellow students on campus they needed a kick in the pants to get to the mission field—who admonished them for not swearing off dating, for not realizing they were in college to "study to show themselves approved unto God"—and somehow married his gospel zeal with a woman's love, without decreasing his passion for souls. The Lord also took my mother's personality and intellect, gave her love for such a man, challenged her to restrain it to the level of true Christian love between friends, yet crowned her willingness to absolutely trust Him by giving her not only more of Himself but also giving her my father, the other great desire of her heart.

God has taught me through their example, and through His visible outworking in their lives, that I can trust His holy will, even when nothing around me looks hopeful or good. And He can use even my failures and pain and worries as part of what He transforms into a life that brings Him full honor and glory.

November 11, 1953: El Oriente

"The Lord, He it is that doth go with thee. He will not fail thee." He has brought us to this place at last, in safety and with no loss of goods. *Our first home!*

"Home." Together at home.
God had brought them all the way home.

And it shall be said in that day,
Lo, this is our God; we have waited for him.

ISAIAH 25:9

EPILOGUE

DECEMBER 1, 1953: It is not raining at the moment, but the fresh-cut bamboo slats are chunked with fresh mud, and the other half of the tent, not yet floored, is slippery gum from an all-night rain on Sunday. We had to get this much of the floor in yesterday, and they are supposed to be bringing more bamboo today, so perhaps we will be fully floored this week.

Betty took matters in her own hands this afternoon while I rested (I am supposed to have had jaundice—almost since the day we arrived, November 11—and am still a part-time bed patient) and put down sticks between the tent and the eight-by-ten mud-floored kitchen, as yet only half walled.

She is there cooking now while I sit at the card table, decked with an aster-flowered tea cloth with a centerpiece of white candle and a graceful-leafed little forest flower set off beautifully in a tin can.

I don't know how many men and women would have endured the kind of waiting and sacrifice that resulted (finally) in my parents' October 8, 1953 wedding—his twenty-sixth birthday. Nor do I know how many would consider marriage off to a successful start if it meant living in the conditions they found themselves—a tent measuring sixteen feet square, pitched amid barely a clearing in the Amazon jungle. Some would see nothing else but the "tin can," not the "flower set off beautifully" inside it.

But after journeying with me through their uncommon love story, I hope what you see in this all-too-common scene from their early married life is the hand of God's blessing. They had given themselves to the Lord; they had given themselves to each other. And while it may seem an absurdly austere beginning, I think we'd trade a lot of our "stuff" for the strength of devotion, love, purpose, and simplicity my parents were experiencing in their tent.

"This is where God has sent us, and this is where we belong," my mother said. *"It is not for nothing that Thou hast brought us here."*

They began married life in Puyupungu, a tiny village that my father's scouting team had located during that three-week exploration in September, deeming it the most promising for gospel influence. With no one else quite in the position to take on the challenge, my parents said yes. It's what led to their saying "I do," sooner than expected.

By late March they'd finished a little thatch house which gave them relief from the elements. They continued serving the Indians, setting up a little school for the children, ministering to them in countless ways, being the light of Christ. But as rebuilding began occurring in Shandia, the decision was made to restore it as their mission's hub, converting places like Puyupunga into more like outstations that they could serve from a single base of operation. With this model taking shape, my parents returned to Shandia, where my father especially could focus on construction. Even my Grandfather Elliot came down to assist in the building project.

The house they eventually built for themselves there is actually the one I remember well. My mother and I lived in it until I was three and a half, before we went to live with the Aucas, and then again from ages six to eight, until we returned to the States. It was my mother's "dream home," luxurious compared to the thatched roof and bamboo walls they'd been accustomed to living in. They had talked and written much about what they needed and wanted in a house, and my father happily built it with the help of local Indians and Grandpa Elliot. It had cement floors, screened windows, and a corrugated tin roof, on which the tropical rains thundered with thrilling regularity. It also contained a kerosene-fueled refrigerator, a wood-burning cast iron stove, and a second story, where my mother's maid lived with her daughter. My mother couldn't have been happier, cooking meals and bread and cakes for her beloved and for me. And since she had a maid, she was able to work at her desk each morning, preparing Bible classes and translating some of the New Testament into Quichia. I, of course, was expected to entertain myself, a childhood task made easier by having the maid's daughter to play with.

Some of my earliest memories involve washing my feet in the bathroom sink, and going to my cozy bed at night. My dad built it for me—a simple, junior-sized bed—and Mama made a pink and white-striped, ruffled skirt that neatly went under the mattress. We kept the bed in our family for many years before carpenter ants destroyed it in our North Carolina garage. But along the way, four of his grandchildren and even one of his great-grands slept in that same bed I'd enjoyed as a child in the jungle.

I was able to go back and see that house again, forty years after my father was killed, at the invitation of my mother. It was rather dilapidated, of course, but still standing and still being lived in, now by an extended family of Quichuas, who were thrilled that we'd come. The man who'd taken possession of it wanted us to go back and tell Americans that they could come down and stay there anytime they liked.

Whether we wanted to or not, they asked us to eat with them. They served us hard-boiled eggs and chicha, a local drink made from chewed, cooked manioc (yes, chewed into a liquid) that is kept in a package made with banana leaves. While sitting there, as my mother was carrying on conversation with them in Quichua, a young blond-haired man in motorcycle garb walked up the trail. He said he was a German, living in Quito, and wanted to know if this was indeed the house that Jim Elliot built. Imagine his surprise to find my mother and me there. He was quite overwhelmed to meet us, and we were thrilled to confirm to him his hopes of seeing my father's house. Isn't that God's perfect ordaining?

But hasn't this whole story been one of watching God at work, waiting on His timing, allowing Him to lay the path that kept them in the center of His will? As I draw it to a close, I again let my parents' own words paint the moods, thoughts, and descriptions of their lives, now as husband and wife, first in Puyupungu, then again in Shandia.

JE (DECEMBER 1, 1953): She is just what I always knew her to be, all woman, with her habit of being surprised and shocked at things I do and say (an amusing habit to me, and an incentive to keep saying shocking things), her tendency to use exaggerated words ("horrible," "awful," in tones of utter disgust), and to feel things strongly and with a love for me that I can neither understand nor appreciate, let alone be worthy of. We have had nothing but harmony, from our wedding night in El Panama to the last time we spoke. . . . The marriage adjustment, if it exists at all, is something that I am going through effortlessly—unconsciously, even. Such is the love we know.

My father took this picture of her in a rare moment of letting her hair down.

EE (MARCH 25, 1954): God has answered prayer again . . . He has provided a house for us! I now sit in the pleasantest living room, at the little desk Jim made months ago. Two sides of the room are windows, looking out over the vast expanse of the Pastaza to the Andes.

One never knows what a good roof and dry floor mean till he has lived in a leaky tent nearly five months! How we thank God for this thatched house, floor six feet off the ground, of boards. Have finished the bedroom and living room, except kitchen to be done today. . . . Praise to Thee, Lord, for good shelter, for money and workmen to build it, for Jim's health and ability to plan, direct, and help in the work.

JE (APRIL 1, 1954): Pause late on a rainy afternoon. Gratefully settled in our home in Puyupungu for a week now. Been a long, but not unendurable five months in the tent. God has been faithful.

EE (APRIL 7, 1954): Life can be very routine—rise at 6:00; breakfast 6:30; clean the house; devotions at 8:00; read, write, or study; cook dinner; radio at 1:30; dinner at 5:30; bed at 8:30. Lord, cause me to remember continually the reason I am here. Cause me to look at the things which are not seen.

And one more prayer I bring—O Lord, give us a son.

EE (APRIL 10, 1954): Jim is out working on a fence to keep the cows off the airstrip. By simply walking across it when it's soft (as it nearly always is), they can cause Jim hours of work smoothing it down.

He works so hard—comes in several times every day, soaked to the skin with sweat (and often rain), mud just saturating his shoes, socks, and pants up to the knee. I love him so much and look for the day when there will be no more airstrips or house-building to think of. (Will that day come, if we carry on a program simi-lar to the work here at Puyupungu?)

Married life is all I had hoped for. Jim is always a thoughtful, loving, and most appreciative husband. He notices little things. He comments on food he likes; he has planted six or seven kinds of orchids which he watches and cares for with great interest; he continues to teach me in the things of God; he is just boyish enough to be lots of fun when occasion warrants; he handles Indians with what seems to me special wisdom; his spirit is so buoyant and cheerful, trusting in God's faithfulness through what, to me, are often very discouraging times. How I praise God for him—no one could ask more of life than to be loved as I am loved.

My father at left, working on their Shandia house.
His father is obscured in the background.

———

More or less finished. This is the house I remember living in.

———

JE (MAY 30, 1954): Betty and I were able to fly out of Puyupungu strip April 21 in separate flights. We waited a day in Shell for Ed and went on to Quito together the twenty-third. Met Dad with much thanksgiving at Puná on Tuesday 8:00 a.m. April 27. . . . We spent a week in Quito getting teeth fixed, attending IMF conference, and meeting people, coming down on truck to Shell with GMUers on May 14. Betty came here, and I went to Shandia to choose a house site. (O, God, may it be the right one!)

EE (JULY 23, 1954): Praise, praise to Him from whom comes every good and perfect gift. I am quite certain that I am pregnant. Jim and I are so happy about it. We have "agreed together as touching one thing"—we've asked God for a son.

JE (AUGUST 8, 1954): In Shandia now for several weeks with Ed and Marilou gone out for a rest. Just Dad, Rob, Betty, and me. Working on the house now, pouring cement mostly, and have finished the floor and walls except for surfacing.

EE (OCTOBER 31, 1954): Don't know how I allow such long intervals to pass between writings. I cannot plead busy-ness, but I have been very disorganized. Living down there in Pete's hot, crowded little shack, eating meals at the McCully's house, etc., did not make for a unified life. But now, thanks be to God, we are in our own home! Jim and I moved up here last Monday, though we continue to eat dinner at midday with the McCullys since we haven't a pipe for our stove yet. I am so grateful to God for this house—so far beyond any house I had ever expected to have. But He gave it to us, and it is His. I want it to be used for His name's sake, and to be a place of peace for the Lord's people, as well as a lighthouse to these who live around us. I wonder if we shall spend the rest of our lives here? I dream of it being filled with children and guests—Lord, let it be.

EE (DECEMBER 6, 1954): Three months to go until the baby is born—it seems a long time. But we thank God for the happy prospect.

EE (DECEMBER 28, 1954): Ten weeks seems a long time for me to wait. It is uncomfortable lying in bed these nights—what will it be in the next two months?

EE (JANUARY 10, 1955): Marj Saint's son was born on December 26. Wonder when ours will come? Wish it would come early! I have asked the Lord for a child that will glorify Him. The thoughts which I'm sure millions of mothers-to-be have had before me beset me now and again—Will he be normal? Will he live and grow nicely? What will labor be like?—but I am at peace, knowing that He is able to keep that which I have committed unto Him, and it is *all His*.

EE (FEBRUARY 9, 1955): If all goes as hoped, we should be parents by three weeks from now. How I long for the day to have Jim's child—what a wonder! I'm sure all the discomfort of the present days will seem completely insignificant. . . . How I pray that I may be prepared in every way for the birth. O, that we might have a son who will grow up to glorify God!

EE (FEBRUARY 23, 1955): I expect to be going to Shell Mera tomorrow to await the baby's birth. How I pray that it may not be delayed at all.

EE (MARCH 6, 1955): On February 27, one week ago today, at 5:20 a.m., Valerie arrived. I had been in labor from 10:30 a.m. Saturday. Dr. Fuller delivered her here in the Saint's house, with Liz, his wife, in attendance. Jim was with me every minute, which meant more to me than he will ever know. . . .

What a joy to hear her first cry, and to see our own daughter! She wasn't red or wrinkled, and her head was perfectly shaped. Dear Jim—he told his mother he thought he would be disappointed if it was a girl, but he wasn't at all. He loved her right away, and took her in his arms. How thankful I am! . . .

O, Lord—this child is one of Thy "perfect" gifts, which comes from the Father of Lights. We give her back to Thee, in gratitude, and ask Thy holy wisdom and love in guiding and caring for her.

What can I say but that they loved me and were thankful.

Clueless as to what a mirror is.

———

The carefree joys of being born in the jungle.

———

The three of us, together, in Shell Mera.

And this is where I think I'll leave them, enjoying this precious moment in their love story—our little family of three, surrounded by friends, by faithful coworkers, swept up together in gratitude to God. He had answered their prayers—all those prayers for a son—with me. I think the Lord must have smiled.

Here, too, is where I fall on my knees in praise, thanking Him not only for knitting my life so uniquely into this story but allowing me to share it with you. May you take from their real lives the confidence and trust that God has designed you, too, for noble service in His kingdom, as You surrender to Him, obey Him, and daily learn to let Him lead where He alone is able to take you. Lo, He is your God. Wait on Him, *devotedly*.

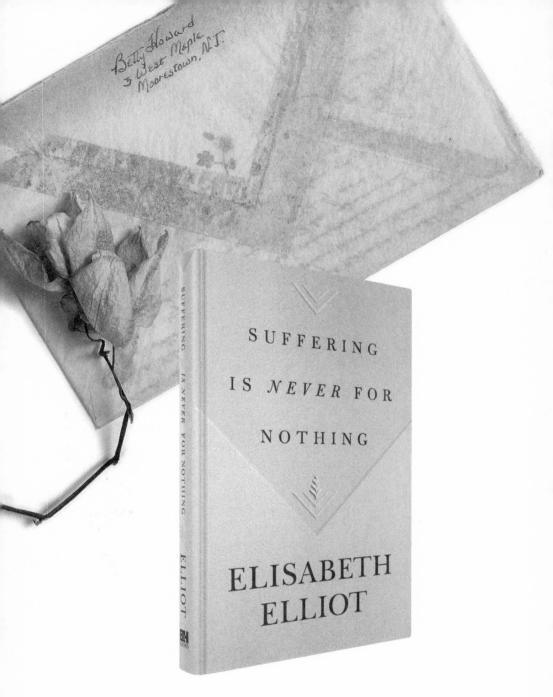

"Love still wills my joy."
–ELISABETH ELLIOT

LEARN MORE *at* ELISABETHELLIOTBOOKS.COM

...y I let answering go until later.

First let me congratulate all the new Howa...
aunts and uncles, the doting grand folks an...
the blessed parents of Katharine Jane. The o...
had reminded me to pray for R. and M. ...
it was this expected news that made me ca...
to hear from you today, partly.

The mail comes late on Thursdays because...
fluke in the delivery system. I had been ...
for a letter from you since Monday (don't ask m...
and had almost concluded that you were, ...
desperate measures" to discipline our correspon...
again. I was rather expecting today's pac...
to contain a certain poem or two I'd asked ...
I somehow (rightly) sensed you wouldn't send ...
So after lunch I headed for mount Tabor ...
close where we discussed the letters that af...
I had difficulty recognizing the exact spot ...
things are much more in a tangle since the fa...
the leaves. This hindered considerably my sear...
those bits of paper into which you rendered th...
much disputed poem of March 22, 1947. I found ...
few pieces, some badly soaked, some only shreds...
rumpled and decomposed. You would ...

your strokes, what is there left for me to say? Judging from what you say, I'm persuaded you know a lot of things about that I don't even know yet, and have access to a barometer of feelings that I've never had a glimpse of. Well, carry on, brother - it's fascinating.

You asked me to write my brother David. I don't see that is necessary. He've never discussed the matter at all, so I'll leave it up to you to defend yourself. He blew in here on Friday morning from Chicago, on his way to New York where he was going. We Sibby a ring that night. He was only here a couple of hours, we had no chance to talk, & of course all he can think of is it.

I think the picture idea is a good one. I had already thought of having mine made for mother but didn't want to commit myself by letting you know, because they might turn out to look just like & then of course I wouldn't have sent you one! But I suppose they can't be worse than the ones you have. I would like to have one of you, though, past the age